LIEUT.-GENERAL SIR HUBERT DE LA POER GOUGH, G.C.M.G., K.C.B., K.C.V.O.

HISTORY

OF THE

SIXTEENTH, THE QUEEN'S, LIGHT DRAGOONS

(LANCERS),

1912 TO 1925.

BY COLONEL HENRY GRAHAM.

The Naval & Military Press Ltd

Published by

The Naval & Military Press Ltd
Unit 10 Ridgewood Industrial Park,
Uckfield, East Sussex,
TN22 5QE England

Tel: +44 (0) 1825 749494
Fax: +44 (0) 1825 765701

www.naval-military-press.com
www.military-genealogy.com
www.militarymaproom.com

*In reprinting in facsimile from the original, any imperfections are inevitably reproduced
and the quality may fall short of modern type and cartographic standards.*

AUTHOR'S PREFACE.

At the request of the Officers of the Regiment I have in this volume brought down the History of the 16th Lancers from 1912 to 1925.

The period includes two important episodes in the Regimental record—one, the Ulster affair in 1914, when the Officers of the 3rd Cavalry Brigade by their honourable and unselfish conduct averted the imminent danger of a Civil War; the other the Great War, in which the Regiment displayed its usual valour and discipline, and gained its usual honour and distinction. Its long Roll of Casualties and rewards is sufficient testimony to the way in which its duties were performed in the Field. In writing the record of the Regiment during the war I have only entered into the details of those actions in which the 16th themselves took part. For the rest enough only is given to enable a reader to follow the general course of the campaign.

I am indebted to Colonel Cecil Howard for the account of the Regiment in India and Egypt and for the Polo Appendix.

HENRY GRAHAM.

TABLE OF CONTENTS.

PREFACE ... ... PAGE iii.

PAGE 1-15. (1912 to 1914).

CHAPTER XXXI.—1912-1914.—Norwich. The Regiment sent to Wigan. Returns 18th April. The Eastern Counties manœuvres. The Regiment moves to Ireland and joins the 3rd Cavalry Brigade at the Curragh. The Home Rule Bill. Unrest in Ireland. Ulster and the Army. Speech of Mr. Winston Churchill. A fleet sent to Lamlash. The Military Plan of Campaign. Sir Arthur Paget's interview with General Officers in Dublin. Second interview with Cavalry and Artillery Officers at the Curragh. Resignations of officers. Brigadier-General Gough, Lieut.-Colonels Parker and MacEwen ordered to London. General Gough telegraphs to Lord Roberts. Interview with the Adjutant-General at the War Office. Intervention of Lord Roberts. His audience by the King. General Gough's interviews with Sir John French and Colonel Seely at the War Office. Complete surrender of the Government. Reinstatement of Brig.-General Gough and the Commanding Officers. Memorandum of assurance given to General Gough.

APPENDIX TO CHAPTER XXXI.—Speech of Lord Roberts in the House of Lords. Some accounts of the Commander-in-Chief's speech to the officers at the Curragh on March 21st.

PAGE 15-22. (28th June to 6th August, 1914).

CHAPTER XXXII.—The War with Germany. Causes of the War. Murder of Archduke Ferdinand. Temperate demands of Austria. Germany's secret preparations. Designs of Germany. Austrian Ultimatum to Servia. Diplomatic efforts to avoid war. Conference proposal abortive owing to refusal of Germany to participate. German High Sea Fleet recalled. Russian mobilisation. German terms for British neutrality. Their rejection. German troops enter Luxembourg. Belgian rejection of German terms and subsequent mobilisation. German Army invades Belgium on August 3rd. Sir Ed. Goschen demands explanation and is handed his passports on 4th. Siege of Liége begins on 5th. British Declaration of War as from 11 p.m. August 4th. Fleet and Army mobilised and Lord Kitchener appointed Secretary for War, August 5th. The Expeditionary Force sent to France. Composition of the Expeditionary Force.

APPENDIX I.—Staff and details of the Expeditionary Force.

APPENDIX II.—Comparative Tables of Organisation. British, French, Belgian, and German Armies.

SUMMARY OF EVENTS, JUNE 28th TO AUGUST 6th, 1914.—June 28th, Murder of Archduke Ferdinand. July 23rd, Austrian Ultimatum to Servia. 25th, Servian reply received. 28th, Austria declares War on Servia. 29th, Russia begins to mobilise. August 1st, Germany declares War on Russia; France begins to mobilise. 2nd, Germans enter Luxembourg. 3rd, German invasion of Belgium; Great Britain orders mobilisation; State of War declared between France and Germany. 4th, British Declaration of War. 5th, Austria declares war on Russia; Siege of Liége begins. 6th, Three of Liége forts destroyed.

PAGE 22-27. (14th August to 22nd August, 1914).

CHAPTER XXXIII.—Embarkation of the Regiment at Dublin, 16th August. Disembarkation at Havre. 18th, Entrains for Jeumont, Detrains 19th August. March to Consolre. Positions of the British, French, and German Armies The progress of the war in Belgium. The Kaiser's Order as to the "Contemptibles". Plans of General Joffre and Von Moltke. Mistakes of Von Kluck. The Regiment joins the 3rd Cavalry Brigade. Dispositions of Sir J. French. Movements of the Cavalry Brigades. The first shot of the Campaign. Encounter at Casteau. The Greys at Peronnes. The 16th at Peronnes in support. The march of the 16th to Elouges.

SUMMARY OF EVENTS, AUGUST 7th TO AUGUST 22nd, 1914.—August 7th, The Germans enter town of Liége; French enter Mulhouse; Russians invade East Prussia. 9th, First troops of British Expeditionary Force land in France. 15th, Remaining forts of Liége destroyed. 19th, Retreat of Belgian Army to Antwerp. 20th, Brussels taken by Germans; Siege of Namur begins. 21st, Japan declares war on Germany; Retirement of French in Alsace and Lorraine; Namur forts destroyed. 22nd, Defeat of the French at Charleroi.

PAGE 27-36. (August 23rd to August 26th, 1914).

CHAPTER XXXIV.—Battle of Mons, August 23rd. Action begun by German Artillery at 10 a.m. Infantry attack by 9th German Corps along the Canal north of Mons at 11 a.m. The attack well held. Retirement from Mons and Binche. Action ceases at night-fall. British Casualties. German losses. Condition of the enemy. News received of disasters to the French Armies. Decision to retreat. August 24th. The Retreat of the 1st Corps. Retirement of the 2nd Corps. German attack on the left flank. Severe fighting at Frameries. The 5th Division reinforced by the Cavalry. Charge of the 9th Lancers. Retirement effected. Moves of the 16th. General position at night-fall. Heavy losses of the 9th Lancers, Cheshires, and Norfolks. Continued retreat of French 5th Army. Orders issued for retreat to Le Cateau. Difficulties of retreat. The Forest of Mormal. The 1st Corps to move by the east and 2nd Corps by west of Forest. Arrival of the 4th Division, which is sent to Solesmes. Positions of the Cavalry Brigades. Movements of the 16th. Unmolested march of the 1st Corps. Combats at night at Landrecies and Maroilles. Difficult position of the 2nd Corps. Orders to continue the retreat on the 26th. Sir H. Smith-Dorrien finds this impossible. His decision to stand and fight. Reluctant acquiescence by the Commander-in-Chief.

SUMMARY OF EVENTS, AUGUST 23rd TO AUGUST 26th, 1914.—August 23rd, Battle of Mons; Germans enter Namur; Austrians driven out of Servia; Japan declares war on Germany. 24th, Retreat from Mons begins. 26th, Battle of Le Cateau; Battle of Tannenberg begins.

PAGES 36-52. (August 26th to September 5th, 1914).

CHAPTER XXXV.—Continuation of the Retreat from Mons. The Battle of Le Cateau. Position of the 2nd Corps. Von Kluck's strength and dispositions. The battle movements of the 3rd Cavalry Brigade. Heavy losses on the left flank. The Lancasters. The line successfully held. Retirement at 2 p.m. Many detached parties left in the firing line. Heavy losses of the Gordons. Cavalry movements. Lieut.-Colonel MacEwen badly wounded. Losses of guns. Casualties of the 2nd Corps. Retreat of the 1st Corps. Rear-guard action at Le Fayt. The Connaughts cut off. Further retreat of the 1st Corps on the 27th. Rear-guard action at Fesmy. Death of Major Charrier. The gallant fight of the Munsters. Retreat of the 2nd Corps on the 27th covered by the 3rd Cavalry Brigade and crossing of the Somme. Position of the Army 28th August. The retreat continued. The 3rd and 5th Cavalry Brigades. Their combats at Essigny and Cirizy. Charge of the 12th Lancers. The German 1st and 2nd Armies. The French 5th and 6th Armies. Casualties from 23rd to 27th August. Battle of Guise. Further retreat on 29th covered by the Cavalry. . The 16th at Chauny. Retreat on 30th to the line Soissons-Compiègne. Formation of the 3rd Corps. Further retreat 30th August, and September 1st. Orders for the march September 1st. Actions at Nery and Taillefontaine. Sir J. French in Paris. Interview with Lord Kitchener. Retreat resumed September 2nd to the line Meux-Dommartin. Further retreat September 3rd. The Marne crossed and retirement to the Grand Morin on the 4th September. Further and final retirement on September 5th. The end of the Retreat from Mons. Marches and Casualties.

SUMMARY OF EVENTS, AUGUST 28th TO SEPTEMBER 5th, 1914.—August 28th, Naval battle off Heligoland. 31st, Defeat of the Russians at Tannenberg. September 3rd, Lemberg taken by Russians. 5th, End of the Retreat from Mons.

APPENDICES TO CHAPTER XXXV.—I.: Mons and Afterwards. II.: Table of Marches

PAGE 52-58. (September 6th to September 9th, 1914).

CHAPTER XXXVI.—Situation on September 6th. French and German Armies. Position of Von Kluck. New orders of the H.Q. German Staff. Action of Von Bülow. Obstinacy of Von Kluck. Orders by General Joffre. Orders of Sir J. French for the 6th. Battle of the Marne. September 6th, Attack by General Maunoury. Attack by French 5th Army. Position at night-fall. September 7th, Advance of the British Army. Cavalry combats. Advance of the French Armies. Heavy fighting in front of Paris all day with no decisive results. September 8th, Continuous fighting between Von Kluck and General Maunoury. The French left thrown back. Advance of the British Army. Combats along the line of the Petit Morin. Position at night-fall. German defeat at Nancy. Retreat of Von Bülow. Von Molke's peremptory order to Von Kluck, who is placed under command of Von Bülow. September 9th, Retreat of Von Kluck. British advance. Crossing of the Marne. General retreat of the 1st and 2nd German Armies and end of the Battle of the Marne.

SUMMARY OF EVENTS, SEPTEMBER 6th TO SEPTEMBER 9th, 1914.—September 6th, Battle of the Marne begins. 7th, Capitulation of Maubeuge; Battle of Nancy. 8th, Retreat of Von Kluck. 9th, End of Battle of the Marne.

PAGE 58-63. (September 11th to September 30th, 1914).

CHAPTER XXXVII.—September 10th, The pursuit. The Cavalry Division at Latilly. Capture of a convoy. Halt at Breny and Roset. The 1st Infantry Division combat near Courchamps. General Gough's Brigade. Action near Chezy, rout of the enemy, capture of prisoners and wagons. The line of positions at night-fall. The 3rd and 4th Brigades at Passy. Casualties and captures. September 11th, Pursuit continued. No fighting. Crossing of the Ourcq. September 12th, Instructions of General Joffre. Special Orders of Sir J. French. Advance of the Cavalry. Passage of the Vesle forced at Braisne, Courcelles, and Chassemy. Failure of attempt to cross the Aisne. Position at night-fall. 3rd Cavalry Brigade at Ciry. French positions along the Vesle and Aisne. Geography of valley of the Aisne. Designs of General Joffre. Positions of German 1st and 2nd Armies. September 13th, Orders of Sir J. French. The crossing of the Aisne at Venizel by the 11th Infantry Brigade. Reconnaisance by Cavalry Division. Position at night-fall. September 14th, Battle of the Aisne. German reinforcements from Belgium and Maubeuge. Failure of attack on the Aisne. Position at night-fall. The 16th billeted at Lime. The French Armies. Definite failure of plan of General Joffre. The casualties. September 16th, The arrival of the 6th Division. Its distribution. Beginning of Trench Warfare. September 16th to 28th, Indecisive attacks and counter-attacks. Formation of 2nd Cavalry Division under General Gough. Extension of the battle line northward.

SUMMARY OF EVENTS, SEPTEMBER 10th TO SEPTEMBER 30th, 1914.—September 10th, Final defeat of Austrians in Galicia. 13th, 1st Battle of the Aisne begins. 17th, Belgian Army retires to Antwerp. 18th, End of First Battle of the Aisne; Commencement of "Trench Warfare"; Bombardment of Rheims. 28th, Siege of Antwerp begins. 29th, Battle of Albert.

PAGE 63-68. (October 1st to December 31st, 1914).

CHAPTER XXXVIII.—October 1st, Extension of Allied line northwards. Movements of the British to the North. The 16th march to Hazebrouck. Situation in Belgium. Landing of the Naval Brigade at Antwerp. Bombardment and capitulation of Antwerp. Landing of the 3rd Cavalry and 7th Infantry Divisions. Attempt to extend the line to Bruges. Advance of the 3rd Cavalry Brigade. Death of Lieut. Macneil. The combat at Mont des Cats. The action at Warneton and failure of attack. Arrival of the Infantry Corps. New position from Albert to Nieuport and distribution of the troops. The Regiment in the trenches. November 5th, The French shelled out of their trenches. Major Dixon's gallant effort to rally them. Casualties of the Regiment on November 5th. First Battle of Ypres. October 15th-21st. Heavy losses. December 2nd, Inspection by the King. The 16th in billets. Formation of two Armies. Distribution of the troops.

SUMMARY OF EVENTS, OCTOBER 1st TO DECEMBER 31st, 1914.—October 1st, Southern forts of Antwerp destroyed. 3rd, Movement of the British Army to the North. 8th, Bombardment of Antwerp. 9th, Capitulation of Antwerp. 19th, Transfer to Flanders completed. 21st, First Battle of Ypres begins. November 7th, Capitulation of Kiaochau. 23rd, Basra taken. December 6th, Defeat of Austrians by Servians. 15th, Belgrade retaken by Servians.

PAGE 68-74. (January 1st to December 31st, 1915).

CHAPTER XXXIX.—Plans for winter campaign discussed. This decided to be impossible Visit of Sir J. French to London. The Government persists in the refusal to send more men or munitions. Description of "Trench Warfare". The Gallipoli expedition. February 13th, The Regiment returns to the trenches. February 21st, Mine explosion under trench, followed by enemy's attack in force. Severe fighting. Heavy loss by the 16th. February 26th, Regiment back to billets. March 12th, Battle of Neuve Chapelle. The Brigade moved up to front but sent back. April 17th, General Kavanagh takes over command of the 2nd Cavalry Division from General Gough. April 20th. Second Battle of Ypres. Bombardment of the town. April 22nd, "Poison gas" used for first time. April 24th, The Regiment returns to the trenches. "Stink shells" first used. May 2nd, the 16th trenches gassed. May 3rd, the 16th back to billets. May 24th, the Regiment returns to trenches. Disaster at Ypres sally-port. French attack in Artois with partial success. July 15th, General Sir Philip Chetwode takes over command of the 2nd Cavalry Division. The shortage of shells. Mr. Asquith's denial. Sir J. French's appeal to the Press for publicity. Mr. Ll. George made Minister of Munitions. Supply of munitions largely increased. Division of Allied line into Sectors. Disposition of Allied Armies. September 22nd, Battle of Nancy and French victory. September 24th, Battle of Loos. Capture of Vimy Ridge and Loos, but with great loss. December 18th, Resignation of Sir J. French, who is succeeded by Sir D. Haig. The casualties of the Allies during September.

SUMMARY OF EVENTS, JANUARY 1st TO DECEMBER 31st, 1915.—January 1st, Decisive defeat of Turks in the Caucasus. 8th, Battle of Soissons. February 19th, Allied attack on

Dardanelles begins. March 10th, Battle of Neuve Chapelle. 18th, Failure of Naval Attack on Dardanelles definite. 22nd, Capitulation of Prezmysl. April 22nd, Second Battle of Ypres; German gas attack 27th, Army landed at Gallipoli. 28th, Beginning of Mackensen's offensive against Russia. May 7th, Lusitania torpedoed. 19th, Coalition Ministry formed. June 1st, Prezmysl retaken by Germans. 3rd, Amara (Mesopotamia) taken. 20th, Defeat of Russians at Rava Russka. 22nd, Lemberg retaken by Austrians. August 5th, Germans occupy Warsaw. 10th, Germans take Novo Georgievsk. 25th, Germans take Brest Litovski. September 25th, Battle of Loos. 29th, Kut el Amara taken by General Townshend. October 3rd, Allies land at Salonika. 5th, Bulgaria joins Germany; Resignation of Venizelos, the Greek Prime Minister. 7th, Austrians and Germans again invade Servia. 9th, Belgrade taken. 11th, Bulgarians invade Servia. 13th, Murder of Miss Cavell. 15th, War declared on Bulgaria. November 22nd, Battle of Ctestiphon. December 8th, Evacuation of Gallipoli begins. 15th, Resignation of Sir John French and appointment of Sir Douglas Haig to succeed him as Commander-in-Chief.

PAGE 74-83. (January, 1916, to December 31st, 1917).

CHAPTER XL.—1916, January 2nd, The Regiment at Wavrans. Trenches. February 9th, Return to billets at Wavrans. Line extended by relief of French 10th Army. Now from Boesghe on north to Corlu eight miles N.W. Peronne. February 21st, Great German offensive at Verdun begins. July 1st, Beginning of 1st Battle of the Somme. Attack by 4th Army. Formation of 5th Army. June 19th, The 3rd Brigade at Sec Bois. November 18th, Battle of Somme ends. The results. The Cavalry not engaged. September 6th, Regiment to Bray. November 8th, To billets at Petits Preaux for winter. 1917.—No serious fighting during winter. German retirement to new Hindenburg line in February. Retreat followed up. The new position. April 5th, The Regiment on reconnaisance. April 19th, To billets Villeroy. Preparations for new attack by 1st and 3rd Armies east of Arras. April 9th, Attack begins. June 6th, Battle ceases. Results of Battle of Arras. French attacks on the Aisne. French line extended. May 23rd, The Regiment to trenches at Lempire. June 27th, Move to Epehy in support to 2nd Army. Preparations for attack on the north. Movements of 4th and 5th Armies. June 7th, Third Battle of Ypres. Operations impeded by bad weather. Results. The 16th in billets July, August and September. Preparations for new attack by 3rd Army. Objectives Bourlon and break through by Cavalry at Cambrai. November 20th, Battle of Cambrai. Initial success at Bourlon. Failure on Schelde Canal. November 20th, German Reserves come up. German counter-attack. The Break through near Gonnelieu. Letter descriptive of action. The 3rd Brigade in support at Masnières. November 23rd, Cavalry withdrawn. November 25th, The 3rd Brigade to Fins and Ribecourt. Dismounted party at Bourlon. December 4th, Camp bombed. December 6th, To billets round Bovelles.

SUMMARY OF EVENTS, JANUARY 1st, 1916, TO DECEMBER 31st, 1917.—January 9th, 1916, Final evacuation of Gallipoli. February 21st, Great attack on Verdun begins. March 10th, Germany declares war on Portugal. April 29th, Capitulation of Kut. May 30th, Battle of Jutland. June 5th, Lord Kitchener drowned. July 1st, Allied offensive on Somme begins. 6th, Mr. Lloyd George Secretary for War. August 6th, Battle of the Isonzo; Italian victory. 27th, Roumania declares war on Austria; Germany declares war on Roumania. 30th, V. Hindenburg succeeds V. Falkenhayn as Chief of General Staff. September 3rd, Invasion of the Dobruja by Germany. October 5th, Retreat of Roumanians from Transylvania. 12th, Germans invade Roumania. November 11th, Death of Emperor of Austria. December 5th, Resignation of Mr. Asquith. 6th, Mr. Lloyd George Prime Minister. 8th, Blockade of Greece. 12th, Tentative proposals for peace by Germany; General Nivelle succeeds General Joffre. 20th, Peace Note from President Wilson. 30th, Allies reply to German Peace Proposals. January 11th, 1917, Allies reply to President Wilson. 31st, Germany announces unrestricted submarine warfare. February 3rd, Submarine sinks United States steamer Housatonic; Diplomatic relations broken off with Germany. March 10th, Russian Revolution begins. 11th, Baghdad taken. 26th, Invasion of Palestine. April 6th, United States declares war on Germany. 9th, Brazil declares war on Germany; Vimy ridge taken by Canadians. October 24th, Defeat of Italians at Caporetto. November 18th, Death of Sir S. Maude in Mesopotamia. 20th, Battle of Cambrai. 26th, Germans evacuate East Africa. December 22nd, Brest Litovski negotiations opened between Berlin and revolutionary Russia.

PAGE 83-95. (January, 1918, to July, 1918).

CHAPTER XLI.—January 20th, the move of the 5th Army to the South. January 1st, the 16th goes into the trenches. January 28th, the 3rd Brigade sent to Amiens. March 1st, to camp at Brie. March 4th, to trenches at Vermand. March 11th, the Brigade returns to Brie. March 13th, the Brigade moves to Grandru. General position at resumption of hostilities. The 3rd and 5th Armies. German Armies and plans. March 21st, Second Battle of the Somme opens. March 22nd, Crozat Canal crossed by enemy.

Orders of General Gough. General retreat of 3rd and 5th Armies. March 24th, Allied Council at Doulens. General Foch appointed C.-in-C. March 25th, Formation of Carey's Force. March 26th, Attack renewed. Further retreat. The 2nd Cavalry Division engaged west of Noyon. March 27th, Withdrawal to Compiègne. March 27th, the 2nd Division to Montdidier area. March 29th, the Division to Cattenchy. March 28th, the 5th Army broken up. General Gough's command ceases. His place taken by General Rawlinson and 4th Army. March 30th, Renewal of Battle. The 2nd Division at Moreville. March 31st, Fighting between the Avre and Luce. The line re-established. April 1st, the withdrawal of the 2nd Cavalry Division. April 5th, Final German attack fails. The line stabilised. End of Second Battle of the Somme. April 7th, the Battle of the Lys. Successes of the enemy. April 21st, Fighting suspended. April 23rd, Tank fighting between the Somme and Ancre. April 25th, the Lys battle renewed. Loss of Mount Kemmel. April 29th, German attack finally defeated. Close of Battle of the Lys. The 2nd Cavalry Division during the Battle of the Lys. April 29th, March of the 2nd Division to Clety. May 5th, the Regiment moves into billets at Longvillers. May 27th, the attack on the French along the Ailette river and Third Battle of the Aisne. June 9th, Attacks on the Montdidier section and at Rheims. June 18th, Termination of major operations. The line stabilised. General result of the fighting from March 21st to June 18th.

SUMMARY OF EVENTS, FEBRUARY TO JUNE, 1918.—February 24th, Brest Litovski Treaty signed; final withdrawal from the war by Russia. March 5th, Roumania makes peace. 21st, Second Battle of the Somme begins. April 7th, Battle of the Lys. 22nd, Zeebrugge harbour blocked. May 9th, Ostend harbour blocked. 27th, Commencement of offensive by Allies; 3rd Battle of the Aisne. June 15th, Defeat of Austrians on the Piave.

PAGE 95-122. (July 18th to November 15th, 1918).

CHAPTER XLII.—New plans for offensive. July 18th, Attack of French on the southern salient. Success of attack. Aug. 8th, Attack by 4th Army. Disposition of Troops. The old Amiens Defence Lines regained. Attack by 1st French Army. August 9th, Attack by 3rd Corps. Fighting by the Cavalry. Attack by 3rd French Army. August 10th, Advance continued. August 18th, Attack by 10th French Army. General retreat of enemy. September 1st, Peronne regained. September 5th, 1st and 4th French Armies cross the Somme. September 12th, Attacks by General Byng and 1st U.S. Army. Further advance by 3rd and 4th Armies. September 24th, Advance resumed. Position of Allied Armies. September 26th, Attack by 4th French and 1st U.S. Armies. September 27th, Attack on Cambrai front. September 28th, Belgian attack. October 2nd, La Bassée taken. October 3rd, General Pershing drives enemy over the Suippe. October 8th, Attack by 3rd and 4th Armies. Cambrai taken. September 4th to 8th, Le Cateau, Laon, and Douai taken. Belgian and French attack. September 19th, General Allenby's victory in Palestine. September 20th, Belgians occupy Bruges. Lille evacuated. September 23rd, Austrian defeat. October 26th, Von Ludendorff resigns. November 3rd, Valenciennes taken. November 9th, Landrecies, Catillon and Quesnoy taken. October 10th, Ghent re-occupied. October 4th, March of the 3rd Cavalry Brigade to Haspres. October 8th, The 16th sent to 22nd Corps, 1st Army. October 10th, The 16th cover advance. German attempts to procure armistice. Applications to President Wilson. Revolution in Germany. November 9th, Abdication and flight of Kaiser. German delegates meet Marshal Foch. Terms of Armistice. November 11th, Armistice signed. Surrender of Mons. The fighting early in the morning of the 11th. The last charge of the 16th. Fighting ceases at 11 a.m. and end of the War. The Regiment withdrawn to Harmignies. November 15th, The state entrance into Mons.

SUMMARY OF EVENTS, JULY-NOVEMBER, 1918.—July 18th. Second Battle of the Marne. September 19th, Decisive defeat of Turkey in Palestine. 26th, Bulgaria sues for peace. October 24th, Decisive defeat of Austria by Italy. 29th, Austria sues for peace. November 10th, Mons retaken. 11th, The Armistice signed. End of the War.

APPENDICES TO CHAPTER XLII.—I.: Summary of Services of the 2nd Cavalry Division. II.: List of Officers commanding Regiment, 1914-1918. III.: Casualty Lists; Officers killed in action during the War; Officers wounded; Names of other ranks killed in action, or died from wounds or other causes. IV.: Honours and Awards to Officers and other ranks. V.: Names of Officers and other ranks mentioned in despatches.

PAGE 122-125. (24th June, 1919, to 24th November, 1920).

CHAPTER XLIII.—Syria and Palestine. Embarkation at Liverpool, 24th June. Landing at Port Said. Kantara. Port Said. Beyrout. March to Rayak. The Regiment sent by train to Homs. Unhealthy conditions at Homs. The camp moved. Evacuation of Syria. The march to Sarona. The Regiment sent by train to Belbeis. Embarkation at Suez, 24th November, 1920. Roll of the Officers.

PAGE 125-136. (December 12th, 1920, to January 17th, 1925).

CHAPTER XLIV.—India and Egypt. The Regiment at Lucknow. Retirement of Lieut.-Colonel St. John, D.S.O. Lieut.-Colonel Howard, C.M.G., to command vice St. John. Visit of the Prince of Wales. Visit of Field-Marshal Sir W. Robertson. Amalgamation with the 5th Lancers, April, 1922. Roll of the Officers. Favourable Inspection Reports. Inspection by the C.-in-C. India, General Lord Rawlinson. Orders to move to Egypt. The horses given over, February, 1924. Memorial tablet placed in the Church. The general health of the Regiment compared with 1890-96. The Regiment leaves for Egypt, relieved by 4th Hussars. Farewell Orders by G.O.C. U.P. District and others. Disembarkation at Suez, 19th March, 1924. Arrival at Cairo. Abbasia Barracks taken over from 9th Lancers. The Regiment remounted. Political disquiet in Cairo. Murder of Sir Lee Stack. His funeral. The Cavalry Brigade Horse Show. Visit of Lieut.-General Sir J. M. Babington. Retirement of Lieut.-Colonel Howard. His farewell order, January 17th, 1925. Lieut.-Colonel G. F. H. Brooke, D.S.O, M.C., to command vice Howard to H.P.

APPENDIX I.—The Officers of the Regiment.

APPENDIX II.—Roll of N.C.O.'s and Privates of the Regiment who obtained Commissions during the War.

LIST OF PLATES.

1.—Page 35: Brigadier-General MacEwen.
2.—Page 61: Lieutenant-Colonel Eccles.
3.—Page 122: Lieut.-Colonel Harris-St. John.
4.—Page 124: Lieutenant-Colonel Howard.
5.—Page 133: Lieutenant-Colonel Brooke.

Groups of Officers.

Page 126.—Inspection by H.R.H. The Prince of Wales.
Page 129.—Visit of Lord Rawlinson.
Page 134.—Officers, Lucknow, March, 1923.
Page 137.—Officers, Lucknow, February, 1924.

War Memorial.

Page 131.—War Memorial, Canterbury.

The History of the 16th, The Queen's Lancers.

CHAPTER XXXI.

1912—1914.—Norwich. The Regiment sent to Wigan. Returns 18th April. The Eastern Counties manœuvres. The Regiment moves to Ireland and joins the 3rd Cavalry Brigade at the Curragh. The Home Rule Bill. Unrest in Ireland. Ulster and the Army. Speech of Mr. Winston Churchill. A fleet sent to Lamlash. The Military Plan of Campaign. Sir Arthur Paget's interview with General Officers in Dublin. Second interview with Cavalry and Artillery Officers at the Curragh. Resignations of officers. Brigadier-General Gough, Lieut.-Colonels Parker and MacEwen ordered to London. General Gough telegraphs to Lord Roberts. Interview with the Adjutant General at the War Office. Intervention of Lord Roberts. His audience by the King. General Gough's interviews with Sir John French and Colonel Seely at the War Office. Complete surrender of the Government. Reinstatement of Brig.-General Gough and the Commanding Officers. Memorandum of assurance given to General Gough.

Appendix to Chapter XXXI.—Speech of Lord Roberts in the House of Lords. Some accounts of the Commander-in-Chief's speech to the officers at the Curragh on March 21st.

In April a strike of the Coalminers in Lancashire took place which was regarded by the Government with some apprehension and the 16th were ordered to Wigan. Sixteen officers and 273 N.C.O.'s and men were sent by train from Norwich under the command of Lieut.-Colonel MacEwen and four officers and 133 N.C.O.'s and men from Weedon. There was, however, no disturbance of any consequence, and on the 18th the Regiment returned to quarters.

In August the Regiment was detailed to take part in the manœuvres and on the 8th A and C Squadrons left Norwich by march route for Salisbury Plain, arriving at their destination on the 17th, having camped at Diss, Ipswich, Colchester, Warley, Woolwich, Aldershot, Hounslow and Overton. D Squadron, five officers and 132 N.C.O.'s and men, came in the same day from Weedon, having billeted en route at Buckingham, Oxford, and Newbury. From the 18th August to the 2nd September the Regiment was engaged in Brigade Training. On the 2nd September the Division moved towards the manœuvre area via Newbury, Henley, Berkhampstead, Hitchin, to Linton. The manœuvre area covered Norfolk, Suffolk, and Cambridge, and the operations ceased on the 20th September, when the Squadrons returned to their respective quarters. On the 16th Captain Lord Holmpatrick was appointed Adjutant from 17th August, 1912.

At the conclusion of the manœuvres the Regiment was ordered to Ireland, and on October 1st proceeded by four trains from Norwich and one from Weedon to Holyhead for embarkation. The troops left Holyhead the same night on two cargo ships, strength 23 officers, 670 N.C.O.'s and men, 470 horses, under command of Major Leny, and after disembarking at Dublin arrived at the Curragh on the evening of October 2nd.

The 16th were posted to the 3rd Cavalry Brigade, the other regiments of this being the 4th Hussars and the 5th Lancers, the last being quartered at Dublin. The Brigade was commanded by Brigadier-General Hubert de la P. Gough, formerly Lieut.-Colonel commanding the regiment.

There were no events of importance during 1913 outside the usual routine duties. Several drafts were sent to the 17th Lancers in India, amounting in all to eight sergeants and 299 other ranks.

In March, 1914, however, the Sixteenth became involved in one of the most remarkable transactions in their whole history.

1914   In 1914 Mr. Asquith found that he was entirely dependent in the House of Commons on the votes of the Irish Home Rule members for his majority, as the Conservatives and Liberals in the House were about equal in number. He therefore found it expedient to bring in a Bill conferring Home Rule on Ireland. The people of the Northern Counties, being loyal, law-abiding and prosperous, naturally objected very strongly to being handed over to the tender mercies of a Dublin Parliament where they would be in a permanent minority. The great majority of the population of Ulster did not wish to sever their political connection with Great Britain, and finding their peaceful protests ignored by the Government, determined, if driven to it, to resist the application of the provisions of the Home Rule Bill by force.

Large quantities of arms therefore were imported by the Volunteer Associations in Ulster, and a formidable force was raised, armed, drilled, and organised, the headquarters of the movement being at Belfast. The Home Rule party was equally active in Southern Ireland, where, under the name of "Hibernians," Volunteer Associations were also armed and drilled with the avowed intention of being used against Ulster if that province resisted the imposition of Home Rule for a United Ireland.

Early in 1914 the Government began to realise the difficulties of the situation. The original Bill had been so far modified that a clause had been inserted excluding Ulster from its provisions for six years from the passing of the Act. Further amendments were promised, but Mr. Asquith refused to divulge what these were before the second reading was passed in the Commons. Meanwhile the Government received repeated warning that any attempt to coerce Ulster by the use of the Army would probably be met by a refusal of the troops to slaughter loyal Ulstermen for the benefit of disloyal Dublin.

With the Liberal Government now it was neck or nothing. To drop, or even to alter, the Bill by excluding Ulster would certainly result in their immediate expulsion from office by the votes of the Home Rulers, and this was to them a calamity of vastly more weight than the danger of a possible or even probable Civil War in Ulster.

On the 16th March the First Lord of the Admiralty, Mr. Winston Churchill, delivered himself at Bradford of a very provocative speech.* He said in it that unless Ulster agreed to accept the Home Rule Bill, coupled with the exclusion of the province from its provisions for six years, troops would be used to compel acceptance, and further, "that bloodshed no doubt is lamentable, but there are worse things than bloodshed, even on an extensive scale." Occupying as he did a comparatively independent position with regard to the Fleet, he proceeded to take steps at once to insure that "bloodshed" if the opportunity was afforded. On the 19th he ordered the 3rd Battle Squadron, less the "Britannia," to proceed at once to Lamlash, and two destroyers to Carrick-

---

* It was this speech that caused Mr. Churchill to be considered the instigator of the whole trouble.

fergus, and the next day two divisions of destroyers were ordered also to proceed to Lamlash and to report there to the Vice-Admiral commanding. On the same day the leaders of the Volunteer movement were threatened with arrest if they did not cease their activities.

A plan of campaign against Ulster was prepared by the Government. The 3rd Cavalry Brigade was to be sent from Dublin and the Curragh, and the infantry of the 5th Infantry Division from the same places was to follow. This force was to occupy the bridges and general line of the Boyne River. The 6th Division was to be moved from the South of Ireland to Dublin and the Curragh. The Army in Ireland was to be reinforced by 10,000 men from England, and Belfast was to be blockaded by the Fleet. Orders were given for reinforcing the garrisons at various depôts of arms, especially at Carrickfergus, Omagh, and Dundalk; finally General Macready was detailed to take over the military command at Belfast, and the Chief Constable there was ordered to report to him.

The ostensible reason for these warlike preparations was the necessity of guarding the arms and stores from possible attacks by the Hibernians and Ulster Volunteers, but these pretended fears were entirely without justification. The Volunteers had a good supply both of arms and ammunition which was being daily augmented by fresh importations, and moreover their leaders were doing all they could to restrain their followers from any overt act of violence, while the Hibernians were naturally unwilling to do anything to embarrass the Government.

But there was a further and much more sinister design behind these movements. There was a wish to provoke the Volunteers to some act of violence that would justify the Government in using the Army to crush once for all the resistance of Ulster to the Home Rule Bill.

The Commander-in-Chief in Ireland, who, not being aware of these secret intentions, was really anxious to avoid an outbreak, was much disquieted by the provocative measures which were forced upon him, and particularly by the appointment of General Macready, who was by no means a " persona grata " in Ulster, and at his request it was not publicly disclosed. As General Macready was fortunately detained for the time in London, he sent Major-General Friend, one of his own staff, to Belfast in his place, who reported that everything was quiet.

The Commander-in-Chief also was very doubtful as to the possible attitude of the Army in the event of active operations being undertaken in Ulster. A memorandum had been already issued defining the duties and responsibilities of soldiers in times of Civil Commotion, which indeed fully justified the ensuing action of the officers, and by the end of March he was so convinced that these provocations would infallibly result in war that in his communications with the officers which followed he several times asserted that " by Saturday (March 28th) the whole country would be in a blaze."

By this time the Government itself was evidently beginning to have misgivings as to the attitude of the Army towards the projected Civil War in Ulster, and in the third week of March Sir A. Paget was instructed by the War Office to ascertain exactly what the officers would do if such an event came about. He therefore ordered the following officers to meet him in Dublin on Friday, March 20th :—

    Lieut.-General Fergusson, Commanding 5th Division.
    Brigadier-General Rolt, Commanding Infantry Brigade, 5th Division.
        ,,   Cuthbert, ,,   ,,   ,,   ,,
        ,,   Gough, Commanding 3rd Cavalry Brigade.

1914

Major-General Friend, i/c Administration H.Q. Staff.
,,   Walker, C.G.S., H.Q. Staff.
Colonel Hill, Commanding Northern Depôts.
General Poultney, 6th Division (not present).

NOTE.—The 5th Division was quartered partly in Dublin, partly at the Curragh, where the Headquarters were. The 3rd Cavalry Brigade consisted of the 16th Lancers and 4th Hussars, with Headquarters at the Curragh, and the 5th Lancers at Dublin.

The 16th were commanded by Lieut.-Colonel MacEwen, the 5th Lancers by Lieut.-Colonel Parker, and the 4th Hussars by Lieut.-Colonel Hogg.

At this interview the Commander-in-Chief made the following remarkable and unprecedented statements to the assembled officers :—

That active operations were to be begun against Ulster. That he had the following instructions from the War Office and the Chief of the Staff to convey to the officers, namely—that officers domiciled in Ulster would be " allowed to disappear " and would be reinstated without detriment at the end of the operations in Ireland, but they must give their word of honour not to fight for Ulster. Officers not prepared to engage in active operations against Ulster from conscientious or other scruples were to send in their resignations at once and would be dismissed the Army. Resignations to be sent in that evening. All the Brigadiers were ordered to go down and deliver this message to the units of their Brigades and to collect and forward the results.

Some conversation followed in the course of which the G.O.C. said that the Fleet was in Belfast harbour, and in reply to a question by Brigadier-General Gough he insisted that the clause about officers domiciled in Ulster was the only concession that would be granted. The General concluded by saying that he was going to meet General Poultney* and the other General Officers of the 6th Division at 2 p.m., when he would explain his plans, and that any officers who were not prepared to carry out his orders were not to attend this meeting.

Generals Fergusson, Rolt, and Gough then left. There was some conversation between them as to what course each would pursue. Finally General Fergusson said that he should obey any orders which he might receive to act against Ulster, Rolt said nothing, and Gough said he should refuse to go.

General Gough then went to the Mess of the 5th Lancers. A number of the officers were collected, including Colonel Parker, to whom the situation was explained. General Gough then returned to the Curragh and issued an order for all the officers of the Cavalry Brigade to attend at the Mess of the 16th Lancers at 3.30 p.m.

When the officers were assembled General Gough made a brief statement of what the Commander-in-Chief of Ireland had said at the Dublin meeting.† He said that he himself intended to resign his commission, but that he declined to give any advice to anyone. The officers must decide each for himself according to the dictates of his own conscience. He then dismissed the officers to their own quarters with a request that their decision might be sent in to the Brigade Office before 5.30 p.m.

In the evening General Gough sent the following report to Dublin :—

" With reference to the communication from the War Office conveyed to me verbally by the Commander-in-Chief this morning, I have the honour to report the result of my interviews with the officers of my Brigade.

" The officers are of unanimous opinion that further information is essential

---

* G.O.C. 6th Division.
† General Gough had said exactly the same things to the officers of the 5th Lancers.

before they are called upon at such short notice to take decisions so vitally affecting their whole future, and especially that a clear definition should be given of the terms ' duty as ordered,' and ' active operations ' in Ulster.

"If such duty consists of the maintenance of order and the preservation of property, all the officers in this Brigade, including myself, would be prepared to carry out that duty, but if the duty involves the initiation of active operations against Ulster, the following numbers of officers by regiments would respectfully and under protest prefer to be dismissed :—

"Brigade Staff, 2 officers.

"4th Hussars, 17 out of 19 doing duty.

"5th Lancers, 17 out of 20 doing duty.

"16th Lancers, 16 out of 16 doing duty.

"3rd Brigade R.H.A., 6 out of 13 doing duty, ' including R.M.'

"3rd Signal Troop R.E., 1 out of 1 doing duty.

"In addition the following are domiciled in Ulster and claim protection as such :—

"4th Hussars, 2 officers.

"5th Lancers, 1 officer.

"3rd Brigade R.H.A., 2 officers."

The number of resignations apparently somewhat discomforted the Commander-in-Chief for he went to the Curragh himself the next morning, Saturday, March 21st.

All the officers of the Cavalry Brigade then at the Curragh were ordered to meet the Commander-in-Chief at the Divisional Headquarters at 11 a.m. About 35 officers presented themselves, including Brigadier-General Gough, Major Kearsley (Brigade Major), Colonel Breeks, commanding the R.H.A. Brigade, Colonel MacEwen, 16th Lancers, and Colonel Hogg, 4th Hussars.

The Commander-in-Chief* then made a long rambling sort of speech. He asked the officers to reconsider their decisions, and stated, in flat contradiction to what he had said to the officers at the Dublin meeting on the previous day, that the resignations would not be accepted and that officers who declined to go against Ulster would be tried by Court-martial.

The General then made a series of disconnected statements to the effect that the troops were being sent into Ulster solely to preserve order, that the talked-of fighting would be merely a sham, that the Cavalry would not be used if any fighting did take place, and finally emphatically declared that all this was done by the direct order of the King, and concluded his speech by asking the officers if they thought he would obey the orders of mere politicians—a remarkable observation which led his hearers to conclude that he was himself not particularly pleased at the part which he was obliged to play. Colonel Breeks was the only officer who made any direct reply to the speech and his remarks were anything but encouraging. General Gough contented himself with saying that he did not see how the resignations could be refused as these had been demanded by the Commander-in-Chief's own order. As no one else said anything the officers were ordered to talk the matter over among themselves and to convey their final decisions to General Fergusson, G.O.C. of the 5th Division, in the course of the day. The Commander-in-Chief then left the room.

The officers then considered the speech, which was generally thought to be unsatisfactory both from the point of view of assurances that no organised

---

* As no notes were made on the spot it is not easy to be certain of the C.-in-C.'s exact words. Two accounts by separate officers are given in the Appendix. They are in substantial agreement.

1914 attack was intended on Ulster. Nevertheless some of the officers of the Artillery and the 4th Hussars, including Colonel Hogg, thought it possible that some pacific arrangement might still be arrived at if any guarantee could be given as to the strictly defensive nature of the projected operations. The 16th officers, however, and the others did not think that this was possible and decided not to withdraw their resignations.

General Gough, with Colonels Breeks, MacEwen and Hogg, then went to see General Fergusson.

The General was sympathetic, but insisted that the officers must give a definite decision at once. He also reiterated the statement* previously made by the Commander-in-Chief that "every movement projected had been expressly sanctioned by the King." Finally the commanding officers agreed to go out and consult their officers again. This they did, with the following result:—

General Gough and the officers of the 16th and 5th Lancers refused to withdraw their resignations. Colonel Hogg and some of the officers of the 4th Hussars and the R.H.A. officers expressed their readiness to withdraw provided that General Gough was satisfied with the validity of the guarantee that the troops were only to be used for the preservation of law and order and were not to initiate Civil War in Ulster. This of course was not so, but all the officers offered to withdraw their resignations if the War Office endorsed the guarantee in writing. Brigadier-General Gough and the commanding officers, except Colonel Hogg, were then ordered to go to London and to report themselves personally at the War Office on the next day.

Brigadier-General Gough then sent a telegram to Lord Roberts. This was as follows:—

"All officers Ireland offered alternative instant dismissal or undertaking active operations against Ulster. I accepted instant dismissal. Practically all officers Cavalry Brigade have done the same, and total about 100 officers in Dublin and Curragh. What is situation in England. What do you advise?"

Brigadier-General Gough arrived in London early on the morning of the 22nd. There he received private information that the War Office people intended to take up the line that there had been a misunderstanding; that the alternatives were not intended to be put; and that he and the other C.O.'s were to be reinstated.

On arriving at the War Office the General found Colonels MacEwen and Parker there. After some conversation it was agreed to maintain their position and to refuse to withdraw their resignations unless they received a positive assurance that they should not be again placed in such a situation or ordered to take part in a war against Ulster.

General Gough was then taken alone into the Adjutant-General's room, where he was received by Sir Spencer Ewart, who was accompanied by General Macready, who had not yet gone to Belfast. He was then asked to give an account of the proceedings at Dublin and the Curragh. After hearing his statement General Ewart asked if he thought an officer had any right to question when he should go, or should not go, in support of the Civil Power to maintain law and order. To this question the General replied, "None whatever," adding that if Sir A. Paget had simply ordered the Brigade to go to Belfast they would all have gone without demur, not knowing why they should be wanted there. The interview then closed.

---

* The wording of this statement is somewhat ambiguous. It might be construed to mean only that the King had sanctioned the projected military operations, but the officers certainly understood that it applied also to the alternative presented to them by the C.-in-C. and the subsequent threats.

Colonels MacEwen and Parker then came in and gave their evidence, as also did Colonel Hill.

1914

All the officers were ordered to remain in London and required to arrange to be within reach of a telephone. Later in the afternoon the officers received an order to report themselves at the War Office at 11 a.m. the next day, the 23rd.

Now, when Lord Roberts received General Gough's telegram sent on the 21st he perceived at once that the dangerous situation of which he had previously warned the Prime Minister and Sir J. French had really arisen. He lost no time in endeavouring to deal with it, but wrote at once to Lord Stamfordham asking for an immediate audience with the King. He had no previous communication with General Gough, but supposed that he was appealed to because he was the Senior Officer in the Army, and because, from his speeches in the House of Lords, he appeared to be in sympathy with the officers.

His Majesty was pleased to accord the audience asked for, and Lord Roberts went at once to Buckingham Palace, where he was received by the King.

When the King learned the nature of Lord Roberts' business Colonel Seely was sent for, it being the constitutional usage that the Sovereign discusses political questions only in the presence of a Minister.

At the conclusion of the audience Lord Roberts went to the War Office, where he had an interview with Colonel Seely on his return from the Palace. Some conversation and explanations ensued, and finally Lord Roberts left an open letter with Colonel Seely for Brigadier-General Gough.

What passed between the various members of the Government during the afternoon and night of the 22nd will probably never be divulged, but at any rate the 23rd found the War Office in a very chastened frame of mind.

General Gough went, as directed, to the War Office at 11 a.m. and found Colonels Parker and MacEwen already there. The three officers had some conversation and agreed among themselves to refuse any offer of reinstatement unless they received a written statement that they would not be called upon to undertake operations against Ulster. General Gough was then shown alone into Sir John French's room. Sir Spencer Ewart, the Adjutant General, was present at the interview.

Sir J. French began by saying that there had been a great misunderstanding. To this General Gough replied that there had been none on his part. Sir J. French, continuing, said that as there had been a misunderstanding, all the officers were to return to their commands as if nothing had happened.

Here was indeed a change from the threats of the previous day! The lion roaring Court-martials and dismissals had become the gentle dove, softly cooing reconciliation and kiss and be friends all round.

General Gough easily perceived that this foreshadowed a complete surrender on the part of the Government, and he was encouraged to persevere in his previous determination to have this surrender in writing. He replied that he was quite willing to return to his command, but that such a grave crisis had arisen that neither he nor the other officers could return unless they received a definite assurance that they should not be asked again to enforce the present Home Rule Bill on Ulster.

Sir J. French then said that he could assure them that no such thing was intended and that the Prime Minister had himself given a similar assurance in the House of Commons.

A long conversation then followed in the course of which Sir John French said that his word ought to be sufficient, suggested "wiping everything off the slate" and going back to Thursday evening. But General Gough adhered firmly to his condition, saying that Sir J. French's word was of course good

1914 enough for him, but that he must have something in writing to show to the officers, and asked what was the objection to putting the assurance in writing that the Government had given verbally. Finally Sir J. French said it was impossible and that the Government would not give it, to which General Gough replied equally firmly that he was very sorry but that he could not return without it.

After a long silence Sir J. French said to Sir S. Ewart, "Well, we can't do anything more for him. You will bear me out that I have done my best for him. He will never know how much I have done for him. Very well, there is nothing for it but to take him before the Secretary of State."

They then all left the room and proceeded to that of the Secretary of State, where they found Colonel Seely with Sir A. Paget.

Colonel Seely received them with considerable "hauteur." He requested all the four officers to seat themselves at his table, taking the chair at the head of it himself. He then delivered a discourse explanatory of the relation of the Military to the Civil Power which seemed to be mostly a repetition of the Manual of Military Law, and then went on to explain that the action taken in Ireland had merely been aimed at the security of stores, etc., and that the Government had reason to fear that grave disorders might break out at any moment in the West and South. Finally he said that the questions put by the Commander-in-Chief Ireland arose out of a misunderstanding, that the putting of hypothetical questions to soldiers was illegal, and that all the officers concerned were to return to their commands.

General Gough at once replied that he would gladly return, but that both he and the two Colonels concerned felt that they could not again run the risk of finding themselves in the very grave situation that had been forced upon them, and therefore that they must have an assurance that they should not be asked to enforce the present Home Rule Bill on Ulster.

To this Colonel Seely replied that the Prime Minister had made a statement already that it was not and never had been the intention of the Government to coerce Ulster, and that the assurance already given by the Army Council ought to be sufficient, but General Gough remained immovable and insisted on having the "assurance" in writing before he consented to return to his command.

This Colonel Seely said was impossible—no Government would allow itself to be dictated to.

A complete deadlock now seemed to have been reached when Sir J. French intervened to ease the situation by saying that General Gough had perhaps not made it clear that he felt that he would not be able to reassure his officers and regain their confidence unless he could show them the authority of the Army Council, feeling that his own assurance would not be sufficient now that so much feeling had been aroused.

This extremely diplomatic suggestion evidently seemed to present a way of escape to Colonel Seely, and General Gough hastened to say that this was precisely what did actuate him in making his request for a written assurance. Colonel Seely then said at last, "Oh, I see," and in turning to Sir A. Paget, "I think it only a reasonable request." To this Sir A. Paget assented. He then went on to say that the Adjutant General would draw up a draft containing the assurance asked for, and that General Gough and the two Colonels would then return to their commands with the full concurrence of the Commander-in-Chief in Ireland.

The conference then broke up and General Gough went back to the waiting room to talk matters over with Colonels Parker and MacEwen.

The three officers returned to the War Office at 4 p.m., and half an hour afterwards General Gough was shown into Sir John French's room. Sir John, who was attended by Sir S. Ewart, handed him the memorandum, which was initialed by the Secretary of State, himself, and the Adjutant General. After reading the document General Gough asked his permission to show it to Colonels Parker and MacEwen, and for a short time to consider it. Leave to do this having been given (very reluctantly and after much hesitation), the General left the room and rejoined the Colonels in the waiting room.

The memorandum was addressed to Brigadier-General Gough, and was as follows :—

" 1. You are authorised by the Army Council to inform the officers of the 3rd Cavalry Brigade that the Army Council are satisfied that the incident which has arisen in regard to their resignations has been due to a misunderstanding.

" 2. It is the duty of all soldiers to obey lawful commands given to them through the proper channel by the Army Council, either for the protection of public property and the support of the Civil Power in the event of disturbances, or for the protection of the lives and property of the inhabitants.

" 3. This is the only point it was intended to be put to the officers in the questions of the G.O.C., and the Army Council have been glad to learn from you that there never has been, and never will be, in the Brigade any question of disobeying such lawful orders.

" 4. H.M.'s Government must retain their right to use all the forces of the Crown, in Ireland or elsewhere, to maintain law and order and to support the civil power in the ordinary execution of its duty.

" 5. But they have no intention whatever of taking advantage of this right to crush political opposition to the policy or principles of the Home Rule Bill.

" 23rd March, 1914."

This memorandum was initialed by the Secretary of State for War, Sir John French, and Sir S. Ewart.

With paragraphs 2, 3 and 4 everyone concerned had always been in perfect agreement, and the last seemed to concede in a few words everything that the officers had been contending for. Nevertheless the officers were not completely satisfied with the wording of the phrase " crush political opposition," which seemed somewhat ambiguous, and knowing by experience the facility, acquired by long practice, with which the War Office could wriggle out of its engagements, and the importance of having their attitude clearly defined, a statement was made out in writing which described exactly what the officers understood to be the meaning of paragraph No. 5 of the memorandum, and with this General Gough, accompanied this time by the two Colonels, returned to Sir John French.

Sir John read the paper carefully and after some consideration wrote at the foot of it, " That is how I read it," and initialed it " J.F."

The officers then thanked Sir J. French and Sir S. Ewart for their kindness and assistance and withdrew.

The paper initialed by Sir John ran as follows :—

" We understand the reading of the last paragraph to be that the troops under our command will not be called upon to enforce the present Home Rule Bill on Ulster, and that we can so assure our officers."

Thus the officers by their steadfast determination, supported as they had been throughout by the patriotic assistance of Lord Roberts, effectually gained the point for which they had contended and fully vindicated their conduct under the most difficult circumstances. Incidentally they averted the danger of

1914 Civil War in Ulster, for all the projected moves of the troops were cancelled, and orders were given countermanding the sending of the Fleet to Lamlash. Moreover, the Home Rule Bill was practically killed, for though the second reading was carried by a majority of 77 in the House of Commons on May 25th, nothing more was ever heard of that ill-omened measure.

The position of the officers all through the controversy had indeed been unimpeachable. They had disobeyed no order, for no order had, in fact, been given, except the order, afterwards admitted by the Secretary for War himself to be illegal, to state what their conduct would be on a purely hypothetical occasion. For answering this in accordance with what they conceived to be the dictates of their honour and their conscience they were accused of mutiny and threatened with Court-martials and dismissal, though they had committed no offence against either Civil or Military Law.

The defence of the officers is admirably set out in the speech made by Lord Roberts in the House of Lords on March 30th, which is given in full in the Appendix to this Chapter.

There were some heated debates in Parliament about the transaction in the course of which the Government tried to shuffle out of their responsibility by reiterating the excuse that what the Commander-in-Chief Ireland had said to the officers was not in accordance with his instructions. Attempts were made, but without success, to force a disclosure of what these instructions really were, but nothing was ever discovered as to even how and when they were given by the Government to its unhappy tool and scapegoat.

On the 26th Mr. Asquith repudiated the "assurance" memorandum given to General Gough altogether, on the ground that it had not been shown to the Cabinet, an assertion flatly contradicted by Lord Morley. This final act of duplicity was too much for even a War Office conscience, and Colonel Seely, Sir John French, and Sir Spencer Ewart all resigned. Some attempts were made to induce Colonel Seely to withdraw his resignation, but he persisted in it, and finally, as Mr. Asquith could not find anyone who would consent to fill the office of Secretary for War under these invidious circumstances, he was forced to undertake it himself, and thus this sordid conspiracy came to an ignominious end. The officers and Lord Roberts were subjected to the most venomous vituperation by the supporters of the Government both in Parliament and the Press, being accused of mutiny, insubordination, and disloyalty to the King. Of course, these people could not understand that the officers, not being politicians, had not bartered away their honour and consciences in return for their pay, but anyone would have thought that even the bitterest partizan would have found something to admire in gentlemen who were ready to resign their profession and livelihood rather than do an act which they thought to be wrong.

APPENDIX TO CHAPTER XXXI.

Ulster and the Army.

Speech of Lord Roberts.

During the week 23rd-30th March, little else than Ulster, the Government, and the Army were talked or written about, and on Monday, 30th, Lord Roberts made the following speech in the House of Lords:—

"My Lords,—We are discussing a subject of the very gravest importance— 1914 graver indeed as regards potential disaster to the nation than anything that has occurred for generations. Is is then with a very real sense of the seriousness of the situation that I rise to make an appeal to your Lordships, and through you to the people of this country—regardless of class or political creed—to make an end of all these idle, but dangerous and mischievous assertions, that the Army is implicated in any political conspiracy, and that it is allowing itself to be used as the tool of one Party in the State. These baseless assertions are being freely made in the Press and in speeches by politicians, and it is sought to substantiate them by equally wild and slanderous charges of disobedience of orders and disregard of discipline.

"My Lords, there is not the smallest justification of any sort, kind, or description, for a single one of these indictments of the Army. Where they are not inspired by a reckless desire to secure a Party score, or by a malicious disregard of truth, they have their origin in complete ignorance of the Army —its sentiments, feelings, and conditions of life.

"I can fairly claim to have some knowledge of these things, and I can tell you, my Lords, with all the conviction produced by 62 years of service in the Army—and I am sure that those of your Lordships who have had the honour of serving His Majesty will bear me out in this—that the soldier does not trouble himself about Party politics; indeed he dislikes politics, his indifference is even tinged with contempt for the unfortunate people engaged in political warfare, as men who are perforce bereft of individuality.

"That, believe me, My Lords, is the general feeling in the Army, and if you add to that the sense of 'esprit de corps' and almost inordinate pride in the Army, is it ever conceivable that soldiers would consent to engage in a political plot, or to assist one Party to secure a political advantage over its opponents? The thing is an absurdity. The man is not living who could seduce the Army to play so despicable a part. And, My Lords, what are those charges of indiscipline and disobedience of orders?

"Your Lordships are fully aware of the facts of the deplorable situation produced by the ultimatum which was suddenly hurled at the troops in Ireland the week before last. I defy anybody to give me a solitary instance of indiscipline or disobedience.

"At the instigation of the Government—or so we must presume until it has been proved to be otherwise—the officers were asked to make their choice between two terrible alternatives. This option was unsought by them. It was deliberately given to them by the Government, acting through General Sir Arthur Paget as its mouthpiece, and they were given but the scantiest time in which to consider the momentous choice that they were commanded to make.

"Now, My Lords, the all-important fact of what I have said—and it cannot be stated too often—is that in exercising the option thus forced upon them, there was obviously no semblance of disobedience of orders. But, My Lords, what of the choice that was put before these officers? Dismiss from your minds the ridiculous fallacy that officers of the Army are a wealthy and privileged class, and consider the nature of the option unexpectedly placed before them. They were to be ready to operate against the men of Ulster—loyal subjects of the King, flying the Union Jack—or to send in their resignations and be dismissed from the Army with consequent loss of their careers and their pensions. This latter meant to all the break-up of a home, the sundering of ties which had bound them for years—the ties of comradeship, love of regiment, and pride in the Army. It meant to all the loss of occupation and the waste of many years of strenuous endeavour—it meant to many, and, My

Lords, I would draw your particular attention to this—the almost total loss of the means of livelihood—and yet, My Lords, the finger of scorn is pointed at the officers who chose this latter alternative. They are made the subjects of false charges, are accused of wishing to dictate to the Government, and are branded as conspirators.

"My Lords, it is high time for the sake of the nation—no less than for the sake of the Army—that these perversions of the truth should cease, and that the Army should be allowed to disappear from the political arena into which it has been thrust—much against its own wish or expectation.

"I know what I am speaking about when I tell your Lordships that the Army, as a whole, had so little considered the political situation, and the atmosphere in which it has its being is so devoid of political elements, that it has never conceived the possibility of finding itself entangled in this manner.

"My Lords, it has, indeed, often surprised me to mark the air of personal detachment with which the Army has regarded this great political struggle; but so it has been, and I say no more than the truth when I state that the Government's ultimatum was like the springing of a mine to the Army.

"My Lords, I need say little more. My desire has been to nail to the counter once and for all the lies that are being told as to officers having disobeyed orders. If any further justification of their action were needed, surely it is to be found in the unexampled and unprecedented course taken by the Government in offering alternatives to the officers. For what, My Lords, does this portend? What is the irresistible implication arising from this course? Why this departure from custom? Surely the only reason and true reason is that the Government realised that they were going to make demands on the Army which they had no right to make, and which the constituted authorities, as revealed in the Army Act and the King's Regulations, gave them no excuse for making. These authoritative works lay down in the most detailed manner what the duties of the military forces are. They are very precise as to the manner in which those duties are to be performed and the penalties for non-performance, they cover the whole field of the possible and even improbable uses to which the Army can be put. What duties then did the Government intend asking of the Army, that led to this novel step? What was contemplated? Obviously something that was not legislated for in the Army Act or the King's Regulations.

"My Lords, I can discover only one answer to this question, and that is in Chapter I. of the Manual of Military Law, where the following words will be found : ' English Law never presupposes the possibility of Civil War and makes no express provision for such contingencies.' "

20th April, 1914.

R.

Speech of General Sir A. Paget.

Brigadier-General Gough's Account.

29th March, 1914.

Notes of interview between the Commander-in-Chief Ireland and Officers 3rd Cavalry Brigade (less 5th Lancers), at the Curragh Camp, on Saturday, 21st March, 1914.

Present : The Commander-in-Chief and A.D.C. (Lieut. Mackintosh), all officers 3rd Cavalry Brigade in barracks (about 35), including self, Major Kearsley, Colonel Breeks, Colonel MacEwen, Colonel Hogg, Major Gillson, Major Compbell, Major Howell, etc.

At 11 a.m. the Commander-in-Chief entered the room and sat at the only table, asking us to sit down, which we did as best we could on available accommodation.

He commenced by saying that he was our friend and asked us to trust him as our General and our Chief, and he would see that we were not placed in any positions which we might object to. He said he did not know why so many officers had resigned, because he had no intention of making war on Ulster, and to prove it he would take us into his confidence and divulge some of his plans. Only moves had been ordered that were necessary to protect stores, etc., and even these moves were precautions mainly directed against the "Hibernians." The depôt at Enniskillen was dangerously exposed to Hibernians; the guns in Dundalk—a low-lying town surrounded by hills peopled by Hibernians—were very exposed, and every soldier would know that guns must have the protection of other arms.

He had moved some troops by sea (he now thought it was a mistake)—merely to avoid their marching through the streets of Belfast. Why should we think military operations were intended against Ulster when everywhere his troops had been received with ovation in Ulster?

As far as the Cavalry were concerned they would not be required to take any serious part in any fighting—not more than one regiment would, anyhow, be employed—he would send one regiment south to maintain order there. A squadron or two might be employed on the lines of communication.

He then went on to say that it was necessary, of course, "to hold the line of the Boyne," while 25,000 troops were being brought over from England. He said he had expected that only a few religious fanatics would accept dismissal.

He said that if officers liked to "indulge in the luxury of sentiment they must pay for it, like other things." He said that no resignations would be accepted. He said that senior officers would be tried by C.M. He said that we must clearly understand that this was the direct order of "the Sovereign," and asked us "if we thought he would obey the orders of mere politicians."

Then, as no move took place, he said we must decide again and let General Fergusson know, and if there was no change, that I and the C.O.'s would "hand over command," cross to London that night and report to the War Office next morning.

Some of these statements were made in the presence only of myself, Major Kearsley, Colonels Breeks, MacEwen, and Hogg.

Colonel Breeks had some words with the Commander-in-Chief, but I have forgotten exactly what they were; they were mainly expressing the resentment felt at the grave decision demanded from officers, apparently for no cause, in a very short time, and with "practically a pistol at one's head."

I remarked that I did not see how resignations could be refused, as they had been demanded from officers by the Chief's own order. Also that though sentiment might be a luxury, men had died for it.

Account Given by the O.C., R.H.A.

"I received an order that the Commander-in-Chief Ireland wished to address all officers of the Cavalry Brigade at 11 a.m. The gist of his statement was as follows:—

"He earnestly desired us to reconsider our decisions. These resignations would not be accepted and that officers who declined to go against Ulster would be tried by General Court Martial. That though operations were about to be initiated against Ulster we were to trust to him that they would be of a purely defensive nature. That in proof of this he called our attention to the moves that had already taken place, which were merely necessary strengthening of exposed garrisons in view of the danger of their being rushed by either Party. That he was about to mass or was making arrangements to mass at least 20,000 men on the Boyne. He also stated that he could do without cavalry and was willing to give a guarantee to the Cavalry Brigade that they, except for scouting purposes, would not be used offensively, merely on the lines of communications. The Commander-in-Chief was most emphatic that any disobedience of these orders was disobeying the King. The officers were then dismissed, and General Gough and myself, Colonel Hogg and Colonel MacEwen, left with the Commander-in-Chief. He repeated some of his arguments and elucidated some points.

"I must confess that the speech was absolutely unconvincing and inconclusive.

"I then went out and consulted with the G.O.C. Cavalry Brigade and O.C. Regiments, telling my officers to meet me later in our Mess.

"Then some differences of opinion arose. Some R.H.A. officers and the O.C. 4th Hussars and some of his officers hoped that, in spite of the unconvincing nature of the Commander-in-Chief's speech, all officers might be able to take his statements as to the strictly defensive nature of the operations at their full value, but others thought that it was impossible for him to give such a guarantee. General Gough and the O.C.'s then went to see General Fergusson, who had been deputed to receive the decisions. We saw a copy of what we understood to be the War Office instructions, in which no mention was made of a choice of action being given to any officers except those domiciled in Ulster. General Fergusson again put the case against resignation before us very fairly strongly, but insisted that a definite decision had to be given at once to the choice put before us by all officers.

"He said that he had received from Sir A. Paget his word that every movement projected and made had been expressly sanctioned by the King, and that he thought this statement was the deciding point. But he had to acknowledge that the massing of 20,000 men on the borders of Ulster was certainly moral coercion to say the least. We agreed to go out and consult our officers again. General Gough and the officers of the 16th and 5th Lancers could not see their way to alter their decisions. Colonel Hogg and some officers of the 4th Hussars were undecided as to the validity of Sir A. Paget's guarantee. General Gough and the other officers commanding went over to the War Office, being superseded in their commands (except Colonel Hogg) and handing over to the next senior. I saw my officers and explained the situation up to date. My officers were of opinion (with the exception of those domiciled in Ulster) that they were prepared to withdraw their resignations on General Sir A. Paget's guarantee, if General Gough was satisfied with it, which he was not. Also they were quite prepared, as were all the cavalry, to withdraw their resignations, if the War Office endorsed the covering letter mentioned above in the sense of

giving a guarantee that the operations were of the purely legal nature of pre- 1914
serving law and order and property and not to initiate Civil War in Ulster.
We decided to wait in hopes that General Gough would be able to arrange
matters at the War Office.

"I deeply regret to say that now the matters are a good deal worse. We all, even myself and the officers who thought with me, think that the King's name has been used to deceive us."

CHAPTER XXXII.

28TH JUNE TO 6TH AUGUST, 1914.

THE WAR WITH GERMANY.

Causes of the War. Murder of Archduke Ferdinand. Temperate demands of Austria. Germany's secret preparations. Designs of Germany. Austrian Ultimatum to Servia. Diplomatic efforts to avoid war. Conference proposal abortive owing to refusal of Germany to participate. German High Sea Fleet recalled. Russian mobilisation. German terms for British neutrality. Their rejection. German troops enter Luxembourg. Belgian rejection of German terms and subsequent mobilisation. German Army invades Belgium on August 3rd. Sir Ed. Goschen demands explanation and is handed his passports on 4th. Siege of Liége begins on 5th. British Declaration of War as from 11 p.m. August 4th. Fleet and Army mobilised and Lord Kitchener appointed Secretary for War, August 5th. The Expeditionary Force sent to France. Composition of the Expeditionary Force.

Appendix I.—Staff and details of the Expeditionary Force.

Appendix II.—Comparative Tables of Organisation. British, French, Belgian, and German Armies.

Summary of Events, June 28th—August 6th, 1914.—June 28th, Murder of Archduke Ferdinand. July 23rd, Austrian Ultimatum to Servia. 25th, Servian reply received. 28th, Austria declares War on Servia. 29th, Russia begins to mobilise. August 1st, Germany declares War on Russia; France begins to mobilise. 2nd, Germans enter Luxembourg. 3rd, German invasion of Belgium; Great Britain orders mobilisation; State of War declared between France and Germany. 4th, British Declaration of War. 5th, Austria declares war on Russia; Siege of Liége begins. 6th, Three of Liége forts destroyed.

But Irish affairs were speedily relegated to oblivion by the advent of the war with Germany.

This had been meditated and prepared for by the Kaiser and his Government for years, with the full approval of the German nation. Indeed no attempt was made at concealment of their intentions, and "Der Tag," as they were pleased to term the day for the beginning of the great war, which was to end by the humiliation of Britain and the final removal of the last obstacle in the way of German World Power, was anticipated with eager exultation, though it suited the majority of the people here, and particularly our Government, to ignore what was impending.

1914   Some few there were, like Lord Roberts, who endeavoured to awaken their country to a sense of the danger, but they were roundly abused by Ministers and their subservient organs in the Press as alarmists and would-be disturbers of the peace, Lord Roberts himself being assailed with a coarseness and virulence both in Parliament and in the newspapers which supported the Government that one can only term simply disgraceful to those who indulged in it, many of whom ought to have known better.

There were two men, however, in the Ministry who did recognise the coming danger, Lord Haldane and Sir E. Grey. Both repeatedly warned their colleagues of it, and did their best to prepare for it, but unfortunately neither imparted their apprehensions to the public, and both were subsequently made the scapegoats for the Government apathy, though it was owing entirely to Lord Haldane's ability in previously, as Secretary for War, perfecting the organisation of an Expeditionary Force that the country was enabled to send out the "Contemptible" Army that really decided the issue of the war.

The Kaiser was driven into the fateful path he followed by both fear and ambition. His colossal self-sufficiency saw himself the master of the world, and he feared the growing power of the Slav States that threatened to block his road to the Empire of the East. The three great obstacles to the realisation of his hopes were Great Britain, France and Russia, particularly the first.

The Kaiser and his Government appear to have decided to begin the war in the spring of 1915, with a surprise attack on England. It was fortunate for us that this plan was changed. Though the German Fleet was certainly no match for ours once our whole naval strength was concentrated against it, it would probably have been able to cover the embarkation and transport of a German Army secretly assembled at Hamburg and the neighbouring ports for a time sufficient to enable it to effect a landing, even though its own destruction was in the end certain. If a force of even three Army Corps had been so landed it is easy to imagine the confusion that would have followed, and we might have been treated to something unpleasantly like a real "Battle of Dorking" before any sort of adequate mobilisation had been accomplished.

Though the war was probably inevitable, it was brought on prematurely by the same cause that has brought on all our wars for the last hundred years, namely, the belief that whatever happened Great Britain would not fight; for the Kaiser, like the Emperor Nicholas of Crimean fame, Arabi Pasha, Mr. Kruger, and other mistaken potentates, believed in the frothy protestations of pacificist politicians and their venal supporters in the Press, to their own eventual undoing.

The trouble in Ireland, and above all the difficulty with the Army over the coercion of Ulster, which the Government falsely called a mutiny of the troops, seemed further deterrents to intervention, and in truth it is very possible that if the German Government had avoided the fatal error of violating the neutrality of Belgium, which it had guaranteed itself in the famous "Scrap of Paper," Mr. Asquith's Cabinet would have kept Great Britain out of the war for the time being, for there were plenty of short-sighted and selfish people, both in the Ministry and outside it, who shamelessly advocated standing aside and profiting by the commercial exhaustion of the combatants.

These things being so, the Kaiser merely waited for the inevitable pretext which was unfortunately soon afforded by the shocking murder of the Archduke Ferdinand, the heir to the Austrian throne, and his morganatic wife, the Duchess of Hohenberg, by one Prinsep at Serajevo, the capital of Bosnia, on the 28th of June.

The Austrian Emperor, justly exasperated at the cruel death of his heir, at once charged the Servian Government with having engineered the assassination. The only real evidence against Servia was that the bombs used had certainly come from the Servian Arsenal, and indeed it is difficult to see what object there could have been for the murder so far as Servia was concerned. There were two parties in Austria. One led by Von Hoetzendorff and the Hungarian Tisza, advocated the suppression by force of the political aspiration of the Austrian Slavs, whereas the Archduke on the contrary desired to content them by giving them a measure of local autonomy.

Austria at first was reasonable enough, and after the first burst of indignation only demanded that Servia should take steps to guard against similar outrages for the future, and as nothing further was done apparently, for the next three weeks it looked as if the storm would blow over. The British Government was fully occupied with its troubles in Ireland. France was busy with the domestic difficulties resulting from the Caillaux scandal, and the President had escaped from the consequent turmoil by going on a tour in the North of France, while the Kaiser ostentatiously absented himself by embarking on his yacht for a cruise in the Baltic.

But this was only a blind. Germany's sinister influence was at work on the senile Austrian Emperor, and the interval was secretly and quietly occupied in completing the preparations for the impending war. The foreign Consuls and governors of Colonies were warned of what was coming, the already large garrisons along the French and Belgian Frontiers were quietly strengthened, and, short of actual mobilisation, the military machine was made ready for the stroke.

The plan of compaign was very simple. England would be neutral. Austria was to keep Russia at bay while Germany overwhelmed France by a surprise attack through Belgium, and when France was finally disposed of, then would come the turn of Great Britain; after Great Britain had been dealt with the united forces of Germany and Austria would be able to compel Russia to accept terms that would effectually check for the future the Slav aspirations in the near East.

The universal complacency was shattered in a moment on July 23rd by the sudden presentation of an Ultimatum to Servia, a definite reply being demanded within 48 hours, while the German Ambassadors notified the approval of Germany of the Austrian demand to all the Great Powers. By the advice of the Russian Government Servia notified the acceptance of all the terms of the ultimatum but two, which she wished to be reserved for further consideration, but no sort of reply would have averted her fate, for war had been decided on both by Austria and Germany, and at 10 p.m. the Austrian Ambassador at Belgrade asked for his passports.

Six days of feverish efforts to avert war by the diplomatists of Great Britain, France, Russia and Italy followed. Sir E. Grey proposed a conference of the Great Powers in London, but this was rendered nugatory by the flat refusal of Germany to take part in it, and on the 29th July Austria declared war on Servia and immediately after the declaration began the bombardment of Belgrade.

After this things moved with cyclonic celerity. Germany recalled her High Sea Fleet and Russia ordered the mobilisation of her Southern Commands. After a midnight Council of War held at Potsdam, at which the Kaiser presided, the Imperial Chancellor made a proposal to Sir E. Goschen, the British Ambassador, which was, in effect, that we should remain neutral in the impending war, Germany in return promising that if victorious, which seemed to be taken for granted, France should not be deprived of any European terri-

1914 tory, and that the neutrality of Belgium should be respected after the war, provided she had not sided with France.

The Russian Foreign Minister had already warned our Government that the one and only chance of averting war was to declare at once that we would stand by France and Russia, and on the 29th the French Government asked for a specific declaration of British intentions, but only obtained an evasive reply from our "Wait and See" Prime Minister, and a personal letter from the French President to King George met with no better fate. On the 30th the British Government rejected the proposal made to it on the 29th.

On the 31st the Kaiser declared a "State of War" in Germany and issued an ultimatum to Russia requiring instant demobilisation. On the 1st August Germany declared war on Russia. On the 2nd the German troops entered the Grand Duchy of Luxemburg, another country whose neutrality had been guaranteed, and some cavalry patrols crossed the French frontier. On the 3rd the German mobilisation began officially.

Meanwhile Belgium had rejected categorically the German demand for a free passage of her armies and had begun to mobilise, and on the 3rd the German advance guard entered Belgium and occupied Gemmich.

In the evening Sir E. Goschen asked for explanations and was promptly handed his passports and the next day, August 5th, the siege of Liége began.

This decisive action by the German Government settled the question of peace or war. The rising indignation of the country at the unprovoked invasion of Belgium and the impudent proposal that Great Britain should connive at the violation of a Treaty to which she was a party silenced the pacificist members of the Ministry. Mr. Asquith himself was no doubt not ill pleased at the chance of getting rid of the Irish mess which he knew the war would give him, and with the willing consent of the King and the full approval of Parliament, a "State of War" was declared, to begin at 11 p.m. on Tuesday, the 4th August, this being the exact time at which Sir E. Goschen received his passports.

Both the Admiralty and the War Office had already made full preparations for the outbreak of war. The Fleet, which had been practically mobilised for review and manœuvres, had been sent direct from the review to its stations in the North Sea, and the Army had been mobilised on the 3rd. On the 5th Lord Kitchener was appointed Secretary of State for War, and on the next day the first of the Expeditionary Force, the Aldershot Division, sailed for France. This Army, which consisted of two Army Corps and a Cavalry Division of five Brigades, was placed under the command of Field-Marshal Sir John French, and its composition was as follows :—

1st Corps.—1st and 2nd Divisions, 15th Hussars, Lieut.-General Sir D. Haig.

2nd Corps.—3rd and 5th Divisions, 19th Hussars, Lieut.-General Sir H. Smith-Dorrien.

To these a third Corps was afterwards added, under command of Major-General Pulteney, consisting at first of the 4th Division only. This was increased by the addition of the 19th Infantry Brigade of four Battalions, originally detailed for the line of communications, which did not join up until August 25th.

The Cavalry Division was commanded by Major-General Allenby. Its composition was as follows :—

1st Brigade.—Brigadier-General Briggs. 2nd Dragoon Guards, 5th Dragoon Guards, 11th Hussars.

2nd Brigade.—Brigadier-General de Lisle. 4th Dragoon Guards, 9th Lancers, 1914 18th Hussars.

3rd Brigade.—Brigadier-General H. Gough. 5th Lancers, 16th Lancers, 4th Hussars.

4th Brigade.—Brigadier-General Hon. C. Bingham. 3rd Hussars, 6th Dragoon Guards, Life Guards Composite Regiment.

Five Batteries Royal Horse Artillery.

In addition there was another Brigade not at first numbered under Brig.-General Sir Philip Chetwode, Bart., consisting of the Greys, 20th Hussars, and the 12th Lancers. This was afterwards the 5th Brigade.

In all about 75,000 men and 250 guns, exclusive of the 3rd Corps. The Expeditionary Force of all arms mustered 160,000 men, but more than half of these had not reached the battle line when the fighting at Mons began.

APPENDICES TO CHAPTER XXXII.

I.

Staff British Expeditionary Force.
August, 1914.

Commander-in-Chief, Field-Marshal Sir J. D. P. French, G.C.B., etc.
Chief of General Staff, Lieut.-General Sir A. J. Murray, K.C.B.
Major-General, Major-General H. H. Wilson, C.B.
Adjutant-General, Major-General Sir C. F. N. Macready, K.C.B.
Quarter-Master-General, Major-General Sir W. R. Robertson, K.C.V.O.

Cavalry Division.

G.O.C., Major-General E. H. H. Allenby, C.B.

1st Cavalry Brigade.

G.O.C., Brigadier-General C. J. Briggs, C.B.
2nd Dragoon Guards (Queen's Bays).
5th Dragoon Guards.
11th Hussars.

2nd Cavalry Brigade.

G.O.C., Brigadier-General H. de B. de Lisle, C.B.
4th Dragoon Guards.
9th Lancers.
18th Hussars.

3rd Cavalry Brigade.

G.O.C., Brigadier-General H. de la P. Gough, C.B.
4th Hussars.
5th Lancers.
16th Lancers.

4th Cavalry Brigade.

G.O.C., Brigadier-General Hon. C. E. Bingham, C.V.O.
Composite Regiment Household Cavalry.
6th Dragoon Guards (Carabineers).
3rd Hussars.

1914

5th Cavalry Brigade.
G.O.C., Brigadier-General Sir P. W. Chetwode, Bart.
2nd Dragoon Guards (Scots Greys).
12th Lancers.
20th Hussars.

I. Corps.
G.O.C., Lieut.-General Sir D. Haig, K.C.B.

1st Division.
G.O.C., Major-General S. H. Lomax.
Divisional Cavalry, A Squadron, 15th Hussars.

2nd Division.
G.O.C., Major-General C. C. Monro, C.B.
Divisional Cavalry, B Squadron, 15th Hussars.

II. Corps.
1st G.O.C., Lieut.-General Sir J. M. Grierson, K.C.B.
He died in the train between Rouen and Amiens, 17th August, 1914.
2nd G.O.C., General Sir H. L. Smith-Dorrien, G.C.B.
Took over command at Bavai, 21st August.

3rd Division.
G.O.C., Major-General Hubert I. W. Hamilton, C.V.O.
Divisional Cavalry, C Squadron, 15th Hussars.

5th Division.
G.O.C., Major-General Sir C. Ferguson, Bart., C.B.
Divisional Cavalry, A Squadron, 19th Hussars.

III. Corps.
Formed in France 31st August, 1914.
G.O.C., Major-General W. P. Pulteney, C.B.

4th Division.
Landed in France 22nd August.
G.O.C., Major-General T. d'O. Snow, C.B.
Divisional Cavalry, B Squadron, 19th Hussars.

6th Division.
Embarked for St. Nazaire 8th-9th September, 1914.
G.O.C., Major-General J. L. Keir, C.B.
Divisional Cavalry, C Squadron, 19th Hussars.

Line of Communication Troops.
2nd Royal Welsh Fusiliers.
1st Cameronians.
1st Middlesex.
2nd Argyl and Sutherland.

These four battalions were formed into the 19th Brigade at Valenciennes, 22nd August, 1914.

1st Devonshire Regiment.

Infantry Brigades.

1st Division.	1st, 2nd, 3rd Brigades	I. Corps.
2nd ,,	4th (Guards), 5th, 6th Brigades	I. Corps.
3rd ,,	7th, 8th, 9th Brigades	II. Corps.
5th ,,	13th, 14th, 15th Brigades	II. Corps.
4th ,,	10th, 11th, 12th Brigades	III. Corps.
6th ,,	16th, 17th, 18th Brigades	III. Corps.

APPENDIX II.

COMPARATIVE TABLES OF ORGANISATION.

BRITISH.

Airplane Squadron.—12 Airplanes.
Cavalry.—Division, 4 Brigades, 9,000 all ranks, 10,000 horses 20 13-pdr. guns, 24 machine guns.
,, Brigade, 3 Regiments.
,, Regiment, 3 Squadrons.
,, Squadron, 4 Troops.
Artillery.—(Horse)—Brigade, 2 Batteries.
,, Battery, six 13-pdr. Q.F. guns.
,, (Field)—Brigade, 3 Batteries.
,, Battery, six 18-pdr. Q.F. guns, or six 4.5 in. howitzers.
,, (Heavy)—Battery, four 60-pdr. guns.
Infantry.—Corps, two Divisions.
,, Division, 3 Brigades.
,, Brigade, 4 Battalions.
,, Battalion, 4 Companies.
,, Company, 4 Platoons.
Machine guns.—Two to each Regiment of Cavalry and Battalion.
Each Cavalry Brigade had 1 H.A. Battery.
Each Infantry Division fifty-four 18-pdr. guns, eighteen 4.5 in. howitzers, four 60-pdr., and one Squadron Cavalry.
A Division mustered 18,730 all ranks and 5,592 horses, 12,165 being Infantry, and in column of route occupied fifteen miles of road.

FRENCH.

Cavalry.—Division, 3 Brigades.
,, Brigade, 2 Regiments and a Machine Gun Section.
,, Regiment, 4 Squadrons, 32 officers, 651 men, 687 horses.
,, Squadron, 5 officers, 145 other ranks, 143 horses.
Artillery.—Regiment (Divisional), 3 Groupes.
,, Regiment (Corps), 4 Groupes.
,, Groupe, 3 Batteries.
,, Battery, 4 Guns.
Infantry.—Corps, two Divisions.
,, Division, 2 Brigades.
,, Brigade, 2 Regiments.
,, Regiment, 3 Battalions.
,, Battalion, 4 Companies, 22 officers, 1,030 other ranks, and machine gun section.
,, Company, 2 Pelotons.
,, Peloton, 2 Sections.
Each Cavalry Division had 1 H.A. Brigade attached of two 4-gun Batteries.
The strength of a Division of Infantry was 15,000 of all ranks, with 36 guns and 24 machine guns.
A Corps had, in addition to the two, or in the case of a Colonial Corps three, Divisions of Infantry, 1 Cavalry Regiment, 1 Field Artillery Regiment, 1 Groupe 155c.m. howitzers, and a Reserve Infantry Brigade of 4 Battalions.

BELGIAN.

The Belgian Field Army, as distinct from the garrisons of Antwerp, Liége and Namur, was organised in Divisions. Of these there were 6 Infantry and 1 Cavalry Division.

1914 Cavalry.—Division, 2 Brigades.
,, Brigade, 2 Regiments.
Artillery.—Battery, 4 guns.
Infantry.—Division, 3 Brigades.
,, Brigade, 2 Regiments.
,, Regiment, 3 Battalions.

Each Infantry Brigade had 6 machine guns and each Division 3 Batteries of Artillery and 1 Cavalry Regiment.

The strength of the Cavalry Division was 4,500 of all ranks, 3,400 horses, and 12 guns.

The strength of the Divisions of the Field Army varied from 25,000 to 32,000 of all ranks owing to many reserve men not having been able to join their own units, with 60 guns and 18 machine guns, and the entire Field Army may be put down as about 120,000 men at the most.

GERMAN.

Flying Detachment.—12 Airplanes.
Cavalry.—Division, 3 Brigades, 5,200 all ranks, 12 guns, 6 machine guns.
,, Brigade, 2 Regiments, 36 officers, 686 others, 765 horses.
,, Regiment, 4 Squadrons.
,, Squadron, 6 officers, 163 others, 178 horses.
Artillery.—Field—Brigade, 2 Regiments, 72 guns.
,, Regiment, 2 Abteilungen.
,, Abteilungen, 3 Batteries.
,, Battery, 6 guns.
,, Heavy (Foot)—Regiment, 2 Battalions.
,, Battalion, 4 Batteries.
Artillery.—Battery, 4 guns 5.9 in. (15 c.m.) howitzers.
,, Horse—Battery, 4 guns.
Infantry.—Corps, 2 Divisions.
,, Division, 2 Brigades.
,, Brigade, 2 Regiments.
,, Regiment, 3 Battalions, 7 machine guns.

A Cavalry Corps contained 2 or 3 Divisions.

A Cavalry Division, 1, 2 or 3 Jäger Battalions, each with 6 machine guns and a mounted machine gun battery, and an Abteilung of H.A., that is 3 four-gun batteries.

An Infantry Division, 1 Cavalry Regiment and a Field Artillery Regiment.

An Infantry Division had 17,500 men, 4,000 horses, 72 field guns, and 24 machine guns.

CHAPTER XXXIII.

14TH AUGUST TO 22ND AUGUST, 1914.

Embarkation of the Regiment at Dublin, 16th August. Disembarkation at Havre. 18th, Entrains for Jeumont, Detrains 19th August. March to Consolre. Positions of the British, French, and German Armies. The progress of the war in Belgium. The Kaiser's Order as to the "Contemptibles." Plans of General Joffre and Von Moltke. Mistakes of Von Kluck. The Regiment joins the 3rd Cavalry Brigade. Dispositions of Sir J. French.

Movements of the Cavalry Brigades. The first shot of the Campaign. 1914
Encounter at Casteau. The Greys at Peronnes. The 16th at Peronnes
in support. The march of the 16th to Elouges.

Summary of Events, August 7th to August 22nd, 1914.—August 7th, The
Germans enter town of Liége; French enter Mulhouse; Russians invade
East Prussia. 9th, First troops of British Expeditionary Force land in
France. 15th, Remaining forts of Liége destroyed. 19th, Retreat of
Belgian Army to Antwerp. 20th, Brussels taken by Germans; Siege of
Namur begins. 21st, Japan declares war on Germany; Retirement of
French in Alsace and Lorraine; Namur forts destroyed. 22nd, Defeat of
the French at Charleroi.

The Army, by arrangement with the French Government, was to have concentrated at Amiens, but owing to the rapid advance of the Germans the greater part of the troops were sent by train direct to the neighbourhood of Mons.

The 16th left the Curragh on August the 14th for Dublin, billeting at Castleknock en route, with the exception of D Squadron, the machine gun section and Headquarters, who started at 5 a.m. and did the march in one day. On the 15th the Regiment embarked on the Leyland S.S. Indian at the North Wall. The embarkation commenced at 11 a.m., but it was not completed until 4 a.m. the next day, Sunday the 16th, as the horses had to be slung on to the lower deck, which had no side ports. The ship sailed as soon as the embarkation was complete.

After a good voyage in fine weather the ship arrived at Havre at 4 a.m. on August 18th, and was berthed at 9 a.m., the delay being caused by there being no pilot obtainable. The disembarkation was accomplished without any difficulty. The Regiment remained on the pier till 10 p.m., when Headquarters and A Squadron were entrained and left for Jeumont. C Squadron and the Gun Section followed at midnight, and D Squadron at 4 a.m. the next day. At 8 p.m. on the 19th the first detachment reached Jeumont, the others at short intervals afterwards, and the whole Regiment bivouaced outside the town in a village square.

Jeumont was a station on the Maubeuge-Charleroi Railway, about 12 miles S.E. of Mons. On the 20th the Regiment marched to Consolre, about five miles further on the Charleroi road, where it went into billets.

By August 21st the general situation was developed sufficiently to permit the strength, positions, and objectives of the several Armies to be determined with some approach to accuracy.

Field-Marshal French's Army was distributed as follows :—

General Allenby was holding the line of the Condé-Mons Canal with four Brigades of Cavalry.

Two Brigades of Horse Artillery were in reserve at Harmignies, five miles S.E. of Mons.

Sir P. Chetwode's Cavalry Brigade was at Binche, with patrols out towards Soignies and Nivelles.

Sir D. Haig's 1st Corps was in cantonments N. of Maubeuge between Mons and Givey.

Sir H. Smith-Dorrien's 2nd Corps was stationed N.W. of Maubeuge and Sars la Bruyères.

The 19th Infantry Brigade was concentrating at Valenciennes.

The 4th Division was en route from England.

1914 The French Armies, which were not yet completely organised, were distributed as follows :—

The 1st and 2nd Armies were across the frontier in front of Luneville and Nancy, from near Sarrebourg to near Delme, 36 miles N.W. of Sarrebourg.

The 3rd and 4th Armies were close to the Belgian frontier, astride the river Chiers, from near Longwy to Sedan.

The Army of Lorraine observed Metz.

The Army of Alsace was at Mulhausen.

The 5th Army, under General Lanrezac, was on the immediate right of the British line. Its disposition was as follows :—

1st Corps on the Meuse, near Dinant, facing East.

10th and 13th Corps along the Sambre, facing North.

18th Corps echeloned to the left rear on the line Gozée-Thuin, 6 and 9 miles South-West of Charleroi.

Two Reserve Divisions N.E. of Maubeuge on the left of the 18th Corps.

To the north of the left flank of the British were 3 Divisions of Territorial troops under General D'Amade. Two of these Divisions were distributed as follows :—

Sixth and Seventh Divisions at Dunkirk, Cambrai, La Capelle, and Hirson.

Three Divisions of Cavalry, under General Sordet, were posted behind the left of the 5th Army, but they had been operating in Belgium and were in a very exhausted condition.

General Gallieni was organising a new Army in Paris, but its formation was not completed until the first week of September.

The German force was organised in six Armies under the supreme command of the Kaiser with General Von Moltke as Chief of his Staff, which were thus distributed :—

Von Marwitz with three Divisions of Cavalry covered the extreme right of the advance.

Von Kluck's 1st Army lay between Grammont and Lille, W. of Brussels, Enghien, Hal, Braine l'Allund, and was moving on Paris.

Von Bülow, with the 2nd Army, was North of the Meuse by Gembloux, and moving on Charleroi.

The Saxons, under Von Hausen, extended from Namur to Dinant.

The 3rd Army, under Duke Albrecht of Wurtemburg, from Dinant to Sedan.

Then came the 4th Army commanded by the Crown Prince, the 5th Army under the Crown Prince of Bavaria, the 6th Army under Von Heeringen, which lay in front of Strasburg, and lastly a detached force opposing the French in Alsace.

The average strength of each Army was about 200,000 men, and the total probably about 1,300,000 of all ranks.

The 1st Army, with which the British Army was chiefly concerned, originally numbered something like 320,000 of all arms, but was now reduced considerably by the Corps left in Belgium. The exact strength of his battle-line at Mons is difficult to estimate, but on September 4th—6th Von Kluck certainly had 5 Corps and 2 Cavalry Divisions when his Army crossed the Ourcq and Petit Morin rivers. At Mons therefore the attack must have been made with at least 200,000 men and 600 guns.

In Belgium the war, as was only to be expected, was going badly enough. The Belgians began to mobilise on the 28th July, but the enemy were upon them long before the mobilisation was completed, for on the 2nd of August the German vanguard was in Luxembourg. On the 3rd Von Emmich was over the frontier with 30,000 men and the next day saw his army in front of Liége.

Liége was taken on the 15th, after its gallant defender, General Leman, 1914 had been buried under the ruins of the last remaining fort, and the Belgian Field Army had been compelled to fall back from the line of the Dyle on Antwerp. Namur, with its garrison of 26,000 men under General Michel, was still intact, but the bombardment by the heavy German guns began on the 20th, and the next day the line of trenches connecting the circle of forts was evacuated by the garrison.

The siege of Liége only lasted eleven days in all. It commenced on the 4th August and in two days the southern forts had been reduced to heaps of ruins by the fire of the German heavy field batteries alone, for Brialmont's elaborate system of "Cupola" forts, now tried for the first time, proved quite unable to withstand the fire of modern artillery, and the Germans never even brought up their heavy siege guns at all. The town was entered by the enemy on the 6th, but the northern forts held out until the 15th.

Short as this period was, it was of incalculable value to the Allies. The guns of Liége commanded the nucleus of the chief railways into the north of France, and though the lines running through Luxemburg were undamaged and were used to their full capacity, the block at Liége was a very serious hindrance to the concentration of the armies moving into France.

The wrath and astonishment of the Germans at the unexpected and partially successful resistance of Belgium was almost ludicrous. That such an insignificant nation should dare for a moment to think of withstanding the will of the Imperial Kaiser and his invincible Armies was quite inconceivable to the German mind, and the delay caused by it greatly disconcerted the Headquarter Staff and materially affected the plan of a surprise attack on northern France before the British Expeditionary Force could effect a junction with the French Army.

The British intervention and the advent of the relatively small force sent into France was resented in much the same way, and on the 19th the Kaiser issued his famous Army Order* directing his generals to wipe General French's "Contemptible little Army" off the face of the earth. The original design of General Joffre, who was in supreme command of the Allied Armies in France, was to maintain the positions which he held from Namur to the Swiss frontier, and to wheel his left wing, consisting of the 5th Army and the British Corps, to the right, pivoting on Namur, against the right flank of the German advance, and to join up with the Belgian Army along the line of the Schelde.

The German plan of campaign was to effect a great wheel of their right, pivoting upon Thionville, and after rolling up the French line to attack Paris.

The command on each side was equally ignorant of the real strength and position of their respective opponents. Sir John French, who was obliged at first to depend on the French Staff for information, was informed that he had only two Corps in front of him, whereas he had in reality at least four, with Von Marwitz and three Divisions of Cavalry in addition threatening his left.

On the other hand, Von Kluck, who commanded the 1st Army, on the right of the German battle line, was equally ignorant of the actual position and strength of the Expeditionary Force. The German Staff had accurate information of its strength and composition and the date of embarkation, but did not know the ports at which it had been landed, thinking, indeed, that the troops had been disembarked at Calais, Boulogne, and Dunkirk, with the

---

* The text of this Order ran as follows:—" It is my Royal and Imperial command that you concentrate your energies for the immediate present upon one single purpose, and that is that you address all your skill and all the valour of my soldiers to exterminate the treacherous English. Walk over the contemptible little army of General French."

1914 intention of joining up with the Belgian Field Army. Even as late as the morning of August 22nd Von Kluck thought that the British were north-west of his right, and he was confirmed in that opinion when he heard that troops of some sort were detraining at Tournai. The general direction of the march of his columns was then south-west, and supposing that these were British troops from Lille, he halted until he had ascertained that they were really two French Battalions retiring in front of Von Marwitz, and it was not until the evening of that day that he learnt from a report of a patrol at Casteau that he had the British Army in front of him. On the night of the 22nd-23rd his left Corps, the 9th, halted with its head just south of Soignies, his 3rd Corps half-way between Enghien and Ath, and the head of the 2nd Corps five miles north-east of Grammont, while Von Marwitz with at least two Divisions of Cavalry was west of Ath. Von Kluck's march had been conducted with great celerity, some of his troops having covered 140 miles in eleven days. One Corps also of Von Bülow's Army lay north of Charleroi on Von Kluck's left, so Sir John French had within striking distance of his position not two Corps as he had been told by the French Staff, but four Corps, numbering at least 150,000 men and 600 guns, against his own force of two Corps and one Brigade with five Cavalry Brigades, totalling about 70,000 men and 300 guns.

On the 21st the Sixteenth joined the other two regiments of the 3rd Cavalry Brigade. A Squadron was sent on to Binche at 5 a.m. and put out patrols in the direction of Fontaine l'Eveque. The Brigade marched soon after 6 a.m., the remainder of the Regiment acting as advance guard, and moved by Merbes St. Marie to Estinne au Val, where it was billeted for the night.

On the 22nd, as the various reports brought in rendered it evident that the enemy was certainly advancing in force, the troops were moved into their positions and occupied an entrenched line extending from Binche on the right, where it was in touch with the 5th French Army, through Mons to Condé on the left. The right was held by the 1st Corps (Haig's), which extended from Binche to the Eastern suburbs of Mons, the left by the 2nd Corps (Smith-Dorrien), the line being along the Mons-Condé Canal from Mons to Condé, which was occupied by a French Territorial Division, but the 19th Infantry Brigade came up in the course of the day and took over the position on the left of the 2nd Corps. Further away the left flank was covered by General d'Amade's three divisions of French Territorials.

The Canal ran nearly due West and East from Condé to Mons, through a line of small mining villages. On each side were many slag heaps, some of considerable height, intersected by a great number of small wet ditches and water-courses. There were seven bridges over the canal, the two principal ones being at Pommeroeul and Ghislain, and except for the slag heaps there was no rising ground within three miles on either side. The bridges were mined, but not destroyed, with the view of a possible counter-attack.

The position of the 2nd Corps was therefore a good defensive one, except that it offered few good Artillery positions, a disadvantage common to both sides, and the country to the north being very wooded the movements of the enemy were well concealed. The left flank, however, was more or less " in the air," for the French Territorials were not in a condition to give much protection, and the Cavalry Brigades could not be spared to cover it.

The British Army thus had a battle front of about 30 miles, along which the whole of the troops were deployed, for Sir John French had no reserve whatever except Allenby's Cavalry. This was, with the exception of the 3rd Brigade, now posted behind the left of the 2nd Corps.

At 5 a.m. on the 22nd the 3rd Brigade moved to Bray and Chetwode's

Brigade to Binche, one Squadron of the Greys being sent on to Peronnes,* to 1914 watch the bridges. This was afterwards reinforced by a second Squadron.

The first shot of the campaign was actually fired by a patrol of the 4th Dragoon Guards which had moved out from Oburg in the direction of Soignies at daybreak, and had met with a picquet of the enemy. About the same time there occurred the encounter at Casteau which gave Von Kluck the first intimation that the British Army was confronting him.

Soon after this the Greys at Peronnes were attacked by a mixed force of Cavalry and Jagers, but the Greys held the place until they were ordered to retire at 2 p.m., after killing or wounding 40 of the enemy, their only casualty being 1 officer wounded.

A troop of the 16th under Captain Tempest Hicks was sent up to support the Greys. It was ambushed by a party of the enemy† hiding among some wheat stooks and Captain Tempest Hicks had his horse shot. The troop then charged and the Germans bolted. Two of the men were slightly wounded, this being the first casualty of the 16th.

The Brigade then came under artillery fire, which was replied to by the H.A. Battery of the Brigade.

A strong mixed force of the enemy then occupied the village of Peronnes, which was set on fire, and at 5 p.m. the Brigade was withdrawn to Binche and Bray, the 16th being rear-guard. At 7 a.m. the Brigade received orders to march to Elouges, a place about five miles south of the Condé Canal and half-way between Condé and Mons. This was a most trying march of over 20 miles along country roads paved with cobble stones. The Brigade did not get in until 3 a.m., the men having then been 22 hours in the saddle. The troops then bivouaced in the fields.

CHAPTER XXXIV.

August 23rd to August 26th, 1914.

Battle of Mons, August 23rd. Action begun by German Artillery at 10 a.m. Infantry attack by 9th German Corps along the Canal north of Mons at 11 a.m. The attack well held. Retirement from Mons and Binche. Action ceases at night-fall. British Casualties. German losses. Condition of the enemy. News received of disasters to the French Armies. Decision to retreat, August 24th. The Retreat of the 1st Corps. Retirement of the 2nd Corps. German attack on the left flank. Severe fighting at Frameries. The 5th Division reinforced by the Cavalry. Charge of the 9th Lancers. Retirement effected. Moves of the 16th. General position at night-fall. Heavy losses of the 9th Lancers, Cheshires, and Norfolks. Continued retreat of French 5th Army. Orders issued for retreat to Le Cateau. Difficulties of retreat. The Forest of Mormal. The 1st Corps to move by the east and 2nd Corps by west of Forest. Arrival of the 4th Division, which is sent to Solesmes. Positions of the Cavalry Brigades. Movements of the 16th. Unmolested march of the 1st Corps. Combats

---

* Peronnes was a village four miles North of Binche.
† These were a party of Jäger attached to the Cavalry.

1914   at night at Landrecies and Maroilles. Difficult position of the 2nd Corps. Orders to continue the retreat on the 26th. Sir H. Smith-Dorrien finds this impossible. His decision to stand and fight. Reluctant acquiescence by the Commander-in-Chief.

Summary of Events, August 23rd to August 26th, 1914.—August 23rd, Battle of Mons; Germans enter Namur; Austrians driven out of Servia; Japan declares war on Germany. 24th, Retreat from Mons begins. 26th, Battle of Le Cateau; Battle of Tannenberg begins.

22nd Aug.   Von Kluck spent very little time in reconnoitring the British position. He was no doubt eagerly desirous of carrying out to the letter the injunction of his Imperial master to wipe out Sir J. French and his contemptibles now that he had, as he thought, the chance, and without waiting to form his battle-line he hurled his divisions into the fight as they came up. He elected to deliver the brunt of his attack on the British right, probably desiring to join hands with Von Bülow, who he knew was engaged with the 5th French Army in the neighbourhood of Charleroi.

23rd Aug.   At 10 a.m. on the morning of the 23rd the batteries of the 9th Corps, posted along the ridge north of Oburg opened the battle and the line of guns was extended, first with those of the 3rd Corps and then with others as the several batteries came up, until the whole 25 miles of the British position was subjected to a furious cannonade from a line of fully 600 guns.

The German ranging was at first bad, but gradually improved until by 1.30 p.m. a superiority of fire had been established. But our men were well covered in the trenches and there were few casualties.

At 11 a.m. Von Kluck's 9th Corps came up and made a determined attack in mass formation on the loop of the Canal north of Mons. The attacking columns suffered very heavily from the steady and well aimed rifle fire with which they were met, and were kept well in check until late in the afternoon, but Sir J. French had never intended to hold Mons and Binche except as an advanced position, and when Von Bülow's 7th Corps came into action against Binche, Sir D. Haig abandoned the place and retired to a prepared position behind it. This movement necessitated a corresponding withdrawal from Mons of the 3rd Division, which was effected after some very stiff fighting in which the 4th Middlesex and Royal Irish suffered severely. West of Mons also the 5th Division, which had been keeping at bay the greater part of two of Von Kluck's Corps, the 3rd and 4th, was also withdrawn to an entrenched position south of the Canal.

Along the line of the rest of the Canal as far as Condé the fighting had been practically confined to a struggle for the possession of the several bridges, for in view of a possible advance in accordance with the original plan of General Joffre, these had not been destroyed, though they had been mined and prepared for destruction, but late in the afternoon, when the superior strength of the enemy clearly demonstrated the hopeless improbability of any offensive movement, the greater number of them were blown up. As darkness came on the firing gradually ceased and the troops prepared to bivouac on the ground they held.

So far the day had gone well for Sir John French. His Army had maintained its positions and repulsed the repeated attacks of the enemy, for, though Mons and Binche had been relinquished, the retirement had been made for tactical reasons only, and the Huns had acquired such a salutary respect for the rifle fire of their opponents that they did not venture to follow them beyond the outskirts of the two towns. The troops, too, had imbibed a supreme contempt both for the field tactics and the shooting of the enemy, and looked forward with confidence to the expected counter-attack the next day.

The British casualties, notwithstanding the tremendous shelling to which the line had been subjected during the whole of the day, only amounted to just over 1,600 of all ranks, in killed, wounded, and missing. Of these 40 only were lost by the 1st Corps, and of the remainder half were incurred by the two battalions of the 8th Infantry Brigade at the Mons Salient where the most severe fighting took place. Two guns only were lost. These could not be removed from a very exposed position on the Canal at St. Ghislain.

No official account of the German losses can be obtained, but Von Kluck's staff tacitly admitted defeat by preparing to meet a counter-attack on the next day.

Bloem, a Company Commander in the Brandenburg Grenadiers, who wrote a description of the battle, writes that he lost all his five company officers and half his men, and that he was the only surviving Company Commander in his battalion, which was a mere wreck, and that the whole Regiment had been shot down, smashed up, only a handful being left. Bloem concludes with these pregnant words :—" Our first battle is a heavy, unheard of heavy defeat, and against the English, the English whom we laughed at ! "

On the German side, too, there was considerable confusion. The 9th and the 3rd Corps, which had been chiefly engaged, had suffered enormous loss, and had lost all stomach for the fight. Von Kluck's 2nd Corps was continuing its march through Grammont and his 4th Reserve Corps, less a Brigade left at Brussels, was at Hal, while Von Bülow's 7th Corps had not ventured to move out of Binche.

But late in the evening the Field-Marshal received the news of a series of disasters that completely changed the situation. Namur had succumbed to the fire of the heavy German artillery. On the 21st the trenches connecting the circle of forts had been abandoned. On the 22nd the eastern forts were reduced to ruins, and the garrison, or what was left of it, to the number of about 12,000 men, had evacuated the place, and Von Bülow's troops had occupied the town, though a few hundreds of determined men gallantly held some of the western forts for two days longer. Then the Field-Marshal received a belated message from General Joffre telling him that Von Kluck was bringing up four Corps instead of two, with Von Bülow's 7th Corps in addition, and finally he learnt that the 5th French Army had been driven by Von Bülow and Von Hausen's Saxons from its positions on the Sambre, and was then actually five miles behind the British right. In face of this accumulation of misfortunes there was no alternative but immediate retreat.

To make the situation worse the offensive of all the French Armies south of the 5th Army had failed, though as yet this was not known to Sir John French. The First and Second Armies were retreating after the battles of Sarrebourg and Morhange ; the Third and Fourth had been compelled to fall back towards the Meuse after the fighting at Virton and the Semoy.

The order to retreat was received late at night by the Division Commanders, greatly to the disgust and astonishment of the rank and file, who were of course not aware of the reasons for it.

The Field-Marshal had already selected a new position to move to in case a retreat should be forced upon him. The right of this new line rested on the great fortress of Maubeuge and extended through Bavai to Jeulain.

As soon as Sir John French decided on the retreat late on the night of the 23rd the movement of the heavy transport and hospital equipment to the rear began and continued during the night, the troops being ordered to be ready to move

1914 at dawn. To cover the retirement the 1st Corps was ordered to make a demonstration on the right towards Binche, while the 2nd Corps fell back from its position along the Condé Canal.

24th Aug. Accordingly at sunrise on the 24th the 1st Divison, covered by the fire of 120 guns, moved forwards along the Mons road towards Bray and Binche. This threat took the enemy completely by surprise, and Von Kluck thought that the British must have been strongly reinforced during the night and that a general counter-attack all along the line was impending. Meanwhile the 2nd Division was well on its way to the south and the 2nd Corps had fallen back to a new line five miles from the Canal before the enemy had realised that a retreat and not a counter-attack was in progress. The 1st Division then in its turn retired, covered by the fire of the whole artillery of the 1st Corps.

By this time the 2nd Corps and the 19th Brigade had formed a fresh battle-line with the right at Frameries and the left resting on Quarouble, near Valenciennes. It was a good position with a clear field of fire, and the advance of the 4th German Corps which had crossed the Canal in pursuit was immediately checked. Von Kluck had now adopted the plan of battle which he ought to have brought into operation on the previous day, which was to use his great superiority of strength to turn the left flank of the British position. Accordingly he began the action with a bombardment by the guns of his 9th and 3rd Corps, and sent his 4th Corps, which had not been heavily engaged in the battle of the preceding day, against Smith-Dorrien's Corps.

This 4th Corps advanced in two columns between Pommereul and Condé against the extreme left of the line which was held by the 5th Division and the 19th Brigade, with Allenby's Cavalry in support. The attack here was beaten off after a stiff fight in which the enemy, who attacked as usual in mass formation, suffered very severely, the German 5th Division being practically destroyed; but the right of the line at Frameries, which was attacked by practically the whole of the German 9th Corps, was very hard pressed, and between 7 and 8 a.m. Sir C. Ferguson, the General Commanding the 5th Division, sent an urgent request for support. General Allenby was ordered to send two Brigades to the threatened flank. The first to come up were the three regiments of the 2nd Brigade, the 4th Dragoon Guards, 9th Lancers, and 18th Hussars, which began a dismounted action against the enemy's infantry at Audrignies at 1,000 yards range. Then General de Lisle, who commanded the Brigade, ordered the 9th Lancers to charge the flank of the advancing mass of infantry with the other two regiments in support. Unfortunately there had been no time to reconnoitre the ground, and the 9th were brought up by some wire fences within 500 yards of the enemy under a heavy fire of all arms. The 9th were shot down in all directions and what was left of the two leading squadrons were forced to take shelter under cover of a railway embankment, where there were already a few men of the 119 Battery R.F.A., with their limberless guns, which they had been unable to get away, all the horses having been shot.

The third squadron of the 9th, commanded by Captain F. Grenfell, had not suffered so severely as the others, having been brought up earlier in the charge by a wire fence, and had halted and dismounted. Captain Grenfell, though badly wounded himself in the hand and leg, determined to save the guns, and with the few gunners left alive and his own men he managed to man-handle them under a heavy fire under cover behind the firing line. Unsuccessful as this charge was, it nevertheless took off some of the pressure on the 5th Division, and enabled it to continue the retirement, which was begun by the whole

Corps about noon, being then engaged with three of Von Kluck's Corps, 1914 covered by the Cavalry. The retreat was not seriously followed up by the enemy, and by 5 p.m. the 2nd Corps was halted in the new position in line with the 1st Corps.

The 3rd Cavalry Brigade was not in action during this engagement. The Brigade left Elounges early in the morning after a halt of less than three hours, and moved to a village about two miles south of that place. At 11 a.m. the 16th were moved again to near Audrignies in support of the 5th Division, and thence, on the general retirement to Bry, where the regiment formed a line of outposts by Wargnies le Grand.

The position at night-fall was as follows:— 24-25

The 84th French Division was retreating from Valenciennes to Cambrai, Aug. and D'Amade had drawn back and was covering a line from Cambrai to Douai.

The 1st Corps held a line from La Longueville to Bavai.

The 2nd Corps from Bavai to Bry.

The 19th Brigade from Bry to Jeulain.

Von Marwitz was 10 miles east of Douai.

Von Kluck's Corps were halted generally on a line about 6 miles from the British outposts.

Von Bülow's 2nd Army was still driving Lanrezac's 5th Army southward, of which the left Corps was near Solre le Chateau 12 miles south-west of Haig's right, with two Divisions at Maubeuge, which last had orders to retire at daybreak.

Sordet's Cavalry Division was trying to move to the left flank of the British line, but was greatly hampered by the block of heavy transport which choked the roads.

Behind the centre of the British position was the Forest of Mormal.

The casualties on the 24th were considerably greater than those of the previous day and were distributed thus:—

Cavalry, 250.   5th Division, 1,650.
1st Corps, 100.   19th Brigade, 40.
3rd Division, 500.

Of these the losses in the Cavalry were chiefly incurred by the 9th Lancers; those of the 5th Division in the fighting, at the close of the engagement, near Audrignies, where the Cheshires lost 800 men out of 1,000 who went into action, and the Norfolks over 250 of all ranks. The order to retreat did not reach the Cheshires, so the regiment continued to hold its position long after the rest of the Division had retired, and though a part of the reserve companies were withdrawn in time and made good their retreat, the remainder were surrounded and after fighting to the last the few survivors, 40 in number, were made prisoners. As intelligence was received that the 5th Army continued its retreat, the Field-Marshal decided to retire again on the 25th to a new position in the neighbourhood of Le Cateau.

The arrangement of the routes for the retirement of the Army presented 25th some difficulties, for close behind the centre of the position was the Forest of Aug. Mormal. This forest, mostly large oak and beech, was nine miles long and three to four miles broad, and there were no made roads through it, nothing but narrow forest tracks. To move the whole Army to the west of the forest entailed a long flank march across the enemy's front, while the retreating columns of the French 5th Army were so close to the east side that there would not have been enough space for it. The Field-Marshal therefore decided to pass the 1st Corps to the East and the 2nd Corps to the west of the wood. The orders for the march were as follows:—

1914 1st Corps to move in two columns.

1st Division to cross the Sambre at Hautmont and thence to Dompierre.

2nd Division to cross at Pont sur Sambre and Berlaimont, and thence to Leval and Landrecies.

5th Cavalry Brigade to cover the retirement.

2nd Corps to move west of the forest by three roads to the line Le Cateau, Caudry, Haucourt.

Cavalry Division, two Brigades and Divisional Cavalry to cover the retreat of the Corps.

Two Brigades and 19th Infantry Brigade to cover the west flank.

The 4th Division arrived at Le Cateau on the 24th from England, and was detrained there and the neighbouring stations. It consisted of eleven battalions of infantry and a brigade of field artillery, General Snow being in command. It was, however, anything but complete, as it had no divisional cavalry or any of its auxiliary equipment. This Division was ordered to move at once to Solesmes to assist in the withdrawal of the 2nd Corps, and further, when the retirement was completed, to move to the left of the Cateau position.

Solesmes was a very important point, being at the junction of four main roads, and the Headquarter Staff rightly feared that there would be great difficulty in dealing with the congestion of the transport, with which every road was blocked, at the place. This in fact did happen and it took over 24 hours of hard work to get the place cleared. The retirement of both Corps was effected with little serious fighting, the enemy being probably quite as tired out as were the British troops. The German Cavalry in particular showed, as usual, very little enterprise, though Von Marwitz had three Divisions wherewith to oppose General Allenby's one.

The 1st and 2nd Cavalry Brigades were posted at Wagnies near Jeulain, with the 3rd and 4th Brigades in support behind their left; the 19th Infantry Brigade being placed well to their left rear again between Sepmeries and Quérénaing. As the retreat proceeded the 3rd and 4th Brigades were moved to Verchain about eight miles south of Valenciennes, and at noon the 16th were sent to Haspres, a village on the Selle River, to help some French Territorials who had got into difficulties there. These troops were part of one of D'Amade's Divisions which were retreating from Valenciennes to Cambrai.

One squadron went on to Haspres and found that the enemy were attacking a French convoy. The other two remained in support at Saulzoir, but both parties came under such a heavy shell fire that the Regiment could do nothing and eventually the 16th rejoined the Brigade. In this affair the machine gun was lost, and Captain Belleville and four men wounded, all being eventually made prisoners. The 3rd Brigade then moved to Catillon, where it was billeted for the night, getting in at 10 p.m., after detaching two squadrons of the 4th Hussars with orders to gain touch with the 1st Corps. The Brigades of Allenby's Cavalry Division were much scattered at the close of the retreat. Part of the 2nd Brigade followed the 3rd to the neighbourhood of Catillon, the 1st was still south-east of Solesmes, and the 4th remained close to the town.

The retreat of the 1st Corps was practically unmolested and the troops reached their billets in and about Landrecies and Maroilles and the line of villages west of Avesnes by 6 p.m. The march, however, was a very fatiguing one, as the day was exceedingly hot and there were constant halts on account of the congested state of the roads, which were used also by parts of the French 5th Army.

Everyone was hoping to have a good night's rest in quarters, particularly as orders had been received to march at 2 a.m. for Busigny, seven miles south-west of Le Cateau, but soon after night-fall the picquets in front of Landre- 1914 cies and Maroilles were driven in. This was preceded by a general flight of the inhabitants, and the supports had great difficulty in getting through to the firing line. The enemy's advance parties actually effected a lodgement in Landrecies itself, and were only ejected by the Guards Brigade after some hand to hand fighting in the streets.

Though this skirmish was really nothing more than an affair of outposts, nevertheless it caused much disquietude to the Headquarters Staff, as there was a quite disproportionate amount of firing which was kept up until daybreak, and it was impossible to be certain what number of the enemy might be hidden in the Mormal Forest. It had therefore the unfortunate result of keeping the 1st Corps under arms all night and depriving the weary troops of their much required rest.

It was afterwards found that the attack on Landrecies was made by the advance guard of the German 7th Division, which had marched along the western side of the Forest and which actually intended to billet for the night in the town, the G.O.C. being quite unaware that it was occupied by the British. The attack on Maroilles was made under similar circumstances by the advance guard of the 5th Division, which had marched through the Forest.

But though things were uncomfortable with the 1st Corps, they were much worse with the 2nd Corps. It was not until 9 p.m. that Solesmes was reported clear and the covering troops withdrawn from the town, which was immediately occupied by the enemy. The 4th Division, which had been posted south of Solesmes, received orders to march at once to the extreme left of the line and to take up a position from Fontaine au Pire to Wambaix, with its reserve Brigade at Haucourt.

The 12th Brigade moved soon after 9 p.m. and the 11th at 10 p.m., but the 10th was not able to march until midnight owing to the congested state of the roads and did not arrive at its destination until 6 a.m. on the morning of the 26th, after a weary march in torrents of rain of 12 miles, while the block of vehicles at Solesmes had merely been transferred to Le Cateau and the neighbouring roads.

At 7.30 p.m. Sir John French sent orders from St. Quentin, where his headquarters then were, for the retreat to be continued on the 26th 10 to 15 miles further to the south-west, the 1st Corps to Busigny, the 2nd Corps to Premont and Beaurevoir, and the 4th Division to Le Catelet. These orders did not reach Sir H. Smith-Dorrien till 10 p.m., and General Allenby an hour later.

The latter went at once to General Smith-Dorrien, and represented to him that if the troops did not march before daybreak the enemy would be on them before they could move off. The other Divisional Commanders all agreed when communicated with, that it would be quite impossible to move before 9 a.m. as it was then 2 a.m., and many of their units were even then only just marching in.

Sir H. Smith-Dorrien decided that there was nothing for it but to stand fast and fight in his present positions. Orders were issued at once to countermand the retreat, but it was not easy to get these delivered to the Brigade and Regimental Commanders in the darkness and general confusion, and some of the units were formed up in column of march before they were received. The immediate consequence was that the positions were very hurriedly taken up, and there was little time for entrenching. Moreover, many regiments had no tools beyond their "grubbers," the regimental equipment having been lost in the course of the retreat from Mons. Under these circumstances the Battle of Le Cateau was fought under very disadvantageous conditions to the 2nd

1914 Corps, especially as, though the Field-Marshal Commanding reluctantly acquiesced in Sir H. Smith-Dorrien's decision, he warned him that he must not expect to receive any help from the 1st Corps.

CHAPTER XXXV.

AUGUST 26TH TO SEPTEMBER 5TH, 1914.

26th Aug. Continuation of the Retreat from Mons. The Battle of Le Cateau. Position of the 2nd Corps. Von Kluck's strength and dispositions. The battle movements of the 3rd Cavalry Brigade. Heavy losses on the left flank. The Lancasters. The line successfully held. Retirement at 2 p.m. Many detached parties left in the firing line. Heavy losses of the Gordons. Cavalry movements. Lieut.-Colonel MacEwen badly wounded. Losses of guns. Casualties of the 2nd Corps. Retreat of the 1st Corps. Rear-guard action at Le Fayt. The Connaughts cut off. Further retreat of the 1st Corps on the 27th. Rear-guard action at Fesmy. Death of Major Charrier. The gallant fight of the Munsters. Retreat of the 2nd Corps on the 27th covered by the 3rd Cavalry Brigade and crossing of the Somme. Position of the Army 28th August. The retreat continued. The 3rd and 5th Cavalry Brigades. Their combats at Essigny and Cirizy. Charge of the 12th Lancers. The German 1st and 2nd Armies. The French 5th and 6th Armies. Casualties from 23rd to 27th August. Battle of Guise. Further retreat on 29th covered by the Cavalry. The 16th at Chauny. Retreat on 30th to the line Soissons-Compiègne. Formation of the 3rd Corps. Further retreat 30th August, and September 1st. Orders for the march September 1st. Actions at Nery and Taillefontaine. Sir J. French in Paris. Interview with Lord Kitchener. Retreat resumed September 2nd to the line Meux-Dommartin. Further retreat September 3rd. The Marne crossed and retirement to the Grand Morin on the 4th September. Further and final retirement on September 5th. The end of the Retreat from Mons. Marches and Casualties.

Summary of Events, August 28th to September 5th, 1914.—August 28th, Naval battle off Heligoland. 31st, Defeat of the Russians at Tannenberg. September 3rd, Lemberg taken by Russians. 5th, End of the Retreat from Mons.

The Divisional Commanders of the 2nd Corps had but small choice in the matter of selecting positions for the fighting line, for it was so late when orders countermanding the retreat reached the Brigadiers that the troops practically were obliged to stand and fight on the ground which they then occupied. Indeed, some battalions did not get the order until they had actually moved off in Column of Route. The 19th Brigade, which had bivouaced in Le Cateau, were well on their way to Reumont, having left the town, which was at once occupied by the enemy, before 6 a.m., and part of the 14th Brigade, which had passed the night on the hill east of Le Cateau, were also formed up ready to march near the south-east corner of the town. When the line was eventually formed the 5th Division held the ground from Le Cateau to Troisvilles, the 3rd Division from Troisvilles, Audencourt, Caudry, the 4th Division Beauvois, Fontaine au Pire, Longsart, with its reserve at Haucourt.

BRIGADIER GENERAL MacEWEN,
Lieut.-Colonel, 1910 to 1914.

Of the Cavalry Division, the 2nd and 3rd Brigades were sent to Mazinghien 1914 and Bazuel respectively to guard the right flank, the 4th Brigade to Ligny, and the 1st to Escaufourt to support the 2nd and 3rd.

On the evening of the 25th Von Kluck had the 2nd Cavalry Corps and his 4th and 3rd Corps in close touch with the British line and ready to strike in the early morning, with three other Corps within a short march. His design was to hold the centre and envelope both flanks of his opponents' line simultaneously. His 2nd Corps was to have joined in the attack on the left flank, but fortunately General d'Amade had been able to concentrate three of his Territorial Divisions in the neighbourhood of Cambrai, while General Sordet's Cavalry had by this time been able to cross to Serauvillers, and though his men and horses were in a very exhausted condition, his force could not be altogether ignored. Von Kluck's 2nd Corps was therefore fully occupied in shepherding the French, though one of his Divisions did manage to reach the battle-field a short time before the action came to an end.

Von Kluck seems to have been very badly served by his Intelligence Department and his Cavalry. It appears from his own Despatches that he thought that the 1st Corps was to the west of the Selle also. In this he was probably misled by the extension of the line by the 4th Division, of whose arrival he was ignorant, though he thought that the 6th Division which had not left England was also present, and being still obsessed with the notion that the Expeditionary Force was based on Boulogne and Dunkirk he concluded that the battle line lay North and South, instead of its being practically nearly East and West.

The morning of the 26th, the anniversary of the Battle of Crécy, was warm and misty, the rain having ceased before dawn. The German artillery, which had been placed in position during the night, opened fire all along the line as it became light enough to see their targets and before many of the battalions had been able to dig themselves in. The German batteries posted about Forest, three miles N.-N.East of Le Cateau were the first to open fire, followed by others which were placed in a carefully hidden position some two miles W.-N.West of Le Cateau, which practically enfiladed the line between Le Cateau and the Roman road. Meanwhile Le Cateau was evacuated and the place was at once entered by the advance parties of the enemy. The 3rd Cavalry Brigade, which had been moved to Bazuel early in the morning, with the H.A. Battery, were moved up to support the right flank, now thrown back nearly to Bazuel itself. The enemy's advance from Le Cateau down the valley of the Selle was checked, and though the right of the line was subjected to a very heavy and continuous bombardment and an enfilade fire, both from the heights on the east side of Le Cateau and from guns which had been dragged up to the hill south of Montay, as well as repeated frontal attacks, it maintained its position for six hours, notwithstanding its heavy casualties.

In the centre, though the 3rd Division was subjected to an intense and destructive cannonade from daybreak to midday, the infantry attack was kept in check with comparative ease all through the day, but on the left flank the attack began badly for the 4th Division.

The Division having no Cavalry of its own, had to depend on General Sordet's patrols for information as to the enemy's movements, and was also much hampered by having no field telegraph, Divisional Signallers, or Field Ambulances.

The French patrols had reported the front to be clear. The troops were formed up preparatory to entrenching, when suddenly a number of machine guns opened fire on the Battalion of the Lancaster Regiment from a well-

1914 concealed position. This was immediately followed by the advent of three batteries, which, galloping into the open ground between Wambaix and Callinières, unlimbered and deluged the unlucky Lancasters with a hail of shells. The men lay down, and returned the fire as well as they could, for some twenty minutes and silenced most of the machine guns, when the enemy's fire having somewhat slackened, the survivors were gradually withdrawn under cover, leaving some 400 men on the ground killed or wounded.

The attack on the left of the 4th Division was made by the 2nd Cavalry Corps and their Jager battalions, but after the first surprise the enemy made little progress, the dismounted Cavalry being very half-hearted fighters, and by 11 a.m. it had been practically beaten off, though their guns kept up a heavy and continuous cannonade. Further east, between Wambaix and Caudry, the Germans brought up battery after battery until the line of guns extended from north of Fontaine to Wambaix, but though the artillery fire necessitated various small retirements here and there to less exposed positions, the infantry attack was not pressed home in the face of the rapid and accurate rifle fire with which it was met.

On the right about Cateau the conditions were much less satisfactory. The casualties were very heavy and many guns were smashed up by direct hits, being now for the most part actually in the firing line owing to the impossibility of bringing up the horses to remove them, and at 1 p.m. General Ferguson reported to Headquarters that he doubted if he could maintain the position much longer in the face of the enfilade fire to which the right of his line was subjected and the pressure of the fresh Division of the 3rd German Corps which was now being thrown into the fight. General Smith-Dorrien therefore ordered the retirement of the whole three Divisions by the roads previously allotted in his original orders, namely, the 5th Division and the 19th Brigade by Bertry and Maretz to Vermand, and by Reumont and Bussigny to Estrées; the 3rd Division by Montigny to Beaurevoir; the 4th Division by Selvigny to Le Catalet, Vendhuille and Elincourt; the Cavalry Division to withdraw by any roads west of the 4th Division. The 4th and 3rd Divisions were withdrawn gradually from the firing line with little difficulty, but it was not so with the 5th Division, particularly on the right flank about Le Cateau, for here the enemy was still pressing his attack with considerable determination.

At 2 p.m. the extreme right was reinforced by two battalions from the reserve, and by 3.30 p.m., as the attack somewhat slackened, the troops were gradually withdrawn from their positions and the retreat commenced.

Unfortunately it was next to impossible to convey orders to many of the company commanders in the firing line, and as these, with the usual obstinacy of the British soldier, never thought for a moment of quitting their position till they got them, numerous platoons and even companies were left behind, and these fought on until they were surrounded and the few unwounded survivors overwhelmed and made prisoners. The Gordon Highlanders were the worst sufferers in this respect, for some 500 with their commanding officer were surrounded and, after a desperate attempt to fight their way through, were eventually obliged to surrender near Bertry.

Colonel Gordon had, however, prolonged his fight until 1.30 a.m., and the resistance of these isolated parties effectually checked the advance of the enemy until nightfall, and very materially facilitated the general retreat, which was practically unmolested, as Von Kluck, as usual, made no use whatever of his Cavalry Divisions.

The 3rd Cavalry Brigade, with the 1st, remained at Bazuel until about 12.30 p.m., when the two Brigades retired leisurely up the valley of the Selle towards St. Soupplet, after the first attempt of the enemy to turn the right 1914 had been stopped. Thence the 3rd moved to Bussigny, covering the retreat of part of the 5th Division. Thence, having marched by Elincourt and Malincourt, it reached Beaurevoir about midnight, where it was joined by two regiments of the 1st and 2nd Brigades, and finding the road blocked by infantry the five regiments moved east of Estrées to Beaucourt, Monbrehan, and Ramicourt. The 16th then moved by Maubrun to St. Quentin, and after marching all night arrived there at midday on the 27th. After drawing rations and forage at St. Quentin, it was hurried off to Itancourt in consequence of a false alarm and finally billeted there for the night. The Regiment did no actual fighting at Le Cateau, and though it was under shell fire most of the day there were only three casualties, Colonel MacEwen and two men being wounded.*

The total losses of the 2nd Corps on the 26th amounted to 7,812 of all ranks, killed, wounded and missing, and 38 guns, including one 60-pdr. which had to be abandoned. Of the guns, some had been wrecked by direct hits, but most had to be left on the ground owing to the impossibility of removing them, the teams being shot down one after another in making the attempt. According to German accounts the prisoners taken were 2,600, which is confirmed by Von Kluck himself. This includes wounded, very many being left on the ground by the 4th Division, which had no field ambulances.

The 1st Corps was on the move long before daybreak, and retiring by alter- 26th nate Brigades to Etreux and the adjacent villages. The march was compara- Aug. tively unmolested by the enemy except for an unfortunate rearguard affair at Le Grand Fayt. Here the 5th Infantry Brigade was held up for some hours by the movement of the French Reserve Divisions across the line of march, and the 2nd Connaught Rangers, which formed the rearguard, came to a halt. About 6 p.m. the battalion became engaged with the enemy, and the greater part of it being deployed in a cramped country covered with small copses and high hedges did not receive the order to retire when the main body moved off. Le Fayt was then occupied by the Germans and the retreat of the Connaughts effectually intercepted, with the result that their commanding officer, Colonel Abercrombie, and nearly 300 other ranks were found to be missing when the scattered parties that got away rejoined the Brigade, which finally went into billets at Barzy, five miles north-east of the 2nd Division.

The 5th Cavalry Brigade retired to Hannapes, on the Oise two miles southwest of Etreux, where it rested for the night. Beyond suffering some slight casualties from long-distance shell fire its march had not been molested.

By arrangement with the Staff of the French 5th Army, which was still in 27th retreat on the east of the 1st Corps, the road to Guise was left to the British. Aug. At 4 a.m. the 2nd Division marched off, covered by the 1st Division, the Cavalry Brigade being sent west of the Oise to guard the left flank as an attack was expected from St. Quentin, which was falsely reported to be occupied by the enemy in force. The retreat was attended by another rearguard disaster precisely similar to that of the previous day.

The Munster Fusiliers and two guns, which formed the rearguard of the 1st Division, under Major Charrier, of that regiment, was cut off and surrounded at Fesmy, and after a gallant fight of 12 hours, in which Major Charrier was

---

* Colonel MacEwen had been already hit by a piece of shell during the retreat, but remained on duty. At Le Cateau he was struck by a bullet in his leg while taking up a position to cover the retirement of General Rolt's Brigade from the firing line. He was removed with some difficulty, and eventually taken in a horse-box to Rheims, contracting pluro-pneumonia from the exposure on the way. His loss was greatly regretted by all ranks, as he never was able to rejoin for service in the field.

1914 killed and the guns wrecked, some 250 men who survived were obliged to surrender after a final bayonet charge, their ammunition being exhausted. They had kept no less than nine battalions of the enemy at bay for six hours before they were overwhelmed and effectually put a stop to any further pursuit of the 1st Division.

The troops arrived at their appointed positions for the night about 10 p.m. after a slow and fatiguing march, for the day was hot and sultry and the single road was choked not only by their own transport but also by the usual multitude of refugees.

The retreat of the 2nd Corps was also continued on the 27th, the 3rd Cavalry Brigade forming a covering screen to the north of St. Quentin. At 10 a.m. the 3rd was joined by part of the 2nd Brigade. At 2.30 p.m. the approach of the enemy's Cavalry was reported by the patrols and the Brigade retired to Itancourt, the 1st Brigade being in support at Grand Seraucourt.

28th Aug. The retreat was not pressed by the enemy, except on the extreme left, where the 4th Division had some rearguard skirmishing, and by dawn on the 28th the whole of General Smith-Dorrien's Corps was practically south of the Somme, 35 miles from Le Cateau.

The position of the whole British Force on the morning of the 28th August was as follows:—

2nd Corps.—1st, 2nd, 3rd Cavalry Brigades in a semi-circle, four miles south of St. Quentin, from Itancourt, through Urvilliers and Grand Seraucourt to Savy.

4th. Cavalry Brigade, on the left of the 4th Division at Rouy.

5th Division and 19th Brigade at Ollezy and Eaucourt, near the junction of the Crozat Canal and the Somme, south-west of the Cavalry Brigades.

3rd Division, on the left of the 5th, at Ham.

4th Division, on the left of the 3rd at Voyenne on the Somme.

All the Divisions had rearguards north of the Somme.

1st Corps.—The 1st Corps, on the high ground south of Guise, from Longchamps to Mont d'Origny, with the Cavalry and 5th Brigade west of the Oise about Hauteville and Bernot.

By this time it was evident that as far as the 2nd Corps was concerned the German pursuit had practically come to an end, and that Von Kluck, thinking probably that the British Contemptibles had been finally disposed of, had now diverted his attention to the French forces collecting on his right. Nevertheless, General Joffre had not yet completed his preparations for the counter-attack which he meditated, and the Field-Marshal ordered the retreat to be continued on the 28th. The day's march, which began at 4 a.m., was conducted in a leisurely manner with frequent halts, and as many men as possible were either sent off by train or carried on carts, all spare ammunition and such equipment that was not immediately required being discarded.

The 5th Division halted at Pontoise, the 3rd at Crissolles and Givry, close to Noyon, and the 4th, which had covered the rear of the Corps at Bussy, Freniche and Campagne, a little to the north of the 3rd Division.

Of the Cavalry, the 3rd Brigade was sent to Jussy with instructions to gain touch with the 1st Corps, the 1st to Berlancourt, the 2nd to Le Plessis, and the 3rd to Cressy near Nesle four miles north of the 4th Division.

The 1st Corps marched off at dawn, leaving the 2nd Infantry Brigade and a Brigade of Field Artillery at Mont d'Origny to cover the movement. About midday a half-hearted attack was made by the enemy, which was easily beaten off, and shortly afterwards the arrival of infantry of General Valabrèque's Reserve Divisions enabled the rear-guard to be withdrawn. The whole Corps crossed the Oise at La Fère and late in the afternoon reached their billets, the 1st Division south of La Fère at Fressancourt and Gobain, the 2nd further west at Audelain and Armigny. 1914

In the course of the day both the 3rd and 5th Cavalry Brigades were engaged with the German Guards Cavalry Division. At 4 a.m. an outpost of the 16th was attacked by a troop of the enemy, which was easily beaten off after losing an officer and four men killed and one man taken prisoner. Soon after dawn the Brigade took up a position about six miles south of St. Quentin between Cerizy and Essigny. About 10 a.m. General Gough learnt from a party of French Infantry, which was retiring southwards from St. Quentin through Essigny, that they had been surprised at Bellenglise by German Cavalry and Artillery, and shortly afterwards his own patrols reported that a Brigade of Uhlans was advancing on Essigny and another column with artillery on Cerizy. About 1 p.m. the advance guard of the former fell into an ambush of the 4th Hussars, who had been moved to Benay to cover the retreat of the French. The Germans were dispersed with some loss, whereupon their main body tried to work round the right flank of the Brigade, but it was stopped by the guns of the H.A. Battery, whereupon the column retired. The 3rd Brigade remained in the neighbourhood of Jussy during the night.

The affair at Cerizy between the 5th Cavalry Brigade and the eastern column of the German Cavalry was more serious. The 5th Brigade had been posted on the west bank of the Oise, and at 10.30 a.m. General Chetwode moved to Moy, a village two miles east of Cerizy. Here the Scots Greys furnished a line of outposts on the high ground in front of the village with the 20th Hussars as support, the 12th Lancers and guns being in reserve at Moy.

About midday the enemy came into sight on the main road from St. Quentin. The advance troop of the Greys was driven in by superior numbers, but the fire of the support stopped any further advance, until about 2 p.m. two squadrons came on in close formation along the eastern side of the road. These, being met by the fire of the Greys, and of two guns that had been sent up from Moy, dismounted. But the burst of the shells stampeded the horses, and the men after a little wild firing followed them.

General Chetwode then sent his other four guns into action and ordered the 12th Lancers, with two squadrons of the Greys in support, to move round the left flank of the enemy and the 20th Hussars to advance along the St. Quentin road against the German right. The leading squadron (C) of the 12th then came on a Brigade of Cavalry advancing on Moy, but their fire obliged the men to dismount, and, the guns coming into action, their horses also were stampeded. C Squadron then mounted and, led by Colonel Wormald, charged. Their lances did deadly execution among the Germans, who fled in all directions, leaving 80 dead and wounded on the ground. The guns then opened fire again with such good effect that the enemy lost another 200 men before they got under cover, and the advance of the brigade was effectually stopped.

In this spirited little action the 12th lost one officer and four men killed, and Colonel Wormald and four men wounded, the other casualties of the Brigade being about 20 in all. General Chetwode, having collected his wounded, retired to Sinceny and Autreville, on the left of the 1st Corps, where he halted for the night.

The position of the German 1st and 2nd Armies on the night of the 28th were as follows :—

On the right cavalry and field guns were in pursuit of General d'Amade. The rest of the 1st Army had moved south-west and across the British front. The 3rd Corps was at Bellenglise close to St. Quentin, the heads of three other

1914 Corps were on the Somme on a front six miles on either side of Peronne, the 9th Corps a march behind on the left.

Of the 2nd Army (Von Bülow) the two Corps on his left were halted in front of the 5th French Army. The 1st Cavalry Corps were moving south of St. Quentin, the 7th Corps was marching to St. Quentin, and the 10th Reserve Corps six miles south-west of Etreux. Subsequently Von Bülow ordered the 10th Reserve Corps and the 7th Corps to march westward to Ham and St. Simon.

Thus on the 28th touch with the British Army was practically lost as the gap between the two German Armies was gradually increasing until they were some 14 miles apart. Furthermore, the two Generals received orders from the Headquarter Staff directing the 1st Army and 2nd Cavalry Corps to march west of the Oise towards the lower Seine and the 2nd Army and 1st Cavalry Corps towards Paris, which in fact confirmed their present movements.

The French 5th Army after the fighting about Charleroi and the Sambre had retreated before the 2nd German Army to the south-west with the intention of reforming its front on the line Laon-La Fère. On the evening of the 28th the 5th Army was facing north and north-west behind the Oise from Vervins to near La Fère, the 2nd German Army being in contact with the whole front and in possession of the bridge at Guise.

The new French 6th Army under General Maunoury was being rapidly formed on the British left, with the Headquarters at Montdidier, and now comprised six Divisions of Infantry and a Provisional Cavalry Division.

The casualties of the British Army from the 23rd to the 27th August in killed, wounded and missing of all ranks were 14,546, and were distributed as under :—

	August 23rd (Mons)	24th	25th	26th (Le Cateau)	27th
Cavalry	6	252	123	15	14
1st Corps :—					
1st Division	9	42	32	61	826
2nd Division	35	59	230	344	48
2nd Corps :—					
3rd Division	1185	557	357	1796	50
5th Division	386	1656	62	2366	76
4th Division	—	—	65	3158	58
19th Brigade	17	40	36	477	108
	1638	2606	905	8217	1180

29th Aug. In order to delay the advance of Von Bülow, General Joffre ordered his 5th Army to attack towards St. Quentin on the 29th, but the change of direction had caused the right wing of the German 2nd Army to be strengthened, the enemy had also crossed the Oise on the evening of the 28th in force, and after driving back General Valabrègue's Reserve Divisions were now threatening the right flank of the 5th Army. The attack in the direction of Peronne was then broken off, and though a counter attack drove the Germans back over the Oise no further progress was made. This action the Germans call the Battle of Guise, and though in reality it was quite indecisive, Von Bülow, for some reason, imagined that he had inflicted a crushing defeat on his opponents, and as Von Kluck himself had reported that he had effectually disposed of Sir J. French, Von Bülow asked him to join up with the 2nd Army and wipe out the French altogether. Von Kluck's right had been engaged all the morning with General Maunoury's Army, and there had been some severe fighting at 1914 Proyart, 10 miles south-west of Peronne, and at Rosières, six miles south of Proyart, but he now changed the direction of the march of his columns with the view of complying with Von Bülow's request.

This move had two effects. It relieved the pressure on Maunoury, freeing him from the danger of having his left flank turned, and it again threatened the line of retreat of Sir J. French.

The 29th had been a day of much needed rest for the British, as far at least as the infantry were concerned, but late in the afternoon reports of Von Kluck's new movement reached the Field-Marshal, and orders were given to General Smith-Dorrien to withdraw the whole of the 2nd Corps south of the Oise. At 6 p.m. the march began. The troops reached their destinations between 9 p.m. and midnight, the 3rd Division moving to Cuts, the 5th to Carlepont, the 4th to the north of Carlepont, a Brigade being left north of the Oise as rear-guard. The 1st and 2nd Cavalry Brigades followed.

But though the Infantry were not engaged, the enemy showed considerable activity all along the front. At 5 a.m. the 16th were driven out of Jussy by a strong force of infantry and machine guns, but were able to keep the enemy off until the bridge over the Crozat Canal had been destroyed. The whole of the 3rd Brigade then retired slowly to Chauny, $6\frac{1}{2}$ miles south-west of La Fère. The 16th casualties this day were two men wounded and one missing. Between 8 and 9 a.m. the 2nd Cavalry Brigade was engaged with a force of all arms coming from Ham, and the Brigade retired to Guiscard. As reports came in that strong columns of the enemy were crossing the Somme at Pargny and Bethencourt, the 4th Division sent up a battalion of infantry to support the Cavalry, but the enemy made no attempt to advance, and the fighting gradually died down.

In the afternoon General Joffre had a conference with Sir J. French at Compiègne, whither Headquarters had been moved from Noyon. As he desired to make a stand on the Rheims-Amiens line he asked that the British Army should remain in line with his 5th and 6th Armies, but the Field-Marshal represented strongly that his men were tired out and in urgent need of rest, and were not in a condition to attack. The French Commander-in-Chief, after hearing the report of the ill success of the 5th Army, reluctantly gave orders for a further retreat to the line Soissons-Compiègne, behind the Aisne, and abandoned his intention to hold Rheims.

This day the 4th Division and the 19th Infantry were formally made into a 30th 3rd Corps under General Pulteney, who had joined from England. Aug.

The 1st Corps moved off at 3 a.m. covered on the east by the 5th Cavalry Brigade and on the west by the 3rd, and halted for the night at Allemant (eight miles north of Soissons) and Passy. The 2nd and 3rd Corps, marching later, halted on the Aisne about Attichy. The 5th and 3rd Cavalry Brigades billeted at Vauxaillon and Fontenoy, and the 1st, 2nd and 4th round Compiègne.

The retreat was unmolested, as also was that of the 5th Army, but General Maunoury had some considerable fighting before he got his army away. He halted eventually on the line Estrées St. Denis (five miles from Compiègne) —Quiry.

On the 31st the retreat was resumed. The 1st Corps halted at Missy and 31st Laversine, the 2nd at Coyolles, south-west of Villers-Cottérets, and Crèpy en Aug. Valois, the 3rd about Verberie at the south-western corner of the Forest of Compiègne. The 5th and 3rd Cavalry Brigades halted near the 1st Corps, the 16th being billeted in Chelles, the 4th at Verberie, and the 2nd west of it at Chevrières in touch with the French 6th Army, now on the line Chevrières-

1914 Beauvais, the 1st and L Battery R.H.A. at Nèry, which it did not reach until after night-fall, having made a wide sweep from Compiègne and Verberie without seeing any sign of the enemy.

There was no fighting this day, except a rear-guard skirmish between the 3rd Hussars (4th Cavalry Brigade) and the German 3rd Hussars (the Divisional Cavalry of the German 3rd Corps), in which the latter suffered somewhat severely. The left of the 5th Army was now at Vauxaillon, 12 miles north of the British right.

The wheel of Von Kluck to the south-west was now fully developed, and General Maunoury's front was practically clear of the enemy. Von Bülow remained halted, apparently waiting for Von Kluck to come up on his right.

1st Sept. On the night of the 31st August orders were issued to resume the march early the next morning, the 1st Corps to La Ferté Milon—Betz, the 2nd to Betz—Nanteuil, the 3rd to Nanteuil—Baron, the Cavalry Division to Baron—Mont l'Eveque.

There had been little fighting on the two previous days, but on the 1st September the enemy fully made up for their previous inaction, for the day began with the extraordinary combat of Nèry, where the 4th German Cavalry Division and the 1st Cavalry Brigade had actually encamped within a mile of each other, neither being in the least aware of this close proximity, the Germans, after a long march, not having arrived at their halting place until late at night. The 1st Brigade was to have marched off at 4.30 a.m., but when the troops paraded there was such a dense fog that the Brigadier postponed the start hoping that this might clear off when the sun rose. The men were busy preparing breakfast and watering their horses when a patrol of the 11th Hussars galloped in with the intelligence that a large body of the enemy's Cavalry was coming up, and immediately afterwards a heavy fire of all arms swept the village from the high ground overlooking it. What with the fog and the surprise the greatest confusion prevailed for some moments. The horses of the Bays broke away and stampeded, and there was great difficulty in bringing the H.A. Battery into action as it was formed up on the road in column of route, ready to march, when the shells began to drop on it. In a few minutes half the officers went down, and five of the guns were put out of action, one only escaping the fate of the rest, and continuing to fire. The three regiments held the outskirts and approaches to the village dismounted, and a report of the situation brought up the 4th Cavalry Brigade from St. Vaast just as the mist began to clear, followed by a battalion of infantry from Verberie and another from Saintines. The guns (I Battery) came into action and speedily silenced the enemy, but not until the one remaining gun of L Battery had ceased fire, having exhausted all the ammunition within reach. The 11th Hussars then mounted and charged into the enemy's line of guns, only to find that the gun-crews had run away into the woods after dragging off four out of the original 12, and that the Cavalry had followed their example. The 11th continued the pursuit for another mile, when they were recalled after taking 75 prisoners belonging to various regiments of the 4th Cavalry Division. The whole Division had in fact been completely routed, for the Brigades fled in all directions, and the Corps was only got together after days of wandering about in the woods, where the four missing guns were afterwards picked up and brought in.

The casualties of the 1st Brigade in all were about 130 of all ranks only, but the unlucky L Battery suffered very severely, losing five officers and 49 men, among them being their gallant Commander, Captain Bradbury, who was awarded the V.C., but died of his wounds before he actually received it.

Colonel Ansell, of the 5th Dragoon Guards, was also killed. The action was over shortly before 9 a.m.

1914

The 5th Division had delayed its march until the issue of the combat of Nèry was decided, and its outposts and subsequently its rear-guard were attacked by the five Jager battalions of Von Marwitz, but these were easily beaten off and the remainder of the march was unmolested.

The 1st Corps marched at 4 a.m. by two roads through the forest of Villars Cottérets, covered on the right by the 5th Cavalry Brigade and on the left by the 3rd, both brigades operating outside the forest. The 3rd had assembled at Malefontaine. The Brigade came into contact with the enemy's advance-guard at Taillefontaine. The 4th Hussars, being rear-guard, were engaged all the morning among the scattered woodlands and had several casualties, including their commanding officer, Lieut.-Colonel Hogg, who was killed. Eventually the enemy was shaken off and the Brigade reached Antilly, where it billeted for the night.

East of Taillefontaine there was a somewhat serious rear-guard action where the 4th Guards Brigade became involved in a combat in the forest with very superior numbers. Eventually the Brigade was withdrawn, but the action lasted until 6 p.m. The Irish Guards lost heavily, and their commanding officer, Lieut.-Colonel the Hon. G. Morris, was killed. Brigadier-General Scott-Kerr was also severely wounded. The Guards Brigade lost over 300 of all ranks, two platoons of the Grenadiers being surrounded and destroyed after fighting till every man of them was down, and the 6th Infantry Brigade, which was also engaged, lost another 100.

Later on it was ascertained that the enemy's loss far exceeded that of the British, and that at the close of the action all further pursuit had to be abandoned.

Covered by their rear-guards the main columns of all three Corps reached their respective halting places late in the evening without hindrance, after a toilsome march averaging 20 miles.

The Field-Marshal returned to Dammartin from Paris at 6.45 a.m. after an interview with Lord Kitchener, in which he successfully asserted his own independence as Commander-in-Chief of the Army in the Field. Orders had already been given out for the retreat to be resumed at 7 a.m. on the 2nd, but Sir J. French was disquieted by the reports which he received which not only showed that strong forces of the enemy were closing in upon him, but that some of the German Cavalry had worked their way through the woods and were then actually in rear of the British line. He therefore, fearing a night attack, gave fresh orders for his weary troops directing them to move off at 1 a.m. The fact was that Von Kluck, having left Von Marwitz and his 4th Reserve Corps to watch General Maunoury, whose army was at Senlis and south of it, was moving south-east with the intention of sweeping up what he thought to be the broken remnant of the British Army before joining Von Bülow. Von Kluck, being entirely ignorant of the true position, was marching right across the front of the British line, and but for the shortened marches which the fatigue of the troops necessitated, would not have come into contact at all. As it was his flanking Cavalry patrols encountered the British Cavalry rear-guards only. Some of the enemy's Cavalry that were reported to be behind the line were probably troops which had wandered away in the woods after the combat at Nèry, for the four guns that had been got away were picked up near Ermononville. These scattered parties made off in various directions and a considerable quantity of abandoned equipment was found littered about the

1914 roads. There was no further contact with the enemy during the retreat except some trifling skirmishes by Cavalry patrols.

2nd Sept. The position on the evening of the 2nd September was as under:—
5th Cavalry Brigade and 1st Corps in the villages just north of Meaux.
3rd Cavalry Brigade, Isles les Villenoy, S.S.W. of Meaux.
2nd Corps, Monthyon—Montge—Villenoy.
3rd Corps, Eve—Dammartin.
Cavalry Division, Thieux—Moussy le Vieux—Le Mesnil Amelot.

The front therefore extended from Meaux to Dammartin. On the right the 5th Army was a march to the north, the left of the infantry being 25 miles away south-west of Fère en Tardinois, and the Cavalry north of Chateau Thierry. From Dammartin the French Provisional Cavalry Division covered the line to Senlis and thence north-west through Creil to Mouy. Behind it lay Maunoury's 6th Army.

After a consultation with the French General Staff, the Field-Marshal issued orders for the retreat across the Marne, and to avoid closing in upon the defences of Paris, the line of march was directed to the south-east.

3rd Sept. The troops marched off between 3 and 4 a.m. covered by the 3rd and 5th Cavalry Brigades. The 1st Division crossed the Marne at Trilport, the 2nd and 3rd at Meaux, the 5th at Isles les Villenoy, the 3rd Corps and the Cavalry Division at Lagny, and by evening the Army had crossed to the south of the river and was distributed along the villages from Juarre westward to Nogent, after destroying all the bridges. The 3rd Brigade had no fighting, but the 5th had a short combat north of Lizy on the Ourcq, but was not followed, and crossed the Marne at La Ferte sous Jouarre. The 3rd passed through the infantry and billeted at Mont-Guichet, crossing the Marne at Germigny.

The 5th Army had also continued its retreat, and after a combat at Chateau Thierry had fallen back across the Marne and was now in line with the British, its left being about ten miles distant. Von Kluck was now rapidly closing in on the 5th Army, the heads of two of his Corps having crossed the Marne at Chezy and La Ferte sous Jouarre.

The Army expected to have a rest on the 4th, but Joffre was not yet ready for his meditated attack, and orders were issued for a further retirement to the line of the Grand Morin.

4th Sept. At daybreak the 5th Cavalry Brigade, with the 3rd in support, advanced eastward to Doue. The patrols of the 5th came into contact with the enemy about midday, and a troop of the Greys which had been sent to Rebais with the expectation of finding French Cavalry there, found it occupied by the enemy and, being taken by surprise, the whole troop was wiped out, only five men escaping. Some skirmishing, principally artillery fire, was kept up until late in the afternoon, when both Brigades were withdrawn, the 3rd to Chailly en Brie, where it billeted for the night. Meanwhile the 1st Corps had marched to Aulnoy and Colomniers, Mouroux and Girmoutiers. The 2nd and 3rd Corps, with the Cavalry Division, did not march until after dark.

This day a new French Army, commanded by General Foch, came officially into being. This Army was, however, no addition to the strength as it had been merely formed out of Divisions brought from the left of the 3rd and the right of the 4th Armies.

5th Sept. In accordance with the original directions of the French Commander-in-Chief, Sir John French ordered a further retirement for the 5th. This march was made in order to give the 6th Army more room for deployment, but in view of the intended counter-attack planned to take place on the 6th the move was superfluous. However, the notification of this last was not received by the Field-Marshal until the troops had completed their march. The 1st Corps halted at Rosoy, the 2nd Corps in and east of Tournau, and the 3rd Corps on the left of the 2nd from Ozoir-la-Ferrière to Brie-Comte-Robert, where it was touching the outer defences of Paris. The Cavalry Division moved to the right rear of the Army to Mormant and the villages north of it. During this move the 3rd Brigade acted as rear-guard and the 5th as last flank guard. The two Brigades encamped at Vilbert. This day the 3rd and 5th Brigades were placed under the command of Brigadier-General Hubert Gough, though they were not formally constituted a Division in Orders until September 16th. Brigadier-General J. Vaughan was appointed to the command of the 3rd Brigade, and so the memorable Retreat from Mons came at last to an end. The retreat had lasted, with only one halt, thirteen days, and the troops had marched some 200 miles, though the actual distance in a straight line is 130. On the average the Cavalry and Artillery only had three hours and the Infantry four hours' rest in 24 hours.

During the 4th and 5th September the Army was reinforced by drafts of men from England, but very little new equipment came up. Both the men and stores were only forwarded under great difficulties owing to the change of the sea Base, which had been transferred to St. Nazaire from Havre and Boulogne at the end of August. Between the 1st and 5th no less than 60,000 tons of stores, 15,000 men, and 1,500 horses had been removed from Havre to St. Nazaire, but the landing and sorting of the stores had hardly begun on the 5th notwithstanding the utmost efforts of the Base Staff, and the lost guns were not replaced.

On the 5th September there were some 20,000 men wanting. Of these about 5,000 stragglers afterwards rejoined their units, leaving a total of killed, wounded, and missing of 15,000, together with 49 guns. By far the greater portion of these losses were suffered by the 2nd and 3rd Corps, for, with the exception of the combats at Landrecies and Maroilles and the three disastrous rear-guard actions at Le Fayt, Etreux and Villers Cottérêts, the Corps had done no serious fighting (the casualties at Mons for the 23rd and 24th August were under 150 of all ranks), and it had lost only two guns, and the loss of the Munsters at Etreux was now made good by the transfer of the Cameron Highlanders to the 1st Brigade.

The new drafts could by no means sufficiently replace the losses of the 2nd and 3rd Corps, which in addition to the guns was deficient of transport wagons, entrenching tools, and other equipment which had been lost or abandoned during the first four days of the retreat.

The Cavalry had on the whole escaped with comparatively few casualties. They amounted altogether to little over 400 of all ranks, and of these 252 were accounted for on the 24th August, the 9th Lancers being the chief sufferers. The 16th themselves were fortunate, for, though the regiment had been under shell fire nearly every day during the retreat, its casualties only amounted to two officers and 13 other ranks wounded.

Generally all the horses were in fair condition considering what they had gone through, but were in want of horse-shoes and shoeing.

On the three last days of August the Russians were decisively defeated by Von Hindenburg at Tannenberg, and in consequence their invasion of North Germany came to a sudden end. This disaster came at a time very inopportune to the Allies in France, for the Kaiser had been so agitated by the invasion of his beloved Prussia that, relying on the sanguine reports he received of the alleged victories over the British and French, he had given peremptory orders to transfer six Corps from the Western to the Eastern Front, and one Corps

1914 was actually being entrained at Thionville when fresh orders were issued countermanding the move.

APPENDICES TO CHAPTER XXXV.

1.—Mons and Afterwards.
2.—Table of Marches.

APPENDIX I.

Mons and Afterwards.

Fortune had presented Von Kluck with one of those golden opportunities that so seldom fall to the lot of a General in the field, and he threw it away by his precipitate action in commencing the battle without any knowledge of the actual position. Either he was in too great a hurry to fulfil the instructions of his Imperial master to wipe out the Contemptible British, or he was himself actuated by a lordly contempt for his opponents; probably by a mixture of both motives, for instead of acting in unison with Von Bülow and the 2nd German Army, and also utilising his great superiority of force by making a flank attack, he began the battle without any reconnaisance of the position and the action speedily developed into a simple frontal attack on the 2nd Corps and the 19th Brigade.

Now the moment that Von Bülow and the Saxons of Von Hausen drove the French 5th Army from their positions on the Sambre, all fear of a counter-attack on the part of the British Army disappeared. It is clear that Von Kluck might have held the front of the 2nd Corps with even one of the four Corps that were in his battle-line, and if he had massed the other three on the left of Sir John French's weak line, he could have created a position that not even the fighting qualities of the British soldier could have prevented from ending, at the best, in a most serious strategic disaster, for the Field-Marshal would have had inevitably to choose between either taking refuge behind the forts of Maubeuge, or being driven pell-mell on to the flank of the retreating French 5th Army. In either case the way to Paris would have been open to Von Kluck.

The whole force of the attack fell upon the 2nd Corps, for the 1st Corps was hardly engaged at all, its total casualties on the 23rd and 24th being less than 200 of all ranks. Two and a half Divisions therefore, some 30,000 bayonets, extended over a front of 16 miles, less than 2,000 men per mile, with 170 guns, met, and defeated, the attack of three German Corps, the 3rd, 4th and 9th, with at least 430 guns, after 12 hours' fighting, inflicting great loss on the enemy with only 1,600 casualties to themselves. Surely one of the finest achievements in the long and glorious history of the British Army.

The victory showed clearly at the beginning of the war the superior qualities of the British soldier, and disposed, once for all, of the boasted invincibility of the German. The battle was won by discipline, coolness, and above all by good shooting. When it came to rifle fire the German troops had no chance at all. Their shooting was bad in the extreme, and their mass attack was helpless under the cool, deliberate, yet rapid, fire with which it was met. It was indeed so rapid and so accurate that the German accounts of the battle always attribute it to machine-gun fire.

The German Cavalry, too, made a very poor show. The men had not been 1914 taught to fight on foot. It depended in that respect on the regiments of Jäger infantry that formed part of every Cavalry Division. These were dragged about with the mounted troops on motor lorries, carts, or any wheeled vehicle that could be got together, and as they were of course restricted to the roads the Cavalry had to conform to their movements. The Cavalry, therefore, were slow, and their reconnaisance feeble. The men's riding was bad, their attack without dash, and in the whole history of the war on no single occasion was there an encounter between the British and German Cavalry in which the latter were not completely worsted. The German also is the worst horse-master in the world, as the Englishman is the best, for the German treats his horse with the same callous brutality that he metes out to every living thing that is unlucky enough to come under his domination. Possibly the inaction of the German Cavalry after Mons and Le Cateau was to be partly attributed to the condition of the horses. Probably Von Marwitz had scarcely a horse without at least a sore back by August 24th.

The Artillery was the best arm the Germans possessed, and next to that the machine gun, to which last a great deal more attention had been paid than had been the case in the British Army. Certainly the German machine guns were more effectively used, for after all there was no very great disparity in numbers when the war began.

The battle of Le Cateau on August 26th was fought under somewhat similar conditions, for here again the 2nd Corps had to resist the attack of six German Divisions. The 2nd Corps had certainly been reinforced by the 4th Division, but this was without its artillery and without its auxiliary services, while to set against it Von Kluck had also been strengthened by the arrival of four Cavalry Divisions on the right of his line. Furthermore, the position had been taken up in haste, there had been no time to prepare any adequate defences, both flanks were uncovered, the right by the retreat of the 1st Corps, and the left by that of the French under d'Amade, though late in the afternoon this last was in some respect qualified by the arrival of the French Cavalry Corps of General Sordet.

Under these circumstances the 2nd Corps fought under every sort of disadvantage; nevertheless, it held its ground successfully for six hours, and eventually succeeded in breaking off the action and effecting a retreat which the heavy loss that had been inflicted on the enemy rendered practically unmolested.

Here again the fight put up by the German Cavalry, which made a dismounted attack, aided by its Jägers, was of the poorest description, and after a brief initial success it was beaten off by the 4th Division with heavy loss, and for the rest of the day remained in hiding.*

Von Kluck was, as at Mons, completely ignorant of the true situation. He thought that the British line faced the East, instead of nearly North, that he had against him the whole British Army, reinforced by the 6th Division, still in England, and that the Army was based on Calais and Dunkirk. Again, as at Mons, in consequence of this mistake, his intended flank attack developed into a frontal one, and again the cool, rapid, and accurate rifle fire of the British soldier proved too much for the courage of the German troops.

Neither Von Kluck, nor any other of the German authorities, give any details of the Battle of Le Cateau, which they style the "Battle of St. Quentin," beyond claiming a complete victory. The German losses are carefully concealed, while those of the British are grossly exaggerated. The German troops

---

* "Cowering among the houses of Wambaix and Cattenières," says Hauptman Wirth.

1914 were told that 12,000 prisoners had been taken, with eight batteries of artillery, but Von Kluck himself confirms the official report of V. Zwehl that the prisoners did not exceed 2,600, including wounded, many of these last having been perforce left on the battlefield. Thirty-eight guns in all were abandoned, of which the greater number had been smashed up by direct hits.

Though the retreat was not followed up by the enemy it was made under great difficulties. The transport had been sent away in good time to the rear, but every road was blocked with ever increasing streams of the hapless inhabitants who were, with well-founded apprehension, flying from the threatened barbarities of their savage invaders, and who took with them as much of their cherished belongings as could be heaped on any sort of wheeled vehicle that could be obtained from a farm wagon to a perambulator. Through this congested mass the retreating troops had to thread their way, but though on each flank and at the rear of every column there might be a ragged fringe of stragglers who had lost their units, the solid core of each Brigade maintained its discipline and order, the men tramping stolidly on in sultry heat or drenching rain, their hearts filled only with sullen resentment at having to retreat before an enemy whom they knew they had beaten in fair fight, and a longing for the moment when the word should be given for them to turn and face him again.

To an onlooker the retreat certainly did look unpleasantly like a rout, for as the evening closed in the formed columns could hardly be distinguished among the crowd of fugitives, while the roadside was strewn with broken vehicles of all sorts, great-coats, valises and equipment that had been discarded by the hot and weary men, and here and there mounds of provision boxes which the Quartermaster-General, finding it impossible in the prevailing confusion to issue rations, had dumped on the road side so that the troops could help themselves as they passed.

But order was soon evolved out of this seeming chaos. The roads were gradually cleared, and by the time St. Quentin was reached on the morning of the 27th, where rations and forage were obtained, all semblance of disorder had come to an end. Thus the British Expeditionary Force, small as it was, had played a decisive part in the campaign, for it had undoubtedly saved the 5th French Army from an attack by Von Kluck on its line of retreat which must have inevitably resulted in irretrievable disaster, it had saved Paris for the present, and it had given the French Commander-in-Chief the much-needed time which he required to mature his plans.

Up to this time the British nation at large had by no means realised the serious nature of the war. The general expectation was that the war would be over in three months. Indeed it was not unusual to hear ultra-sanguine people saying that when peace terms were settled we must not be too hard on the poor Germans, who had been unwillingly dragged into the war by the Kaiser and his entourage!

But on the Sunday after the battle of Mons the " Times " published a special edition purporting to give a full account of the battle and the retreat. This, embellished as it was by the lurid pen of the writer, gave a very rude shock to the public complacency, and its effect was enhanced by the verification of the report of the fall of Namur to which a quite undue importance was attached.

The military censors had cut out a good deal of the worst of this report, and there was some surprise at the Government giving permission to publish it at all, but the authorities were probably by no means averse to giving the nation a tonic that might make it take the war a little more seriously and do something to dispel the " business as usual " folly. This it most certainly did with most salutary results.

APPENDIX II.

1914

Mons and the Retreat.

Length of Marches, 20th August to 6th September.

	1st Corps.		2nd Corps.		3rd Corps.	
	1st Div.	2nd Div.	3rd Div.	5th Div.	19th Bgde.	4th Div.
Advance—						
Aug. 20	8½	—	2	2	—	—
,, 21	13	—	21	21	—	—
,, 22	22½	20	17	17	—	—
Battle of Mons—						
Aug. 23	—	22	5	5	7	—
Retreat—						
Aug. 24	17	14	15	10	13	—
,, 25	15½	24	25	24	19	6
Le Cateau—						
Aug. 26	15	16	14	15	40	10
Retreat—						
Aug. 27	23	15	17	23		21
Aug. 28	21	20	27	20	17	20½
,, 29	Rest	2	25	12	15	14
,, 30	10	23		4	Rest	12½
,, 31	18	12	15	15	19	15
Sept. 1	19	19	15	12	14	11½
,, 2	18½	21	13	14	13	9½
,, 3	16½	18	10	18	22	17½
,, 4	11½	8	Rest	Rest	Rest	Rest
,, 5	15	16	16	16	14	14
Miles	244	250	237	216	193	151½

Note that many units much exceeded these distances.

CHAPTER XXXVI.

September 6th to September 9th, 1914.

Situation on September 6th. French and German Armies. Position of Von Kluck. New orders of the H.Q. German Staff. Action of Von Bülow. Obstinacy of Von Kluck. Orders by General Joffre. Orders of Sir J. French for the 6th. Battle of the Marne. September 6th, Attack by General Maunoury. Attack by French 5th Army. Position at night-fall. September 7th, Advance of the British Army. Cavalry combats. Advance of the French Armies. Heavy fighting in front of Paris all day with no decisive results. September 8th, Continuous fighting between Von Kluck and General Maunoury. The French left thrown back. Advance of the British Army. Combats along the line of the Petit Morin. Position at

1914 night-fall. German defeat at Nancy. Retreat of Von Bülow. Von Molke's peremptory order to Von Kluck, who is placed under command of Von Bülow. September 9th, Retreat of Von Kluck. British advance. Crossing of the Marne. General retreat of the 1st and 2nd German Armies and end of the Battle of the Marne.

Summary of Events, September 6th to September 9th, 1914.—September 6th, Battle of the Marne begins. 7th, Capitulation of Maubeuge; Battle of Nancy. 8th, Retreat of Von Kluck. 9th, End of Battle of the Marne.

6th Sept. The situation on the morning of the 6th September, 1914, was as follows:—

FRENCH ARMIES.—1st Army, General Dubail. Facing nearly due east from Belfort, on the south, to Nancy.

2nd Army, General de Castelnau. Nancy to opposite St. Mihiel.

3rd Army, General Sarrail, disposed on a salient of which the apex was Verdun, the right wing facing N.E. and the left bent back facing N.W.

4th Army, General de Langle de Cary. Across the Marne facing Chalons.

9th Army, General Foch, facing the St. Gond Marshes.

5th Army, General Franchet d'Esperey (who had replaced Lanrezac), facing north, Sezanne to Provins.

6th Army, General Maunoury, Meaux to five miles north of Dammartin.

BRITISH ARMY.—Mormant to Brie Comte Robert, facing north-east.

GERMAN ARMIES.—7th Army, V. Heeringen, facing General Dubail.

6th Army, Prince Ruprecht of Bavaria, facing de Castelnau.

5th, German Crown Prince, facing Sarrail.

4th, Grand Duke Albrecht, facing de Langle de Carey.

3rd, V. Hausen, facing Foch.

2nd, V. Bülow, facing Franchet d'Esperey, on a line from Vertus, half-way between Epernay and Gond and Montmirail, on the Petit Morin.

1st Army, V. Kluck. The outpost line of the 1st German Army extended in a wide semi-circle from Esternay on the Grand Morin through Villières St. George, Vaudoy and Montcerf to Crècy, and thence northwards through Meaux and St. Soupplets to Nanteuil. The 4th Reserve Corps and a Cavalry Division were posted north of Meaux and left in observation of the French 6th Army, while the other Corps were now on the march nearly due south, with the heads of their columns crossing the Grand Morin. South of the river covering the advance were the 1st Cavalry Corps and part of the 4th.

Thus the 1st, 2nd, 3rd, 4th, and even part of the 5th German Armies were inside a salient, Von Kluck with the 1st Army being in an especially dangerous position, for Sir J. French's refusal to stand and fight sooner had really materially favoured the plan of the French Commander-in-Chief, and had brought him well within the trap that the latter had set for him.

On the 4th some understanding of the true position seems to have been arrived at by Headquarter German Staff, which appears to have been better served by its Intelligence Department than were the Generals in the Field. Von Molke did not share Von Kluck's obstinate obsession that he had broken up the British Army, and that it might be now a negligable factor as far as any offensive action went. A new set of orders were issued in which the 1st and 2nd Armies were directed to cease their advance southward and to remain facing Paris and the French 6th Army, the 1st between the Oise and the Marne, the 2nd between the Marne and the Seine. The 4th and 5th Armies were ordered to attack in a south-easterly direction, and the 6th and 7th to take the offensive as soon as possible.

On receipt of this order, Von Bülow, who had shown more capacity so far than any other German General, and who distrusted Von Kluck's optimism, 1914 at once began to change front to the west, partly by moving his left forward, and partly by throwing his right back.

Von Kluck had obstinately persisted in his advance south-east up to the last moment. On the morning of the 5th September his 2nd Corps was crossing the Grand Morin between Crècy and Mouroux, his 1st Corps, moving from Rebais, had crossed the river. He had placed his 2nd Corps and 9th Corps at the disposal of Von Bülow in anticipation of the intended attack on the 5th French Army, and with the exception of his 4th Cavalry Division on his extreme left, the whole of his Cavalry was across the Grand Morin. He therefore hesitated to obey Von Molke's order, which indeed it was not easy in his present position to comply with.

But the French 6th Army was daily gaining strength, and by the 5th September General Gallieni, who commanded the Paris garrison, and General Maunoury had between them upwards of 150,000 men within striking distance of Von Kluck's right flank.

On the afternoon of the 5th September there was a collision between the opposing forces north of Meaux, and the reports that reached Von Kluck of the French strength there were very disquieting. This coming on the top of the new orders, at last induced him to desist, at any rate for the time, from his move to the south.

On the 5th General Joffre's orders to begin the offensive on the next day 5th were received at the British Headquarters. These were, in brief, that the 6th Sept. Army should move on Meaux; the British, facing east, was to attack in the general direction of Montmirail, on the front Changis—Coulommiers. The 2nd Cavalry Corps (French) was to connect the British right with the 5th Army. The 5th Army was to attack to the north, the 9th Army to cover the right of the advance of the 5th, behind the St. Goud Marches, the 4th and 3rd Armies were to act in concert, the 4th to hold the enemy while the 3rd attacked any German troops moving west along the east side of the Argonne.

The Field-Marshal in the evening then issued the operation orders for the next day as follows:—

The Army will advance eastward with the view of attacking. The left will be covered by the 6th French Army also moving east, the right by the 5th Army moving north.

The 1st Corps will march by Guignes—Chaumes—Fontenoy—Marles to Lumigny, with the left on Lumigny, the right on La Chaplle Iger.

The 2nd Corps by Coubert—Tournau to Villenouve le Comte, with left on Villeneuve, right on La Houssaye.

The 3rd Corps by all roads west of 2nd Corps to neighbourhood of Bailly, facing east.

Cavalry.—Cavalry Division to guard left flank and front of 1st Corps on line Jouy le Chatel, connecting with 5th Army, and Coulommiers in contact with the 3rd and 5th Brigades. The 3rd and 5th Brigades will act independently under Brigadier-General H. Gough, covering the 2nd Corps, in contact with the Cavalry Division on the right, and 6th French Army on left.

Early on the 6th, therefore, the memorable Battle of the Marne began with 6th an attack all along the line. Maunoury attacked with seven Divisions of Sept. Infantry along the line Crècy, Meaux, Douy, Nanteuil, and Von Kluck, now fully alive to the danger to his right, issued orders for his 2nd and 4th Corps to march at once to the assistance of the 4th Reserve Corps and for the Cavalry now south of the Grand Morin to recross the river and cover the movement. Meanwhile the 5th Army attacked Von Kluck's 3rd and 9th Corps, driving

1914 them in confusion across the Grand Morin, and but for the intervention of Von Bülow the two Corps would have been entirely routed.

The result of these movements was that a wide and increasing gap was created between the 1st and 2nd German Armies, and into this gap was thrust the British Army, and though contact was established soon after the march began it was only with the German Cavalry screen, for away behind it the airplane reconnaisance reported the main columns to be moving north. The gap between the 1st and 2nd German Armies was found to be covered only by Cavalry and their attached Jager battalions. The British Cavalry Brigades were at first met by some opposition, chiefly artillery fire, and the march of the 1st Corps was held up for a time about Vaudoy, when the 3rd and 5th Brigades were sent in support of the left rear of the Corps, but the enemy made no serious attack, and on the 2nd and 3rd Corps coming up into line the march was resumed. The final position taken up for the night was:—

Cavalry Division, Jouy le Chatel.
1st Corps, Vaudoy—Tonquin—Pezarches.
3rd and 5th Cavalry Brigades, Pezarches—Lumigny.
2nd Corps, Lumigny—Faremoutiers—Mortcerf—La Celle sur Morin.
3rd Corps, Villiers sur Morin—Villeneuve Le Comte—Villeneuve St. Denis.

The heads of the 2nd and 3rd Corps were thus at the Grand Morin, and the 1st Corps and Cavalry a little behind the line on the right rear.

No orders for a further move were issued on the 6th pending the receipt of further instructions from General Joffre, but the troops were ordered to be formed in column of route and ready to march at 8 a.m.

7th Sept. The Cavalry, however, were early in the field, and reported that the enemy were still in retreat. There were a few trifling skirmishes, the only two of any note being a charge of 30 men of the 9th Lancers on a Squadron of Cavalry met with near Dagny. The 9th rode right through the enemy's line, and then back again. Colonel Campbell, who led the charge, was wounded, but the troop retired to Moncel without being followed. And another combat near Faujus, between a squadron of the 18th Hussars and a weak squadron of Guard Dragoons, which was practically wiped out, 63 being killed and wounded, and only three getting away.

At 11 a.m. a message came in from General Joffre to the effect that the 5th Army had been successful in the engagement of the 6th and directing a further advance, which was immediately commenced in the general direction of Rebais, covered by the Cavalry. The 3rd Brigade met with some opposition, the bridges over the Grand Morin east of Coulommiers being held by parties of the enemy, but these were soon driven off by the guns, and the 3rd and 5th Brigades, supported by a Guards Brigade, crossed the river, and halted for the night on the west side of Rebais.

The 2nd and 3rd Corps also crossed the river and halted just north of it.

During the 6th there had been heavy fighting between the 6th French Army and the 1st German Army on the north, and the 5th Army and Von Kluck's two Corps, supported by Von Bülow, on the south-east, and both had been more or less successful. The 5th Army had by the evening got three Corps across the Grand Morin and these were now on the line Charleville, seven miles south-east of Montmirail, while General Maunoury had advanced after a hard fight to some five miles west of the Ourcq River and was on the line Penchard—Etreprilly—Betz, while the enemy was moving his guns to the west bank of the river. On the morning of the 7th Von Kluck seems to have begun to realise that a victory over Maunoury was not so easy a matter as he expected, for he sent an urgent message to Von Bülow asking him to send back the two

Corps which he had left under his orders in the direction La Ferté Milon (on 1914 the Ourcq) and Crouy. This request Von Bülow complied with, and the two Corps, which had both, and especially the 9th, been very severely handled by the French in the fighting on the previous day, marched accordingly. Von Bülow, who was now getting anxious, went on with his movement of wheeling his line to the west. These movements combined to widen the gap between the 1st and 2nd Armies, to clear the way for the advance of the French 5th Army, and to bring his left into collision with Foch and the 9th Army. Von Bülow also sent several messages to Von Kluck urging an immediate retreat across the Ourcq in order to reduce the gap between them.

To all this Von Kluck paid no attention. A furious battle between his Army and the French raged all the 7th September, each side being continually reinforced, the French by General Gallieni from Paris, and the Germans by the troops withdrawn from the south, each General throwing the Brigades and battalions into the fight as they came up. No progress was made by either Army, and at night both were much in the same positions as they were in the morning.

The battle re-commenced under similar conditions on the morning of the 8th and continued all day with varying fortunes, the front of both armies being gradually extended northwards as fresh troops came up; but in the afternoon one of Von Kluck's Brigades which had been left in Brussels unexpectedly arrived on the left flank of the French line and Maunoury was obliged to throw back his left wing to meet this new attack. This greatly encouraged Von Kluck and again he took no heed of Von Bülow's repeated messages of warning that the British were now across the Marne, not only between the two armies, but well behind the left of the 1st. 8th Sept.

Orders had been issued on the evening of the 7th for the advance to be resumed at daybreak on the following morning, and the Cavalry moved off at 4 a.m., covering the front of the 1st and 2nd Corps, the 3rd and 5th Brigades' objective being that part of the Petit Morin between La Tretoire and St. Cyr. The Cavalry advance drove in the enemy's outpost line without any difficulty, but the line of the Petit Morin, which afforded good defensive positions, was found to be strongly held by dismounted Cavalry and Jager, with a plentiful supply of artillery and machine guns, and no further advance was possible until the Infantry Divisions came up.

The fight for the river lasted all day. The German Cavalry for once fought well, their positions were well chosen, and it was not until late in the afternoon that the action came to a close in torrents of rain with the British Army well across the river and the enemy in full retreat.

The troops halted for the night south of the Marne in the following positions :—

Cavalry Division, Replouges.
1st Corps, Basseville—Hondevillers—Boitron.
2nd Corps, Les Feuchieres—Rougeville—Orly.
3rd Corps, Grand Glairet (one mile west of Jouarre).
3rd Cavalry Brigade, Grand Glairet.
5th Cavalry Brigade, between Gibraltar and Rebais.

The casualties in this action amounted to about 600 of all ranks killed and wounded. The 16th did no actual fighting during the day, but were extensively shelled, particularly between 8.30 and 10 a.m., and were fortunate in getting off with only three casualties, two killed, 1 wounded. Five hundred prisoners and 12 machine guns were taken.

On the right the 5th French Army had continued to make good progress,

1914 the most of it having crossed the river, Montmirail and Marchais being now occupied.

The German Headquarter Staff had been more concerned for some days with the battle going on in front of Nancy than with affairs on the western front, this indifference being confirmed by Von Kluck's sanguine reports.

The German 6th and 7th Armies had been engaged in a most determined attempt to break the French line between St. Mihiel and Epinal since the 3rd September. The battle lasted five days, and being fought under the personal observation of the Kaiser himself, who, confident of victory, had made preparations for a triumphant entry into Nancy, it was pressed to the utmost regardless of losses. By the 8th, however, the attack had been finally repulsed by General de Castlenau and the 2nd French Army with frightful slaughter.

The Headquarter Staff then had more leisure to attend to the proceedings of the 1st and 2nd Armies. Von Bülow, now thoroughly alarmed by the increasing dangers of the situation, decided on an immediate retreat on his own part. Having notified Von Kluck of this, and finding him still obstinate, he sent an urgent message direct to Von Molke, who both agreed to the retreat of the 2nd Army, ordering the 3rd and 4th to conform, and sent a peremptory order to Von Kluck to break off the battle with Maunoury and to retire at once to the line of the Aisne, while to make certain he was placed directly under the command of Von Bülow, who was his senior in the Army.

9th Sept. In the afternoon of the 9th, therefore, Von Kluck commenced his preparations for a retreat in the direction of Soissons by giving orders for a withdrawal first of his left, then his centre, and lastly his right, which was to cover the movement. On the 10th Von Bülow, now in command of both the 1st and 2nd Armies, issued the following order :—" The 1st Army on the 11th September will retire behind the Aisne and, covered by the Aisne Valley, will close on the right of the 2nd Army. The passages over the Vesle Valley at Braine and Fismes are being blocked by the 2nd Army with a mixed brigade at each place."

Orders had been issued on the previous evening for the advance to be continued at 5 a.m., and early in the morning the 1st Cavalry Brigade moved to Charly and Nogent, where it seized the bridges over the Marne, while the 4th Cavalry Brigade occupied the bridge at Azy, further east, and three miles below Chateau Thierry. This being effected without any opposition, the two Brigades crossed the river and moved to Mont de Bounal, three miles north of Nogent, where it took up a position to cover the passage of the 1st Corps. This having been effected by 10 a.m., after a short halt, the 1st Corps continued the march to Le Thiolet and Coupru. The 2nd Corps crossed the Marne at Nanteuil and Saacy without fighting, but a mile further north at La Limon the German rear-guard offered a strong opposition to a further advance and considerable fighting ensued. But little progress was made and when night came on the troops had only reached the Chateau Montreuil road, where the heads of the columns halted. The 3rd Corps met with even more effective opposition, for it found the enemy holding the north bank of the Marne in force, and all the bridges destroyed except the railway viaduct near La Ferte sous Jouarre. Some pontoon bridges were with difficulty thrown over the river under a destructive fire, and eventually some battalions were got across, but at night-fall ten of the sixteen battalions of the 3rd Corps were still on the south side.

The positions at night were as follows :—
Cavalry Division, Lucy le Bocage—Domtin.
5th Cavalry Brigade, La Baudière, just west of Domtin.
1st Corps, Le Thiolet—Domtin—Coupru.

2nd Corps, Bezu—Caumont.

1914

3rd Cavalry Brigade, Grand Mont Merrin (south of Marne).

3rd Corps, Luzancy—Juarre—Chamigny.

The line therefore extended from Chateau Thierry through Bezu and La Ferte sous Jouarre to Jouarre. The left of the French 5th Army had reached Chateau Thierry and was in line with the British.

This day C Squadron of the 16th was attached to the 4th Infantry Division as Divisional Cavalry.

And so ended in victory the memorable Battle of the Marne, which may be said to have commenced with the return to the offensive on the 6th of September.

Tactically the end was unsatisfactory, but strategically the results of the victory were of such importance as to rank it among the decisive battles of the world, for with it the German surprise attack on France came to an ignominious end, and all fear of another siege of Paris vanished once and for ever.

The brunt of the battle fell on General Maunoury and the 6th French Army, which had maintained a desperate struggle for three days against Von Kluck. The British Army did little actual fighting, comparatively speaking, during the action, its influence being more moral than physical, but it was its appearance on Von Kluck's left rear that compelled him to break off his battle with Maunoury and begin a retreat that ended on the line of the Aisne.

Here, as before at Mons and Le Cateau, the British Army played a decisive part, a part altogether out of proportion to its insignificance compared with the other forces engaged. On the 5th September the battle line of the Allies from Verdun to the Oise covered a front of nearly 200 miles. Of this the British front occupied but 20, yet it was the British Army that was the deciding factor in the Battle of the Marne, a striking example of what can be accomplished by discipline, training and efficient leading.

CHAPTER XXXVII.

September 11th to September 30th, 1914.

September 10th, The pursuit. The Cavalry Division at Latilly. Capture of a convoy. Halt at Breny and Roset. The 1st Infantry Division combat near Courchamps. General Gough's Brigade. Action near Chezy, rout of the enemy, capture of prisoners and wagons. The line of positions at night-fall. The 3rd and 4th Brigades at Passy. Casualties and captures. September 11th, Pursuit continued. No fighting. Crossing of the Ourcq. September 12th, Instructions of General Joffre. Special Orders of Sir J. French. Advance of the Cavalry. Passage of the Vesle forced at Braisne, Courcelles, and Chassemy. Failure of attempt to cross the Aisne. Position at night-fall. 3rd Cavalry Brigade at Ciry. French positions along the Vesle and Aisne. Geography of valley of the Aisne. Designs of General Joffre. Positions of German 1st and 2nd Armies. September 13th, Orders of Sir J. French. The crossing of the Aisne at Venizel by the 11th Infantry Brigade. Reconnaisance by Cavalry Division. Position at nightfall. September 14th, Battle of the Aisne. German reinforcements from Belgium and Maubeuge. Failure of attack on the Aisne. Position at

1914 night-fall. The 16th billeted at Lime. The French Armies. Definite failure of plan of General Joffre. The casualties. September 16th, The arrival of the 6th Division. Its distribution. Beginning of Trench Warfare. September 16th to 28th, Indecisive attacks and counter-attacks. Formation of 2nd Cavalry Division under General Gough. Extension of the battle line northward.

Summary of Events, September 10th to September 30th, 1914.—September 10th, Final defeat of Austrians in Galicia. 13th, 1st Battle of the Aisne begins. 17th, Belgian Army retires to Antwerp. 18th, End of First Battle of the Aisne; Commencement of "Trench Warfare"; Bombardment of Rheims. 28th, Siege of Antwerp begins. 29th, Battle of Albert.

Sir J. French did not wait for further instructions from the French Commander-in-Chief, but on the evening of the 9th gave orders for the troops to pursue the retreating enemy with the utmost vigour.

10th Sept. The forward march began at 5 a.m. and by 8 a.m. reports came in that the Germans had vacated the Ourcq and Marne valleys. The Cavalry Division met with some opposition at Latilly, but the enemy retired when the guns came into action. Again at 11 a.m. the Division came up with a strong German rear-guard escorting some 500 wagons, which were captured after a brief artillery duel. After this encounter the Division advanced without further fighting to Breny and Roset, billeting for the night at these two places.

On the left of the Cavalry the 1st Infantry Division found the enemy in position just beyond Prièz, two miles north of Courchamps. After a rather sharp combat lasting over four hours the Germans were driven off and retired through Chouy.

Further west, General Gough's Brigades located a strong force of the enemy moving north from Brumetz upon Chezy. This was at once attacked, and the advance guard of the 1st Division coming up the Germans were routed with the loss of 150 killed and wounded and 350 prisoners. The 12th Lancers captured another 300, with 30 wagons and four machine guns, and the advance guard of the 3rd Division 600 more.

West of the 3rd and 5th Divisions the 3rd Corps met with no opposition. The Army halted for the night generally on the line La Ferté—Milon—Neuilly—St. Front—Rocourt, the 3rd and 4th Cavalry Brigades being billeted about Passy.

The casualties for the 10th amounted in all to about 350, most of them having been incurred in the combat at Priez. Eighteen hundred prisoners were taken and a considerable amount of transport.

The general position found Conneau's Cavalry Corps at Fère-en-Tardinois on the right of the British Cavalry, one Corps of the 6th Army abreast of the 1st Corps, the remainder near the Marne, and the 6th Army engaged in wheeling to the north with its right flank near Milon.

11th Sept. The orders for the 11th were to continue the pursuit north-westward. The troops marched off at 5 a.m. covered by the Cavalry. Some wounded and stragglers were picked up, but the whole Army reached its positions for the night without any fighting. These were across the Ourcq for the three centre Divisions with the 1st and 4th Divisions in echelon behind each flank, covered by the Cavalry, which halted about five miles short of the Vesle. The 3rd and 5th Brigades billeted about Villemoutoire.

12th Sept. Instructions were received from General Joffre on the evening of the 11th to continue the pursuit on the front Bazoches—Soissons. The advance to be supported on each flank by the 5th and 6th Armies, General Maunoury being ordered to endeavour to outflank the German right wing. Sir John French's 1914 special orders were to seize the bridges over the Aisne and to occupy the high ground north of that river.

It had rained heavily the whole of the 11th and the 12th was even worse. The roads were in consequence in terribly bad condition. The low clouds and mist made air reconnaisance nearly impossible, nevertheless there were signs that the German retreat was nearing its end and that masses of troops were being concentrated on the line of the Aisne.

The Cavalry moved off early with the intention of pushing forward beyond the Vesle. The French Cavalry had already got possession of the bridge at Bazoches, but the only one on this part of the British front which remained undestroyed was one of the two at Braine, and this was held by Cavalry and Infantry. The whole three regiments of the 1st Brigade were dismounted and made a vigorous attack on the place and succeeded in driving the enemy out of it after a two hours' fight. Meanwhile the 1st Infantry Division had crossed at Bazoches, and the advance guard of the 2nd Division had contrived to get across the river at Courcelles, and the retreating Germans, being caught between the two fires, were all either killed or captured, 130 unwounded being taken prisoners.

Meanwhile the 3rd and 5th Cavalry Brigades further to the left had crossed by the bridge at Chassemy, which was intact. It was held by a small party of the enemy who were easily cleared out of the way by the 4th Hussars. The 3rd Brigade then moved to the higher ground north-east of Chassemy, whence the 4th Hussars were sent with two guns to seize the bridge over the Aisne at Vailly, but found it destroyed and Condé was found to be strongly held by the enemy. While the Hussars were thus employed the 5th and 16th Lancers fell in with two companies of German infantry moving south from Brenelle, of whom 70 were killed and the remainder, about 100 in number, made prisoners.

The march had been much delayed by the weather and the bad condition of the roads, and finally the troops were obliged to halt for the night on the line Longueval—Courcelles—Chassemy—Braine—Buzancy. The 3rd Brigade was billeted round Ciry. The 16th had two casualties this day—1 killed, 1 wounded.

The French 5th Army had now reached the line of the Vesle from Beaumont, 10 miles west of Rheims, to Fismes, where there had been some severe fighting before the town was taken. On its left flank, in contact with the British right, was Conneau's 2nd Cavalry Corps. On the left Maunoury's 6th Army, along the line of the Aisne from Soissons to Compiègne, and preparing to force a passage across the river.

The geography of the valley of the Aisne offered many advantages to the 13th defence, and more difficulties to the attack. The river slow and sluggish, and Sep about 200 yards wide, and now swollen to its full capacity by a week's almost continuous rain, flowed with many bends along a valley from one to two miles wide. This valley was bounded by a succession of steep promontories between which ran deep ravines bordered by woods and dense copses. These heights afforded excellent positions all along the north bank, which commanded and in places enfiladed the whole valley, where the flat meadows, mostly grass, afforded no cover, and offered no positions for artillery. The guns of the attack therefore, which were compelled to find their positions on the heights of the south bank of the river, were too distant for effective fire, whereas the guns of the defence swept at their ease the whole extent of the valley and the river at short range. The spur or promontory at Chivres, really the key of the German position, dominated Condè and its bridge, and gave a flanking fire along the river both east and west. On this spur the enemy had placed 18 heavy guns,

1914 and it was the failure to storm this position which really decided the battle of the Aisne.

General Joffre's plan was for the 6th Army to extend along the west bank of the Oise, which joins the Aisne at Compiègne, and with General Bridoux's Cavalry Division on his left flank, to turn Von Kluck's right. But Maunoury was also ordered to keep in close touch with the British left, and unless the enemy could be driven some way back above Soissons the two orders were incompatable as he had not enough men to occupy a line as extensive as this movement required.

There was now a gap of 16 miles between the 1st and 2nd German Armies, from Berry au Bac to Ostel.* Von Bülow, fearing that Von Kluck was placing his Army in exactly the same difficulty that he got into on the Ourcq, wished the latter to retire to the east and so to reduce the distance between the two Armies, but Von Kluck, with his usual obstinacy, ignored these orders and determined to fight where he was. And indeed it looked as if history was in this instance really going to repeat itself, for the advance of the British on the present front would have brought Sir J. French's Army directly into the gap between the 1st and 2nd German Armies and on the left rear of the former, just as it did during the battle of the Marne.

The Field-Marshal's orders for the 13th were that the heads of the three Corps should attain a line about five miles beyond the Aisne, namely, Lierval (seven miles north-east of Vailly)—Chavigny (five miles north of Vailly)—Terney ($4\frac{1}{2}$ miles north of Soissons).

The 11th Infantry Brigade (3rd Corps) had contrived with much difficulty to cross the river, on the left of the line, at Venizel during the night of the 12th-13th over the bridge at that place which had only been partially destroyed, and at daybreak occupied a position on the edge of the plateau north of St. Marguerite to Crouy.

The Cavalry Division moved off at daybreak, and soon afterwards the advance patrols reported that the bridges at Villers and Bourg were destroyed, but that those over the Aisne Canal to the south of it were intact, and that the aqueduct which carries the canal over the Aisne was practicable though damaged. Eventually after considerable fighting, during which an attack on the Chivres position was repulsed with loss, part of the Army managed to get across the river, by pontoons, rafts and half-destroyed bridges.

The position at night-fall was unsatisfactory. On the north bank were the Cavalry Division, 1st Division and 5th Infantry Brigade, between Paissy and Vernauil; then after a gap of five miles, two Brigades of Infantry near Vailly, then another gap of three miles to Missy, occupied by two battalions, and the 4th Division and two Brigades at St. Marguerite and Crouy. On the south bank were two Brigades at Vieil Arcy, Dhuizel, St. Mard; the 3rd and 5th Cavalry Brigades and a Brigade of Infantry about Braisne, and the 13th Brigade, less the two battalions across the river, south of Missy. The 16th had been left at Ciry, but were shelled out of it and had to take cover at a farm near by. Casualties, one wounded.

On the right the 5th, 9th, and 4th French Armies had made fair progress, but on the left the 6th Army had met with difficulties similar to those with which the British had been confronted, though some Divisions were able finally to cross the river at Soissons, Vic, and Berneuil.

Orders were issued in the evening directing a further advance, to the line Laon, Fresnes, 12 miles west of Laon, the Cavalry Division to cover the right

---

* Eleven miles north-east of Soissons.

and the 3rd and 5th Brigades the left. The 3rd and 5th were further ordered to follow the 2nd Corps, and to cross the river as soon as the bridges were clear behind them.

The 14th September was a day of hard fighting, heavy loss, and great disappointment. Though it was not yet known by the British Headquarter Staff, the gap between the 1st and 2nd German Armies had been filled by the arrival on the battlefield of fresh troops. Maubeuge had capitulated on the 7th September, and the German 7th Reserve Corps, which had been besieging the place, less five battalions left as a garrison and prisoners' guard, were sent off as soon as possible to the assistance of Von Bülow. These, after a march of 40 miles in 24 hours, arrived at Laon on the night of the 13th. This Corps was intended to be the nucleus of a new Army.

On the 13th September the Belgian sortie from Antwerp had come to an end, and the Belgian Field Army had been obliged to retire within the defences of the city. Thus a number of the troops operating in Belgium were set free, and these, with what men could be spared from the armies on the extreme left, were at once sent to the assistance of Von Bülow. Thus in the afternoon of the 13th, in addition to the 7th Reserve Corps from Maubeuge, the equivalent of two full Brigades joined the new 7th Army. On the 14th two more battalions from Maubeuge came in with three batteries, and on the 17th a Brigade from the 12th Corps. Other reinforcements followed until the gap between the 1st and 2nd Armies was filled up. The Cavalry were withdrawn behind the battle line soon after the fighting began. The 1st Corps alone made any progress, and that only at a great cost, its casualties amounting to 3,500. The other Corps on the left failed completely in their attacks and gained no ground at all, but the losses were less severe, those of the 4th and 5th Divisions being slight, and of the 3rd Division under 1,000.

The positions at the close of the day were:—

1st Corps.—Right resting on the Chemin des Dames; left close to the Aisne near Chavonne.

4th Cavalry Brigade.—Paissy in rear of the point of contact with the French 5th Army.

1st and 2nd Cavalry Brigades between Chavonne and Vailly.

2nd Corps.—Two Brigades in front of Vailly. Then came a gap of $3\frac{1}{2}$ miles in front of Condè and the Chivres promontory, from Missy to Crouy. The gap was covered by a battalion, a battery of 6in. howitzers, and the 3rd and 5th Cavalry Brigades, on the Chassemy heights opposite Condè.

The 16th moved into billets at Lime in the evening, where the Regiment remained until October 2nd. The casualties this day were one killed and Captain Tempest-Hicks wounded.

On the right the 5th Army had made some progress but not much, the left having been checked by strong counter attacks when attempting to effect a lodgement on the Chemin des Dames, but the 1st Corps on the right had re-occupied Rheims, and the battle line ran straight from Rheims to Craonille, being everywhere in close contact with the enemy. On the left Maunoury was across the Aisne from Soissons to Attichy, with his extreme left at Nampcel, but the enemy was well entrenched all along his front and he was unable to make further progress. Thus the plan of outflanking Von Kluck had definitely failed, for on the 15th the German right was extended by the arrival of the 7th Cavalry Division from Alsace and the 9th Reserve Corps from Antwerp.

The total of the casualties during the Battle of the Aisne, from the 12th to the 28th September, amounted to 561 officers and 12,980 other ranks killed, wounded, and missing.

1914   Thus by this unlucky reinforcement Von Kluck was saved. Had the arrival of these fresh troops been even a day later the 1st German Army would certainly have been compelled to leave its position on the Aisne and the Battle of the Marne would have been exactly repeated. Such a retreat might have had the most far reaching consequences and might easily have led to the enforced retirement into Belgium of both Von Kluck and Von Bülow and a considerable change in the conduct of the war.

16th Sept.   On the 16th September the 6th Division, which had been delayed by the change of Base from Havre to St. Nazaire, came up in rear of the 3rd Corps, and was temporarily broken up and distributed by brigades among the first five Divisions. The 17th and 18th Brigades went to the 1st Corps, the 16th to the 2nd Corps. The 17th Brigade became Corps Reserve, thereby replacing the 1st Cavalry Division which had daily sent 500 dismounted men into the trenches at Chavonne.

The fighting had by the 16th September really become the "Trench Warfare" that was destined to last for so many weary years, though as yet no one recognised its true nature. Both sides were hard at work entrenching themselves, and for this the Germans were better prepared than the Allies, for, warned by the events of the Russian-Japanese War, they had done some peace practice in the art. The British soldier had so far not got beyond field entrenching, and the Army was unprovided with barbed wire, except what could be collected locally, periscopes, telephones or indeed any of the accessories of trench warfare, and the French were even worse off as their trench work afforded little protection even against rifle fire.

From the 16th to the 28th there were a succession of attacks and counter-attacks, none of which gave any decisive advantage to either side or in any way changed the situation, and a great deal of artillery practice with no great results. Nevertheless there were over 2,000 casualties during these days. The Cavalry did no fighting beyond some dismounted work in the trenches, with the exception of the 2nd Cavalry Division, which was sent to assist the French 5th Army on the 20th with two brigades of the 1st Corps. The 16th had no casualties since those of the 14th.

On the 16th the 3rd, 4th and 5th Brigades were formally constituted the 2nd Cavalry Division under command of Major-General Hubert Gough, but the 4th Brigade did not join until October 12th. On the 17th Captain Riddell came in with 185 men and 226 horses, and on the 15th C Squadron rejoined.

Both the French and the Germans were busily engaged in extending the battle line northwards. A new French Army, the 10th, was being rapidly got together under General Maudhui at Arras, while the Germans moved up two Corps from their left to oppose it. There was some hard fighting in this quarter for some days but without any advantage to either side, and eventually both became stationary and entrenched in the positions they were holding.

Meanwhile Von Marwitz with his Cavalry had reappeared on the extreme north flank, but his work proved as inefficient as usual and he was so severely handled between Lens and Lille that the 14th Corps had to be sent to extricate him. The 4th German Cavalry Corps did indeed get as far as Ypres, but were forced to retire to Bailleul the next day (8th October).

The whole front, which now extended from the Swiss frontier to within 30 miles of Dunkirk, had in fact become "stabilised," a word of evil portent destined to be used but too often in succeeding years. The actual trenches from the right of the British Army near Craonne ran along the valley of the Aisne to Ribecourt on the Oise and thence northward by Arras and Lens to Bethune.

LIEUT.-COLONEL CUTHBERT JOHN ECCLES.
1914-1918.

CHAPTER XXXVIII.

OCTOBER 1ST TO DECEMBER 31ST, 1914.

October 1st, Extension of Allied line northwards. Movements of the British 1914 to the North. The 16th march to Hazebrouck. Situation in Belgium. Landing of the Naval Brigade at Antwerp. Bombardment and capitulation of Antwerp. Landing of the 3rd Cavalry and 7th Infantry Divisions. Attempt to extend the line to Bruges. Advance of the 3rd Cavalry Brigade. Death of Lieut. Macneil. The combat at Mont des Cats. The action at Warneton and failure of attack. Arrival of the Infantry Corps. New position from Albert to Nieuport and distribution of the troops. The Regiment in the trenches. November 5th, The French shelled out of their trenches. Major Dixon's gallant effort to rally them. Casualties of the Regiment on November 5th. First Battle of Ypres, October 15th-21st. Heavy losses. December 2nd, Inspection by the King. The 16th in billets. Formation of two Armies. Distribution of the troops.

Summary of Events, October 1st to December 31st, 1914.—October 1st, Southern forts of Antwerp destroyed. 3rd, Movement of the British Army to the North. 8th, Bombardment of Antwerp. 9th, Capitulation of Antwerp. 19th, Transfer to Flanders completed. 21st, First Battle of Ypres begins. November 7th, Capitulation of Kiaochau. 23rd, Basra taken. December 6th, Defeat of Austrians by Servians. 15th, Belgrade retaken by Servians.

Both the Germans and the Allies now turned their attention seriously to the 1st urgent necessity of occupying the Channel ports and the neighbouring seaboard. Oct. The Germans indeed would have done this before, but the unexpected resistance of the Belgians had locked up so many troops in Belgium that none could be spared for this purpose. The German Staff also, for some weeks after the war began, being under the delusion that the British Army was based on Boulogne and Ostend, naturally thought that these ports would be occupied and protected in such strength that it would be useless to attempt to seize them except with a force much stronger than could be spared.

To foster this idea there had been some demonstrations made by the British Government along the coast in compliance with a request of General Joffre. Thus on the night of September 19th a Brigade of Marines and the Oxfordshire Yeomanry had been disembarked at Dunkirk, and there were other minor landings made from time to time at various places along the coast. These did at first cause some alarm to the German Staff, but the futile nature of the operations were soon recognised and they were disregarded.

Sir John French perceived very clearly the very great importance of preventing the seizure of the Channel ports by the enemy, and as the position on the Aisne was now stationary, he represented to both his own and the French Government the advisability of transferring his Army to the northern flank of the battle-line, where it could be directly based on a seaport, thereby very materially shortening his lines of communications.

After some discussion the transfer was agreed to, and on the night of the 1st October the move began. Every possible precaution was taken to conceal the movement from the enemy. The troops marched by night, and the men were strictly confined to their billets during the day. The 2nd Corps was the first withdrawn, the 1st Corps extending its line to Vailly and the 3rd to Missy. The 2nd Cavalry Division marched by road on the night of the 2nd, the 1st

1914 Division on the night of the 3rd. The 3rd Corps gave over its trenches to the French on the 6th, and the 1st Corps on the night of the 12th, the whole evacuation being completed on the 15th. The infantry were entrained at Compiègne and the three neighbouring stations. The whole movement was so ably conducted that it remained entirely undiscovered by the enemy for days, and indeed was not realised by the Germans until the Cavalry Divisions were encountered on the Lys.

The 16th marched by Courcelles to Thezy, having joined up with the Brigade at Rubescourt en route. The 3rd Brigade reached Thezy on the 5th, and after halting there for the 6th, marched again by Vaux (just north of Amiens), Maisecourt, St. Hillaire to Hazebrouck, where the Brigade halted for the night. During the 8th and 9th the 2nd Corps detrained at Abbeville and marched towards Bethune. On the 11th the 3rd Corps detrained and marched towards Bailleul and Armentieres. On the 19th the 1st Corps detrained and marched towards Ypres. The Headquarter Staff on the 13th arrived at St. Omer.

With the move of the British Army to the northern flank of the Allied line the war entered into an entirely new phase. The Germans were now in full occupation of the whole of Belgium south of the Schelde, and the Belgian Army had been withdrawn within the circle of the outer line of the defensive works protecting Antwerp.

29th Sept. At the end of September the siege of the city began to be pressed in earnest by General Von Besseler, and by the 29th two of the outer ring of forts had been silenced. As it was evident that under the fire of the German heavy artillery Antwerp would inevitably speedily share the fate of Liège and Maubeuge, the Belgian Government began to prepare a new base at Ostend with the intention of moving the five Divisions of the Field Army to the west of the Schelde. The British Government was then officially informed that the Field Army, 65,000 men, would retire on Ostend as soon as the outer ring of forts was lost unless immediate assistance was afforded by either England or France. The War Office had at this time only one Division, the 7th, and two weak Brigades of Cavalry to dispose of, and Lord Kitchener was not at all inclined to allow this small force to be shut up in Antwerp. There were, however, a certain number of untrained troops, designated the "Naval Division," at the disposal of the Admiralty, and the First Lord, Mr. Winston Churchill, suggested that these should be sent direct to Antwerp, and that the Brigade of Marines already in Belgium should join them there.

As it was of the utmost importance that Antwerp should hold out as long as possible in order to give Sir J. French and his Army time to take up the new positions in front of Ypres, Mr. Churchill's suggestion was adopted.

Lord Kitchener had previously sent Colonel H. G. Dallas (formerly of the 16th) to Antwerp on special duty as his representative, and that officer now received instructions to press upon the Belgian Ministry the urgent necessity of delaying the withdrawal of the Field Army to the last moment consistent with its safety, promising at the same time that the 7th Division and two Brigades of Cavalry should be sent to its assistance. These representations induced the Belgian Command to delay the final withdrawal for upwards of a week and two of the Divisions were detailed to take part in the actual defence of the forts in conjunction with the Naval Division, which, if too weak to be of any material assistance, would, it was expected, encourage the Belgians to prolong the defence.

Ultimately it was decided to send the 7th Division to Bruges with the intention of co-operating with the French and Belgians in an attempt to force

Von Besseler to raise the siege or, at the least, to remove his heavy guns. General Joffre, for his part, agreed to send a Division of Territorials, a Brigade of Fusiliers Marins, and 2,000 Zouaves. Altogether, this force made up the respectable total on paper of 53,000 men, and if it had really been got together in time might very well, by threatening Von Besseler's left flank, have compelled the Germans to raise the siege, and by so doing have materially changed the course of the war, as Von Besseler had only the equivalent of five Divisions himself. Meanwhile the siege was vigorously pressed and by October 2nd four more of the forts had fallen. Mr. Winston Churchill had previously arranged to go to Dunkirk on some Admiralty business, but he was now directed to proceed to Antwerp with instructions to encourage the Belgian authorities to prolong their resistance for at least another ten days. He arrived at Antwerp on October 4th, and the same day the Marine Brigade under command of General Paris came in from Ghent.

1914

On the 6th October the Belgian troops were driven across the Nethe closely followed up by the enemy, and as the German guns now being brought over that river were within five miles of the city, the surrender of Antwerp became only a matter of days. In the afternoon of the same day the two Brigades of the Naval Division which had landed at Dunkirk detrained at Antwerp, and were at once sent into the trenches. On the morning of the 7th the 7th Division disembarked at Zeebrugge.

Mr. W. Churchill, with characteristic modesty, now asked to be placed in command of the whole force engaged in the Antwerp operations, but his request was curtly refused by Lord Kitchener, who doubtless thought it wiser to give that office to a professional soldier in preference to a gentleman whose only knowledge of military matters had been acquired in the dubious position of newspaper correspondent during the Boer War. Mr. Churchill was informed that Sir A. Rawlinson, who had been already sent to Bruges, was in supreme command of the relieving force, and that General Paris was in command of the troops actually in Antwerp.

The general situation on the evening of the 7th October was as follows:—

7th Oct.

At Antwerp the garrison with two Belgian Divisions and the British Naval Division were holding the line of the inner forts.

The rest of the Belgian Field Army was moving away from Antwerp between the coast and Ghent.

The 7th Division was at Bruges.

Of Sir John French's Army, the 2nd Corps was nearing Abbeville, the 3rd Corps entraining at Soissons, and the 1st still on the Aisne.

The Allied Cavalry Divisions covered a line from Lens to Hazebrouck, opposed to three German Cavalry Divisions.

On the 8th the 3rd Cavalry Division,* under Major-General the Hon. J. Byng, disembarked at Ostend and Zeebrugge, and the same day the Marins Fusiliers from Paris reached Ghent, this being the only part of the promised French contingent that arrived before the capitulation of Antwerp.

Von Besseler had summoned the city to surrender on the 6th under a threat of bombardment, and this was commenced at 11 p.m. on the 7th.

On the 8th October three more forts of the inner circle were destroyed, and

---

* The 7th Division, under command of Major-General T. Capper, comprised three Brigades of Infantry and the usual Divisional troops. The 3rd Cavalry Division consisted of two Brigades, of which one, the 6th, had only two Regiments, the 1st Royals and the 10th Hussars. The other, the 7th, was made up from the three Regiments of the Household Cavalry. Brigadier-General Kavanagh, who afterwards commanded the 2nd Cavalry Division, was in command of the 7th Brigade.

1914 as the whole of the Belgian Field Army was now safely out of the place, with the exception of one Division, and it was evident that the defence could not be maintained more than a few hours longer, this Division was ordered to follow the rest of the Army and General Paris gave orders for the Naval Brigades to be withdrawn across the Schelde in the evening in conformity with his instruction he had received when he took over command.

The roads and the streets were everywhere blocked by crowds of the inhabitants of Antwerp, who, terrified by the bombardment, and realising that the surrender of the city was imminent, were seeking safety either by crossing into Holland or by following the troops into France. The Belgian Division got away safely, but the Naval Brigades were not so fortunate. In the darkness and confusion it was next to impossible to get the orders and directions for the march to the several Brigade and Regimental Commanders. In the end some 1,500 men of the 1st Brigade were obliged to cross the frontier into Holland. The rear guard lost 300 men who were cut off and made prisoners, together with some 600 others, mostly stragglers from the 1st Brigade, and 400 Belgians.*

The greater part of the Belgian garrison troops got across the Schelde during the night of the 8th and the morning of the 9th and followed the Field Army, but 18,000 were forced to cross into Holland. On the morning of the 10th the city formally capitulated.

The 7th Division (with the 3rd Cavalry Division) was placed under the command of Sir J. French on the 9th,† who gave it the designation of the 4th Corps. General Rawlinson covered the left flank of the Belgian Army during its move to the area Dixmude—Nieuport—Furnes, and arrived at Ypres on the 14th. Those troops of the Naval Division that had escaped from Antwerp were re-embarked and sent back to England. Mr. Churchill himself left Antwerp on the 6th and returned to England, and Colonel Dallas escaped in the very last hour.

This Antwerp enterprise, the first " side show " attempted by the War Cabinet, cannot be called a success. Though the arrival of the Naval Brigade certainly encouraged the civil population to hope for further help from England, the Military Command had no such illusion and carried out the evacuation of the Field Army, already decided on, without any delay, knowing that General Rawlinson had strict orders not to enter Antwerp. The presence of Mr. Churchill and his levies did not indeed delay the capitulation for a single hour.

Sir J. French was anxious to extend his line so as to cover the ports of Zeebrugge and Ostend, and made urgent representations both to the War Office and to the French Government as to the desirability of doing this, pointing out that the Germans could easily send the parts of submarines to Zeebrugge and put them together there, but this probability was scoffed at by the War Office, and the suggestion also was coldly received by the French. Nevertheless, the Field Marshal persevered in his design and as soon as the Cavalry Divisions arrived these were directed to reconnoitre, and if possible to occupy, the line of the Lys River pending the completion of the move of the Infantry Corps.

On the 11th October the 16th was on outpost covering the line Morbeque—

---

* The casualties of the Royal Naval Division were altogether:—7 officers, 50 other ranks killed; 3 officers, 135 others wounded; 37 officers, 1,442 others interned; 5 officers, 931 others prisoners.

† General Rawlinson had been operating independently under orders from the War Office. Indeed, the first intimation of the landing of the 7th Division was given to Sir J. French by General Joffre.

Hazebrouck. Early next morning the Brigade moved forward to Borre, the 1914 16th forming the Advance Guard.

The Brigade came into contact with the enemy shortly after leaving Hazebrouck, and the 16th had a rather busy day. On reaching Boore two officers' patrols were sent out, one on to Mont des Cats, the other to Godevwaers-Velt.

The first of these, which was in charge of Lieutenants Aris and MacNeil, was ambushed, and in the fight that followed Lieut. MacNeil was shot by a German officer who had been knocked off his horse. Lieut. Aris drew his revolver and tried to shoot the German but his weapon missed fire, and in the struggle that followed he was himself shot before the German was disposed of. MacNeil died shortly afterwards, but Aris recovered. Another patrol which was sent to Flétre was also ambushed and lost two men killed.

The Brigade halted at Caestre to water and feed and then moved off to attack the Mont des Cats, which was reported to be held by the enemy, the 16th moving to Thienhook, and the rest of the Brigade to Flètre. From Thienhook the 16th rode across country to Kruystraete, coming under a heavy fire while crossing an open space.

The enemy were found to be holding the Trappist monastery and the woods on either side. Two squadrons were sent to attack the place, the third being kept in reserve, but the fire from the windows of the building was too heavy and continuous for much to be done without serious loss and the assault was held up pending the arrival of the guns. When these came up a bombardment of half an hour drove the garrison out of the place, which was immediately occupied. Inside three dead Germans were found and a wounded officer, who turned out to be Prince Max of Hesse. He died the same night. The 16th then moved off and bivouaced for the night at Flètre, Thiancourt, and Caestre.

By the evening of the 15th the outpost line was established south of Messines. There were several small encounters with the enemy during these two days and a few casualties, Lieut. Cross and two men being wounded on the 15th.

At 11 a.m. on the 16th orders were received to send a squadron with the machine gun to Warneton, and for the Regiment to join the rest of the Brigade at Gapaard. At 4 p.m. the Regiment was ordered to proceed to Warneton and to clear out the enemy in order that the Engineers could build a bridge over the river Lys.

On arriving at the place late in the afternoon D Squadron with the machine gun was found to be holding the south-west corner of the village, but unable to make any further progress as the place was prepared for defence and strongly held. C Squadron was then sent up dismounted, but was also held up by a barricade at the cross-roads in the centre of the village.

The road down which the attack had to be made was slightly curved about 150 yards from the barricade, which could not be seen until the curve was passed.

Eventually a gun was sent up from E Battery which, when it got dark, was man-handled down to the curve, while three troops were formed in column on the road behind it.

Everything being ready, the gun was shoved round the curve and had fired six shots at the barricade when, without waiting to see the effect, the storming party rushed forward, and finding the barricade still standing began to pull it down under a heavy fire from the cross-roads and houses.

The following account of what followed is taken from the diary of an officer of C Squadron :—

K

1914 "As soon as we started pulling it down the Germans opened fire from the houses. We pushed a maxim up into the window of a house, some of us stood in the street and fired, others tried to break into the houses on either side, and the noise and crackling of a burning house was appalling. After about 10 minutes of this the Germans retired round the corner towards the bridge. On looking round the corner we found another barricade about 70 yards away. They opened on us with a maxim and started throwing flares, while our gun began shelling from over our heads."

The attack was unable to take the second barricade though the fight was prolonged until orders to retire were received at 11.30 p.m.

It was then found that two wounded men had been left in the square behind the first barricade. Three men volunteered to go back and bring them in, F.S.S. Glasgow, Lance-Corporals Chapman and Boynton, which they managed to do, though the square was swept by the fire from the enemy's maxim in addition to rifle fire. The rest of the wounded were brought off safely by the troops engaged who retired by the side lanes.

By this time General Gough had arrived with the 4th Hussars and a Squadron of the 5th Lancers, but information had been obtained that the whole line of the Lys was strongly held by the enemy, with an Army Corps in support, so the attack was broken off and the 16th retired to Messines, which was reached at 2 a.m. The enemy began shelling the outside of the village just as the Regiment moved off.

The casualties were slight considering the amount of firing, being only one man killed and Lieut. Clarke and six men wounded. F.S.S. Glasgow and Lance-Corporals Chapman and Boynton received the D.C.M. Three men who were too severely wounded to be removed had to be left, in charge of Captain Johnson, R.A.M.C., and his orderly, Corporal Ridman.

17th Oct. On the 17th the Brigade marched to Kemmel, where the 16th remained in billets till the 19th, when the Regiment moved to Comines, forming a line of outposts along the Canal to Houthem. The 1st and 2nd Cavalry Divisions were now holding the enemy, who were apparently concentrating for an attack in force, along the line Frelingham—Wervieq, the 4th Brigade being near Warneton, the 3rd at Comines, and the 5th at Wervieq.

During the last week the Infantry Corps had been coming into line, the 1st Corps being the last to do so on the left flank. The 1st Corps was only just in time and only occupied the positions alloted to it after some hard fighting. The 1st Corps had orders to march through Ypres to Bruges, but having met with very strong opposition were finally compelled to retire to the position given below. On the failure of this movement the Field-Marshal abandoned his attempt to extend his line to Zeebrugge, this being clearly impossible with the force he had.

21st Oct. On the 21st October the position of the Allied line, from Albert on the south to Nieuport on the north, was as follows:—

Albert, Arras, Vermelles to La Bassée, the French 10th Army (3rd Corps), under General Maudhui.

La Bassée to Laventie (six miles), 2nd Corps, Sir H. Smith-Dorrien.

Laventie to Messines (one mile), French Cavalry Corps, under General Conneau.

Armentières to Messines (12 miles), 3rd Corps, General Pulteney.

Messines to Zandevoorde (four miles), Cavalry Corps and 3rd Division, General Allenby.

Zandevoorde to Zonnebeke (six miles), 4th Corps, General Rawlinson.

Zonnebeke to Bixchoote (seven miles), 1st Corps, Sir D. Haig.

North of Bixchoote to Nieuport on the sea (20 miles) were the Belgians, 1914 1½ Corps, and a mixed force of French, equalling about eight Divisions.

Opposite the British 3½ Corps were massed 6½ German Corps.

This line was entrenched and prepared for defence, and the Cavalry were dismounted and sent into the trenches along their own front.

On the 22nd the 7th Indian Brigade came in, and was posted as reserve to the Cavalry Corps.

Trench duty as far as the 16th were concerned may be considered to have commenced on the 20th. On the 21st one man was killed, and from that time there were daily casualties in the trenches. From the 22nd to the 29th continuous attacks were made by the enemy, which were beaten off with comparative ease, but on the 30th the enemy attacked in force and there was very severe fighting all along the front held by the Cavalry Corp of five Brigades, which in fact had to keep at bay no less than four Divisions of Cavalry and a Jager Brigade of the enemy for some 48 hours. On this day Major Campbell, Lieut. Lord Wodehouse and eight men were wounded, and one man killed. On the 31st part of the line was taken over by Conneau's Cavalry.

The fighting continued without cessation from November 1st to the 5th, 1st Nov. when the trenches were subjected all day to intense shelling. The trench on the left of the 16th was held by the French Cavalry. This trench was practically destroyed by the shell fire and the French driven out of it. A gallant attempt to rally them was made by Major Dixon, who was killed while doing so, but the line was restored by the Bays, who came up and replaced the French. At 11 p.m. the 16th were relieved by the 9th Lancers and went into billets, where the Regiment remained until the 12th. The casualties on the 5th were Major Dixon, Captain Onslow and 10 men killed, and Lieut. Davies and 13 men wounded.

On November 1st the enemy launched a determined attack on the 1st and 2nd Corps and the 9th French Corps. The battle, known officially as the First Battle of Ypres, culminated on the 10th in an assault made by the Prussian Guard Division under the personal observation of the Kaiser. The 1st Corps was very hardly pressed and had to be from time to time reinforced from the 3rd Cavalry Division. Ultimately the attack was defeated with great loss to the enemy, and on the 12th the fighing died out. The casualties in this battle, which extended from the 15th October to the 21st November, were heavy, for the 1st and 2nd Corps alone had 517 officers and 13,000 other ranks killed, wounded, and missing, of whom 127 officers and 1,666 men were killed.

The 7th Division also had some very severe fighting between Zonnebeke and Zandevoorde before the 1st Corps came up, losing over 8,000 Infantry out of the original strength of 12,000. Indeed, but for its most fortunate presence there can be little doubt that the line would have been broken at this point.

This was the last serious action of the winter, and beyond the incessant shelling of the trenches the front remained quiet until the attack on Neuve Chapelle on the 11th March, 1915.

On the 13th November the 16th were moved to Dramoutre, where the horses 13th Nov. were left and the men sent on foot to Wolvergheim. Here they did duty in the trenches until the 20th, when they were relieved by the French and marched through Ypres to Brisleu, where they met the horses.

On the 2nd December the Brigade was inspected by the King. On the 7th 2nd Dec. the Regiment went into billets at Vieux Berquin, where it remained until February 12th, 1915.

On the 24th December the Army, which had now been brought up to its full 24th Dec. strength by drafts from England, was re-organised, two Armies being formed.

1914 The 1st Army, under Sir D. Haig, comprised the 1st and 4th Corps and the Indian Corps; the 2nd Army, under Sir H. Smith-Dorrien, the 3rd, 4th and 5th Corps.* The Cavalry Corps under General Allenby remained independent.

The front in Flanders and Northern France, which remained practically unchanged until March, 1915, was now established as follows :—

On the extreme left to Dixmude, the Belgian Army.

South from Dixmude, the 9th French Corps and Allenby's Cavalry Corps. South of these Sir H. Plumer's 5th Corps.

Then just west of Whytechaete and Messines, the 2nd Corps.

Then astride of the Lys in front of Armentières, Pulteney's 3rd Corps.

Then from Estaire to west of Neuve Chapelle Rawlinson's 4th Corps, the Indian Corps being between Estaire and La Bassée.

The total casualties of the British Army incurred during the period 14th October—30th November, 1914, were 2,368 officers and 50,529 other ranks, of whom 614 officers and 6,794 other ranks were killed. In addition the Indian Corps lost 4,627 other ranks, of whom 552 were killed.

The grand total of casualties from the commencement of the campaign amounted to 3,627 officers and 86,237 other ranks.

The greater part of this loss fell on the infantry of the first seven Divisions, which originaly numbered only 84,000.

The re-inforcements sent out up to the 10th November were about 110,000 of all ranks.

The losses of the enemy are not known with accuracy, but are reckoned officially at 135,000 of all ranks during the period 15th October—24th November. This was probably much under the actual numbers. It certainly does not include wastage of troops not actually engaged in the fighting.

CHAPTER XXXIX.

January 1st to December 31st, 1915.

Plans for winter campaign discussed. This decided to be impossible. Visit of Sir J. French to London. The Government persists in the refusal to send more men or munitions. Description of "Trench Warfare." The Gallipoli expedition. February 13th, The Regiment returns to the trenches. February 21st, Mine explosion under trench, followed by enemy's attack in force. Severe fighting. Heavy loss by the 16th. February 26th, Regiment back to billets. March 12th, Battle of Neuve Chapelle. The Brigade moved up to front but sent back. April 17th, General Kavanagh takes over command of the 2nd Cavalry Division from General Gough. April 20th, Second Battle of Ypres. Bombardment of the town. April 22nd, "Poison gas" used for first time. April 24th, The Regiment returns to the trenches. "Stink shells" first used. May 2nd, the 16th trenches gassed. May 3rd, the 16th back to billets. May 24th, the Regiment returns to trenches. Disaster at Ypres sally-port.

---

* The 5th Corps, commanded by Sir H. Plumer, had been sent out at the end of November.

French attack in Artois with partial success. July 15th, General Sir 1915. Philip Chetwode takes over command of the 2nd Cavalry Division. The shortage of shells. Mr. Asquith's denial. Sir J. French's appeal to the Press for publicity. Mr. Ll. George made Minister of Munitions. Supply of munitions largely increased. Division of Allied line into Sectors. Disposition of Allied Armies. September 22nd, Battle of Nancy and French victory. September 24th, Battle of Loos. Capture of Vimy Ridge and Loos, but with great loss. December 18th, Resignation of Sir J. French, who is succeeded by Sir D. Haig. The casualties of the Allies during September.

Summary of Events, January 1st to December 31st, 1915.—January 1st, Decisive defeat of Turks in the Caucasus. 8th, Battle of Soissons. February 19th, Allied attack on Dardanelles begins. March 10th, Battle of Neuve Chapelle. 18th, Failure of Naval Attack on Dardanelles definite. 22nd, Capitulation of Prezmysl. April 22nd, Second Battle of Ypres; German gas attack. 27th, Army landed at Gallipoli. 28th, Beginning of Mackensen's offensive against Russia. May 7th, Lusitania torpedoed. 19th, Coalition Ministry formed. June 1st, Prezmysl retaken by Germans. 3rd, Amara (Mesopotamia) taken. 20th, Defeat of Russians at Rava Russka. 22nd, Lemberg retaken by Austrians. August 5th, Germans occupy Warsaw. 10th, Germans take Novo Georgievsk. 25th, Germans take Brest Litovski. September 25th, Battle of Loos. 29th, Kut el Amara taken by General Townshend. October 3rd, Allies land at Salonika. 5th, Bulgaria joins Germany; Resignation of Venizelos, the Greek Prime Minister. 7th, Austrians and Germans again invade Servia. 9th, Belgrade taken. 11th, Bulgarians invade Servia. 13th, Murder of Miss Cavell. 15th, War declared on Bulgaria. November 22nd, Battle of Clesiphon. December 8th, Evacuation of Gallipoli begins. 15th, Resignation of Sir John French and appointment of Sir Douglas Haig to succeed him as Commander-in-Chief.

There was considerable discussion at the Allied Headquarters about plans for a winter campaign, but it had to be finally recognised that without more men, and especially more munitions, such as guns and their ammunition, any further advance in the north was impossible in the face of the superior forces massed by the enemy in front of the allied line. General Joffre then turned his attention to his armies in the south, meditating an attack in the Rheims area.

On the 20th December Sir John French went to London, and was then definitely informed that at present he could not hope to receive any further reinforcements and that any troops that could be spared were to be employed in making diversions on other fronts. The Field-Marshal strongly protested against these ideas, pointing out that one of the first principles of military strategy was to concentrate the whole available strength at the decisive point, now certainly the Western Front. He also pressed upon the Government the urgent necessity of increasing the supply of shells, heavy guns, and machine guns, but to all these requests a flat refusal was returned, and he was told that he was to further economise his expenditure of shells and to confine himself to "Trench Warfare." About this time also came into use the silly catchword "War of Attrition." Unfortunately the "attrition" was by no means confined to the enemy, who could afford it much better than the Allies, for in addition to the daily long list of casualties from shell and rifle fire the malady known as "Trench Feet" now made its appearance, and over 20,000 men were invalided from this cause alone during the first three months of 1915.

1915 "Trench Warfare" in fact consisted, as far as the troops were concerned, in crouching in shallow trenches and dismal dug-outs, waist deep in mud and water, in one of the most detestable countries and vilest climates in Europe, under an incessant rain of shells to which it was impossible to make any effective reply on account of the shortage of shells, of which the enemy had an apparently inexhaustible supply. The guns had to be carefully rationed, and at first were allowed 20 rounds per gun per day. But this proved far in excess of the supply and had to be soon reduced to 10, and ultimately actually to six, for a reserve had to be kept to meet a possible attack.

It was in vain that the Field-Marshal addressed complaints, remonstrances, and requests to the War Office. Not only was no attention paid to these, but he got no reply even until the 19th January, when he received a flat refusal to increase the supply accompanied by an accusation of permitting a too lavish waste of ammunition.

The fact was that the War Cabinet was now occupied solely with preparations for the projected expedition to Gallipoli, an insane scheme which apparently originated in the fertile brain of the same amateur strategist who was at the head of the Antwerp fiasco, and a project which was foredoomed to failure as the folly of its conception was fully equalled by the fatuity of its execution, and which eventually cost the country the equivalent of more than two Army Corps.

12th Feb. On February 12th the Regiment received orders to return to the trenches, and next day 20 officers and 291 other ranks were sent to Ypres on motor lorries to relieve the 3rd Cavalry Division, the remainder being left with the horses. The Regiment remained in billets in Ypres until the 19th, when the men went into the trenches, the squadrons being lined up with D Squadron on the left, A. Squadron centre, C Squadron on the right, each with one troop in the rear as support. During the 19th and 20th nothing particular happened except the usual shelling, from which there were several casualties, Lieut. Thornton and three men being wounded and one man killed, but the 21st was an unusually disastrous day for the Regiment.

The enemy's trenches ran parallel to those of the 16th at a distance varying from 15 to 50 yards only. In front of the right of D Squadron was a deep ditch which ran from the German trench to that occupied by the Squadron. It had been suspected for some days that the enemy was running a sap at the bottom of this ditch, and a close observation had been kept on it, but no sign of anything of the sort had been discovered. It turned out afterwards that the enemy had really run a sap half way down it, but had turned off at a sharp angle and continued the sap underground until it ran under the centre of the trench of D Squadron, and that three mines had been placed at the end of it.

It was afterwards ascertained from prisoners that the mines had been laid some days before the 16th took over the trench, but that the explosion had been delayed with the intention of catching the relief when they were taking over on the 18th, but the opportunity had fortunately been missed.

At 6 a.m. on the 21st one mine was fired, followed immediately afterwards by the other two, with the result that the trench was completely destroyed. The enemy followed this up with a strong attack on the trenches on each side of that held by D Squadron. There was of course much confusion and a hand to hand combat, in which the enemy was finally driven back by A Squadron and the reserve troop of D with a machine gun. A counter-attack was made by the three reserve troops. They were unable to regain the lost trench, and a request for help was sent to two companies of French Infantry which were in support of the left section of the trench, but these refused to move without orders from their own commanding officer, and when he came up he was unfortunately killed while giving the order to advance. No further attack was made until 9 a.m., when the line was reinforced by a squadron of the 20th Hussars and another Company of French infantry from the supporting line. The French were stopped at once by the heavy fire they were met with, all their officers and half their men being shot down in a few minutes. The 20th got a little further when they were brought up by an enfilade fire and the attack was broken off. No further attempt was made to regain the lost trench, but a new one was dug in rear of it.

This was the worst day which the 16th had during the whole of the war. When the roll was called it was found that Major Neave, Captain Nash, Lieuts. Beech, King and Cross, and seven men were killed, and Lieut. Patrick and 29 men wounded. In addition Lieut. Ryan* and 11 men were missing, in all seven officers and 47 other ranks killed, wounded and missing.

On the 22nd the trenches were repaired under a continuous rifle fire, three men being wounded. On the 23rd the Bays took over the trenches and the troops returned to Ypres and then went into billets. On the 26th the Regiment rejoined the 3rd Brigade at Hazebrouck and went into billets, where it remained until the 23rd April, for, though the 3rd Cavalry Brigade was sent up in support on the 12th March during the attack on Neuve Eglise, it was sent back to Estaires by General Rawlinson and replaced by the 5th Brigade, as the action was over.

The attack on Neuve Chapelle was made during the 10th, 11th and 12th March. Neuve Chapelle itself was captured and held, but the ridge of the hill looking over Lille, which was the chief objective, was recovered by the enemy. The fighting was of a very determined description and the casualties on both sides great. Those of the British amounted to close on 13,000, of whom 190 officers and 2,300 other ranks were killed. The enemy's loss was estimated at not less than 20,000, including 2,000 prisoners. The partial failure of this attack was attributed to the reserves being brought up too late to consolidate the first successful advance, and the Staff were much blamed in consequence; but in this, as in many future attacks, the enemy put up such a heavy artillery barrage behind the first line that it was next to impossible to bring the reserves up closer, and in addition the supply of shells was completely exhausted hours before the end of the action.

There was no further fighting of consequence after this until the 17th April, when the second battle of Ypres may be said to have begun by a German attack on the place known as "Hill 60." This was beaten off after some hard fighting.

On the 15th April General Kavanagh took over command of the 2nd Cavalry Division, vice Gough.

On the 20th Ypres was bombarded and much damage was done to the town, and on the 22nd the Germans used poison gas for the first time. The French troops between Pilkem and the Canal were the first sufferers from this barbarous invention and were driven out of their trenches on to the Canadians at Langemark Road. This caused a gap of nearly four miles in the line through which the enemy broke, but the Canadians soon stopped the advance and on the next day the line was re-established.

On the 24th the 3rd Brigade returned dismounted to the trenches along the Canal north-west of Ypres, where they had their first experience of "stink

---

* Lieut. Ryan was blown up, and landed in a German trench, where he was made a prisoner.

1915 shells," which fortunately proved more disagreeable than deadly, their chief effect being to produce a temporary blindness. This day Ypres was again bombarded and another attack made on the Canadians at St. Julien preceded by gas. This was again repulsed.

1st May The Brigade was still in the trenches at Wiltge. This day Lieut. Brown was severely wounded by shrapnel. On the 2nd at 5 p.m. the trenches in front of the 16th were first gassed and then attacked, but the enemy were driven back as the gas took effect principally on the supports, who were obliged to vacate their shelters. The gas fortunately for the most part passed away on the flank of the 16th. This was followed up by very heavy shelling, and the 5th and 4th, who were sent forward to occupy the trenches abandoned by the infantry, had over 100 casualties. The 16th had one killed and one wounded only.

3rd May On the 3rd the Regiment left the trenches and went into billets, where it remained till the 12th, when it returned to the trenches north of Ypres. On the 20th the Regiment again went into billets. The casualties from the 15th to the 20th were one man killed and three wounded.

12th May On the 12th the line had been somewhat shortened and reinforced by the 1st and 3rd Cavalry Divisions. The next day the line held by the 10th Hussars, the Life Guards and the Sussex Yeomanry was so severely shelled that the troops were driven out of their trenches. The shelling was followed up by an attack in force, which was repulsed by a bayonet charge, and the enemy's trenches were taken by the yeoman, who passed the night in thoroughly looting them, but they returned at daybreak to their own trenches. The 3rd Cavalry Division suffered very heavily in this fighting, losing 90 officers (out of 150) and 1,200 other ranks. The 1st Division got off comparatively lightly.

24th May On the 24th another gas attack was made and though the trenches were successfully held there were considerable losses, the 9th Lancers being the chief sufferers. The 16th were sent up to Ypres, and when crossing the pontoon bridge from the sally-port in order to get to the trenches the Regiment was badly shelled by two guns which the enemy had trained on the bridge as soon as the head of the column came into view. Colonel Eccles, Lieutenant Lord Holmpatrick, and Captain Macglashan, the surgeon, and nine men were wounded and two killed before the troops could be withdrawn behind the shelter of the ramparts. When it was dark, about 9 p.m., the Regiment succeeded in crossing the bridge and marched via Zillebeke to Hooge Woods, where it took over the trenches of the 11th Hussars.

The next two days were occupied in trench digging under continuous shelling, during which five men were killed and three wounded. On the 29th the Regiment was relieved by the Blues and went back to Vlamertinghe and thence to Ste. Marie Cappel.

During May there had been much fighting on other sections of the Allied line. On the 9th May the French made an attack in force in Artois, the objectives being Lens, Douai, and Soissons, and in order to hold the enemy to his positions other attacks were made between Festubert and Bois Greniers. Some of the enemy's front trenches were taken after much fighting and heavy loss, but the gains were inconsiderable and few were held.

After the 24th May the fighting died out and the usual "Trench Warfare" re-commenced. No offensive movements of any consequence were made by either side until the 24th September.

The 16th remained in billets at Ste. Marie Cappel until July 1st, when seven officers and 200 men were detailed to dig trenches near Dickebushe, the party

being relieved every week. On the 14th Headquarters moved to Broxelles. 1915
The Regiment were billeted in various places until the 30th September.

On July 15th Major-General Sir Philip Chetwode took over command of the 2nd Cavalry Division.

During the winter military operations had been greatly hampered by the increasing scarcity of munitions, shells and high explosives and the want of heavier guns and machine guns, while the troops were disheartened and exasperated by the incessant shelling that they were subjected to, to which no adequate reply could be made.

Not only were the remonstrances and requests of Sir J. French entirely disregarded by the War Office, but he had the further mortification of seeing every day train-loads of ammunition passing behind his lines on the road to Marseilles for shipment to Gallipoli. The climax was reached when an order was sent from the War Office on May 20th to send away 20 per cent. of the reserve of shells which had been with difficulty accumulated for use in the expected summer offensive.

Some of the facts about the shortage of shells had already leaked out notwithstanding the censorship, and the public was getting a little uneasy about the situation. On April 20th Mr. Asquith made his extraordinary speech at Newcastle, in which he flatly denied that there was any want of ammunition at all. It is impossible to conjecture what could possibly have induced even the most hardened politician to make such a statement. The Prime Minister could not plead ignorance, as Sir John French had repeatedly brought the facts to his knowledge both personally and by letters. It was indeed equivalent to saying that he did not believe that the Field-Marshal was speaking the truth.

The Field-Marshal now took the unprecedented course of seeking the aid of the Press, which he did through the medium of Colonel Repington, the "Times" Correspondent, though he was well aware that he was risking his professional future by doing so. The result was that such a storm was raised in the country that the Cabinet was compelled to take action—the Ministry of Munitions was created to take over the responsibility for all war material and Mr. Lloyd George was placed at the head of the new department. Whatever the faults of that gentleman may be, a lack of energy is certainly not one of them, and by September the weekly supply of shells was fully 30 times greater than it had been in May.

The Allied line was now divided into three sectors, each under the command Sept. of a French General. The northern sector, which ran from the sea to Com- 1915. piègne sur Oise, was commanded by General Foch; the central sector, from Compiègne to Verdun, by General de Castelnau; the right sector, from Verdun to the Swiss frontier, by General Dubail.

The disposition of the Armies on the northern sector was as follows, from left to right:—

From the sea to Boesinghe, on the Ypres Canal, the Belgian Army and a French Corps under General Hely d'Oissel.

From Boesinghe to Armentières, the 2nd Army under General Plumer.

From Armentières to Grenay, west of Lens, the 1st Army under General Sir D. Haig.

From Grenay to Arras, the French 10th Army under General d'Urbal.

From Arras to the Somme, the 3rd Army under General Monro.

The strength of the British battle line now amounted to about 600,000 bayonets, that of the French about 2,000,000.

It was decided that an attack should be made by de Castelnau in the Champagne area, the objective being the German railway communications at the

L

1915 junction at Vousièrs, while the British were to make a subsidiary attack in the Loos area in order to hold the Germans in their positions.

22nd Sept. The attack of de Castelnau began on the 22nd and lasted till the 29th. Though the objective was not fully attained still a considerable extent of ground was gained and very heavy losses were inflicted on the enemy, 25,000 prisoners and 150 guns being taken.

The battle, known as the Battle of Loos, in the northern sector began on the 24th. The main attack was made by the French 10th Army and the 1st Army, by the first upon the Vimy Ridge, by the latter on the line La Basseé, Haines, Hulloch, Loos.

Subsidiary attacks were also made by the 2nd Division from Givenchy, by the Indian Corps from Neuve Chapelle, by the 3rd Corps from Bois Greniers, and the 5th Corps from Ypres. The Cavalry Corps, less the 3rd Division, were kept in reserve at St. Pol and Bailleul les Pernes. The 3rd Division was posted behind the 4th Corps as reserve to the 1st Army.

The battle lasted over six days. The general results were as follows :—

The French 10th Army captured and held the Vimy Ridge.

The 1st Army captured Loos after very severe fighting and heavy loss, taking 3,000 prisoners and 25 guns.

The other attacks, which were not pressed, accomplished nothing of importance.

The 16th were not engaged in this action, but the 3rd Division was sent dismounted into the firing line.

1st Oct. On the 1st October Colonel Eccles rejoined the Regiment. On the 2nd Captain Graham and 33 men per squadron were sent dismounted to Vermelles to clean up the battlefield. The detachment rejoined on the 4th, and the same day Colonel Campbell was promoted Brigadier-General to command the 5th Cavalry Brigade.

The Regiment remained in billets at various places until the 2nd January, 1916.

After the Battle of Loos the enemy made several counter-attacks at various points of the Allied line, which were defeated, chiefly by artillery fire, with considerable loss, but the line as established after Loos remained practically unchanged during the rest of the winter and fighting was confined to the usual " Trench Warfare."

15th Dec. On the 15th December Sir John French resigned the command and returned to England. He was succeeded by Sir D. Haig, who was replaced by Sir C. Monro in the command of the 1st Army.

In December the Indian Infantry Corps left France, and the Cavalry Brigades were broken up and formed into battalions of infantry.

The casualties in the fighting during September were very great. The British lost upwards of 45,000 men up to October 1st, and the French about 120,000.

CHAPTER XL.

January, 1916, to December 31st, 1917.

1916.—January 2nd, The Regiment at Wavrans. Trenches. February 9th, Return to billets at Wavrans. Line extended by relief of French 10th Army. Now from Boesghe on north to Corlu eight miles N.W. Peronne.

February 21st, Great German offensive at Verdun begins. July 1st, Be- 1916 ginning of 1st Battle of the Somme. Attack by 4th Army. Formation of 5th Army. June 19th, The 3rd Brigade at Sec Bois. November 18th, Battle of Somme ends. The results. The Cavalry not engaged. September 6th, Regiment to Bray. November 8th, To billets at Petits Preaux for winter. 1917.—No serious fighting during winter. German retirement to new Hindenburg line in February. Retreat followed up. The new position. April 5th, The Regiment on reconnaisance. April 19th, To billets Villeroy. Preparations for new attack by 1st and 3rd Armies east of Arras. April 9th, Attack begins. June 6th, Battle ceases. Results of Battle of Arras. French attacks on the Aisne. French line extended. May 23rd, The Regiment to trenches at Lempire. June 27th, Move to Epehy in support to 2nd Army. Preparations for attack on the north. Movements of 4th and 5th Armies. June 7th, Third Battle of Ypres. Operations impeded by bad weather. Results. The 16th in billets July, August and September. Preparations for new attack by 3rd Army. Objectives Bourlon and break through by Cavalry at Cambrai. November 20th, Battle of Cambrai. Initial success at Bourlon. Failure on Schelde Canal. November 20th, German Reserves come up. German counterattack. The break through near Gonnelieu. Letter descriptive of action. The 3rd Brigade in support at Masnières. November 23rd, Cavalry withdrawn. November 25th, The 3rd Brigade to Fins and Ribecourt. Dismounted party at Bourlon. December 4th, Camp bombed. December 6th, To billets round Bovelles.

Summary of Events, January 1st, 1916, to December 31st, 1917.—January 9th, 1916, Final evacuation of Gallipoli. February 21st, Great attack on Verdun begins. March 10th, Germany declares war on Portugal. April 29th, Capitulation of Kut. May 30th, Battle of Jutland. June 5th, Lord Kitchener drowned. July 1st, Allied offensive on Somme begins. 6th, Mr. Lloyd George Secretary for War. August 6th, Battle of the Isonzo; Italian victory. 27th, Roumania declares war on Austria; Germany declares war on Roumania. 30th, V. Hindenburg succeeds V. Falkenhayn as Chief of General Staff. September 3rd, Invasion of the Dobruja by Germany. October 5th, Retreat of Roumanians from Transylvania. 12th, Germans invade Roumania. November 11th, Death of Emperor of Austria. December 5th, Resignation of Mr. Asquith. 6th, Mr. Lloyd George Prime Minister. 8th, Blockade of Greece. 12th, Tentative proposals for peace by Germany; General Nivelle succeeds General Joffre. 20th, Peace Note from President Wilson. 30th, Allies reply to German Peace Proposals. January 11th, 1917, Allies reply to President Wilson. 31st, Germany announces unrestricted submarine warfare. February 3rd, Submarine sinks United States steamer Housatonic; Diplomatic relations broken off with Germany. March 10th, Russian Revolution begins. 11th, Baghdad taken. 26th, Invasion of Palestine. April 6th, United States declares war on Germany. 9th, Brazil declares war on Germany; Vimy ridge taken by Canadians. October 24th, Defeat of Italians at Caporetto. November 18th, Death of Sir S. Maude in Mesopotamia. 20th, Battle of Cambrai. 26th, Germans evacuate East Africa. December 22nd, Brest Litovski negotiations opened between Berlin and revolutionary Russia.

On the 2nd January, 1916, the Regiment was sent to Wavrans, where the Jan. horses were left, one man being detailed to look after three horses. The 2nd Cavalry Division was posted at and about Vermelles and the dismounted troops

1916 went into the trenches. The 16th took their turn in the trenches until the 9th February, when the Regiment went into billets, first at Vermelles and finally at Wavrans, where it remained until the 19th June.

During January and February a number of minor attacks were made by the enemy at various places with the intention of diverting attention from the preparations that were being made for the impending great offensive against Verdun. The 16th casualties during this period were one man killed, and Lieuts. Hays and Davies and five men wounded.

During the third week in February the ground hitherto held by the French 10th Army was taken over. The British line then extended uninterruptedly from Boesinghe, five miles north of Ypres, to Corlu, eight miles north-west of Peronne.

On the 21st February the attack on Verdun began. The Germans had massed an army of 230,000 men and an enormous number of guns for this attack, and these were continuously reinforced by Divisions drawn from the reserves on other sections and from the Eastern front during the battle, which

April lasted without intermission until the 19th April, and resulted in the complete defeat of the Germans. The fighting was of the most desperate description, for the enemy pressed the attack quite regardless of losses, and the French fought with even more than their usual courage and determination. The losses on both sides reached unprecedented numbers, the German casualties amounting to at least 200,000 and those of the French to quite half that number.

May On the 3rd May the fighting at Verdun was recommenced and lasted until the 30th June, by which time the French counter-attack had finally regained all the ground that had been previously lost and the German attack came to an end.

1st On the 1st July the first battle of the Somme began with a general bombard-
July ment along the whole line. Great preparations had been made in the rear of the line for the attack by Sir H. Rawlinson's 4th Army with Sir Hubert Gough's 5th Army, then in process of formation, in reserve. This last Army at this date consisted chiefly of the Cavalry Corps. The 16th joined up with the rest of the 3rd Brigade at Sec Bois on the 19th June.

The battle lasted, with occasional breaks for the purpose of consolidating gains, until November 18th, tanks being used for the first time. The result was the gain of a great semi-circle the base line of which extended from Beaumont Hamel on the north to Chilly on the south, a distance of 25 miles, with a maximum depth of eight miles in the centre. In addition 38,000 prisoners were taken, with 29 heavy and 96 field guns, 136 mortars, and 514 machine guns. The Cavalry Corps took no part in the action, and the only casualty which the 16th had during these months was on the 26th September, when Captain Tempest Hicks was wounded.

On September 6th the Regiment marched to Bray sur Somme, and eventually on November 8th went into billets at Petits Preaux for the winter.

Jan. During January there was no serious fighting in the northern sector, though
1917. there were some minor local attacks made to rectify the line in several places, and the Regiment remained in billets until 5th April. On February 9th a Pioneer Battalion was formed and sent to Bethune under the command of Lieut. Allen. On March 1st Lieut.-Colonel Eccles was invalided home and Captain Cheyne took command of the Regiment, but was replaced the next day by Captain Shannon when the Pioneers rejoined.

The results of the Somme battle and the fighting at Verdun had caused much disquiet to the German Staff. In addition to the heavy loss in men and guns, sections of the German line from Arras to Soissons had been rendered untenable and a new set of entrenchments behind it had been constructed in case 1917 of a possible retreat. This new line was called by the Germans the Siegfried, and by the British the Hindenburg line, as it was supposed to have been made under the supervision of that hero.

At the beginning of February it became evident that a retirement to the new Feb. line was being commenced and a general advance in pursuit was ordered.

A series of rear-guard actions followed, but the advance was greatly retarded by the state of the roads, which had not only been destroyed by the enemy as far as the time permitted, but were also broken up by a thaw and wet following a prolonged frost.

Under these circumstances the enemy's withdrawal took place without serious molestation, and by April 7th the German Armies were established on the new line and the retreat came to an end.

The new line ran from just east of Arras, which was little more than a mile within the British lines, by Bapaume and Soissons, being about five miles east of the two towns and a mile west of St. Quentin.

The 3rd Cavalry Brigade marched from their billets on the 5th April and April. was employed in a reconnaisance of the enemy's line. Beyond some shelling there was no actual fighting, but the weather was atrocious, with frequent snowstorms, and shelter was difficult to find as every village had been carefully destroyed. On the 11th April the Regiment bivouaced in a field in a snowstorm. Neither rations or water could be obtained and the horses were two days without any, with the result that 19 died and 28 had to be left behind when the Regiment moved off. On the 19th the Regiment again went into billets, finally at Villeroy, where it remained until the 12th of May. The casualties in this operation were two men wounded.

Meanwhile preparations were being made for an attack by the 3rd and 1st Armies on the German positions east of Arras between Croisilles, south-east of Arras, and Givenchy en Gobelle at the northern end of Vimy ridge, on a front of 15 miles. The German position included about five miles of the new Hindenburg system of trenches.

The French were to begin the attack, called the second battle of the Aisne, on the 16th April, and the battle of Arras was intended to support this action.

To ensure secrecy the greater part of the troops and their supplies were massed for the attack in the great catacombs and cellars under the city of Arras, where they were secure from observation, and for three weeks before the infantry attack the enemy's trenches were bombarded by the heavy artillery. On the 9th April the infantry attack began with the capture of that part of the Vimy ridge still held by the enemy by the Canadians commanded by Sir J. Byng. The Battle of Arras continued until the 6th June and resulted June. in a gain of front extending for 18 miles with an average depth of four miles. Twenty thousand prisoners, 257 guns, 227 trench mortars, 464 machine guns, and a large amount of stores of all kinds were taken. The French attack on the Aisne was also successful, the Craonne plateau and the Chemin des Dames being taken. On the 20th May the French line was again extended to the Omignon River, thus re-occupying the line vacated in February.

On the 12th May the Regiment marched by Peronne to the camp at Mar- May. quais, whence 11 officers and 317 men were sent dismounted into the reserve trenches at Epehy. On the 23rd the Regiment moved to camp at Bouchy and the dismounted troops went into the trenches at Lempire. On the 21st June June. the trench occupied by A Squadron was blown in, one man being killed and two wounded. On June 27th the Regiment returned to Epehy in support of the 2nd Army.

1917   The action at Arras having accomplished its objective, the Commander-in-Chief now returned to his original intention to undertake a vigorous offensive
June in the northern flank of the line. Very careful preparations were made for this, and the disposition of the several Armies was materially altered. General Rawlinson's 4th Army was moved from Peronne to Nieuport, Sir Hubert Gough's 5th Army to Ypres, and General Plumer's 2nd Army to the Lys. The Belgian Army was at Dixmude, and the 1st French Army between the Belgians and the 5th Army. The primary objectives of the coming attack were the Messines and Wyteshaete Ridges.

What is known as the Third Battle of Ypres began at daybreak on the morning of the 7th June with the firing of nineteen great mines which had been laid along the front from Hill 60 to the northern end of the Messines Ridge. The explosion was at once followed by an infantry attack on the nine miles of trenches between St. Yves and Mount Sorrel, which resulted in the capture of Oost-taverne and Gapaard and the evacuation in consequence of all the forward positions of the enemy. Some successful minor operations fol-
27th lowed, and on the 27th July the French and the 5th Army crossed the Yser
July Canal.

31st   On the 31st July the French and the 5th Army renewed the attack on a
July front of 15 miles between Steenstraat and the Lys. The result was the advance of the whole line, 6,000 prisoners and 25 guns being taken. Further operations were held up for two weeks by a succession of storms and heavy rains.

Aug.   On the 15th August the Canadians attacked and took Hill 70 with 1,700 prisoners, and on the next day a second attack was made from Ypres in which Langemarck was taken with 2,000 prisoners and 30 guns.

After some minor operations a further advance was attempted by both the
Sept. 5th and 2nd Armies. Operations were greatly impeded by the continuous rain which turned the whole front into a sea of mud, but on the 26th Polygon Wood was taken and held notwithstanding repeated counter-attacks by the Germans, who had been reinforced by Divisions transferred from the Russian front.

Nov.   Finally on the 6th November Paschendaele was taken by the Canadians after some very severe fighting and the operation came to an end. From the 31st July to the 6th November 24,000 prisoners were taken with 74 guns, 138 trench mortars, and 940 machine guns.

The 16th remained in billets at various places during July, August, September and October with the exception of the week from July 1st to the 8th, when the Regiment went into the trenches from Epehy, and had no casualties.

On the 16th Major-General Greenly took over the command of the 2nd Cavalry Division. On the 20th November the Brigade marched to Villers-Faucon.

Though it was so late in the season, and the troops had been much tried, both by hard fighting and the unusually bad weather, it seemed to the Allied command to be of the utmost importance to continue the operations on the Western Front in order to prevent reinforcements being sent from the German Armies to the Italian front, where affairs were going very badly for the Italians after their decisive defeat at Caporetto. Furthermore, as it was known that the enemy was being reinforced from the Russian front it was desirable, if an attack was to be made at all, to make one as soon as possible. As the enemy had been compelled to concentrate most of his reserve troops in front of Paschendaele Sir D. Haig decided to attack in the direction of Cambrai, where he would have the advantage of dryer ground where tanks could co-operate with the infantry without the difficulties that hampered their action in the muddy valleys in front of Ypres.

Opposed to Sir J. Byng in the area selected for the operation, from Bulle- 1917
court to the Oise, was the 2nd German Army commanded by Von Marwitz.*
This consisted of eleven Divisions; of these there were three Divisions in the
front line in the area about to be attacked, with three more in reserve.

The attack was limited to a front of six miles, from the east of Gonnelieu
on the south to the Canal du Nord opposite Hermies, while subsidiary attacks
were to be made east of Epehy and between Bullecourt and Fontaine les
Croisilles. It was to be made by the 3rd Army, now commanded by Sir J.
Byng, who had replaced Sir E. Allenby when he was transferred to Palestine
in June. Sir J. Byng had nine Divisions of Infantry, of which six were in
line on the front of the main attack, two on the left in the Bullecourt area,
and one in reserve, together with a large force of tanks. As there was a possibility, and indeed an expectation, of effecting a breach in the enemy's line by
means of the tanks sufficient to allow of the passage of the Cavalry, four
Divisions, the 1st, 2nd, 4th,† and 5th Cavalry Divisions, were placed at
General Byng's disposal.

The principal objective was to capture the commanding position of Bourlon
Wood and village on the north, and after forcing the passage of the Canal
and covering the right flank of the advance by the capture of Crèvecœur and
Rumilly, to wheel the line to the north-east. The Cavalry Corps was then to
move as quickly as possible on Cambrai with the view of raiding the enemy's
lines of communication.

Sir D. Haig reckoned that it would take about 48 hours for the enemy to
bring his reserves into action, and that in that time he might be able to accomplish his objective, which was a combination of the seizure and holding of the
Bourlon position and a Cavalry raid.

Every precaution was taken to prevent any warning being given of the impending attack. The troops were assembled by night in the trenches and the
tanks concealed behind woods and copses, chiefly under cover of the Havrincourt Forest, and there was no preliminary bombardment. At 6.20 a.m. on
the 20th November the Infantry Divisions, preceded by a long line of tanks, 20th
attacked on a front of six miles east of Gonnelieu to the Canal du Nord oppo- Nov.
site Hermies, subsidiary attacks being made from Epehy, Bullecourt, and
Croisilles. The attack was so far successful that at noon the 5th Cavalry
Division was sent forward to cross the canal at Masnières and Marcoing, but
the enemy's resistance was still unbroken at these points, and being unable to
get further the troopers were dismounted and joined the infantry line.

The results of the day's fighting were the capture of the German first line,
the Siegfried line and its reserve trenches, and parts of the last line to a depth
of $4\frac{1}{2}$ miles on a front of five miles with 5,000 prisoners. But neither Rumilly
or Crèvecœur were taken, nor were the crossings of the Scheldt Canal made
good.

The next morning the attack was resumed. Flesquières and the ridge there, 21st
Anneux, and Cantaing were taken and held, and the outskirts of Bourlon Nov.
Wood reached, and late in the afternoon Fontaine-notre-Dame. The Canadian
Cavalry Brigade tried to cross the Canal at Masnières but failed, though a
squadron of Fort Garry Horse did manage to cross by a temporary bridge and
breaking through the enemy's line charged and captured a field battery. The

---

* Formerly Commandant of the Cavalry Corps. This seems to have been broken up and
the troopers drafted into Infantry Corps. There were no signs of any German Cavalry
during the fighting at Cambrai.

† The 4th Cavalry Division was comprised of the Mhow, Lucknow, and Sealkote Brigades.
The 5th of the Canadian, Ambala, and Secunderabad Brigades.

1917 squadron was eventually withdrawn after most of the horses had been killed. The 1st Cavalry Division and the Ambala Brigade were held up at Noyelles, where they fought on foot with the Infantry, and at night the 5th Division was withdrawn as the Rumilly attack was abandoned.

22nd Nov. The 22nd was occupied in consolidating the gains and in bringing up reliefs. On the 23rd the battle was renewed. Bourlon Wood was finally cleared of the enemy, but little progress was made elsewhere, and all hope of a "breakthrough" by the Cavalry was given up, to the great disappointment of the troops.

24th Nov. By the 24th the German Reserves were coming up in force and there were strong counter-attacks. Bourlon village was taken but afterwards retaken by the enemy after severe fighting; the Wood, however, was held, and also the hill. There was now a pause in the battle of a week. The general results of the operations so far were the occupation of the Bourlon heights, the clearing of 60 square miles of territory, and the capture of 10,000 prisoners and 142 guns.

But the German Staff was by no means disposed to allow Sir D. Haig to retain his gains without a further struggle. Sixteen fresh Divisions were brought up to reinforce Von Marwitz, and on the 30th he attacked all along his line with 24 Divisions, the chief weight of the attack being directed against the flanks of the British line, at Bourlon and Mœuvres on the north and on the southern flank on the line Masnières—Bonavis—Gonnelieu—Villers-Guislain.

On the northern section the German attack was fairly well held and the enemy had no success, though the fighting was severe and the casualties heavy, but on the southern flank the British line was driven in from Masnières to Vendhuille. There was a thick fog early in the morning which covered the advance of the enemy, and the situation was only saved by the valour of the 29th Division which held Masnières. Nevertheless the Bonavis Ridge was lost, and with it La Vacquerie, with 18 field guns, Gonnelieu, Villers Guislain and Gouzencourt, and Gauche Wood, three miles north-west of Vendhuille.

The 4th Cavalry Division had been withdrawn to Athies and the 5th to Monchy, and these were at once sent back to fill the gap in the line between Gouzeaucourt and Vendhuille, which they succeeded in doing, and a Brigade of Guards with a number of tanks retook the St. Quentin ridge and Gonnelieu, but on the 1st December the 29th Division evacuated Masnières after beating off nine attacks in succession as the loss of the Bonavis position made the place untenable. There was much fighting on the 2nd and 3rd, but the occupation of La Vacquerie necessitated the evacuation of Marcoing, and on the 4th Sir D. Haig gave up Bourlon and retired to the Flesquières ridge. By the 7th the new line was established. The front now ran from the Canal du Nord $1\frac{1}{2}$ miles north of Havrincourt, north of Flesquières and Ribecourt, along Welsh ridge to a point $1\frac{1}{2}$ miles north-east of La Vacquerie, thence west of Gonnelieu and Villers Guislain to Vendhuille, where it rejoined the original line.

It was fortunate that the Germans either did not recognise the extent of the success of their attack south of Gouzeaucourt or had no reserves at hand to push their advantage further, for there was nothing to stop them until the Cavalry Brigades came up.

The following letter, written by an officer of one of the Indian Lancer Regiments that had been sent back to near Peronne to rest after the failure of the attack on the 23rd, shows that the German counter-attack might have had very serious consequences, for it is certain that if the enemy's Cavalry had been effectively used a real "break-through" of the line would have been quite feasible, and though no doubt it would have been soon held up by the reserves, much damage might have been done before it was checked. Fortunately the enemy did not realise the extent of the success they had gained and the opportunity vanished very speedily.

The account referred to begins :—

"It was an awful rush that morning. At about 8 a.m., after having heard the most awful bombardment going on towards the north, we suddenly got the order to march at once. Half the regiment was out at exercise, but we managed to collect things and got off. We trotted off full bat for about 12 miles without stopping, not knowing in the least what had happened except that the Huns had done a proper break-through somewhere to the north.

"After going for $1\frac{1}{2}$ hours in the direction of the noise we had orders to stop, and the Brigade halted for a short time in a ravine. While there we saw one of our balloons brought down over our heads by a Hun airplane, and a lot of rather panic-stricken wounded Tommies began coming through going west. None of them knew what was going on, but we didn't wait there long as we got orders almost at once to mount and ride north-west and drive back any Huns we met. That was the first news we had really that they had got right through with no one in front of them.

"The British Regiment of the Brigade was told off to clear a wood and we were told to work on their left and fill the gap between them and the Guards, who were told off to counter-attack a village about two miles from the left of the wood. We then went off and after going about a mile we came on the tanks, which were on their way to join the Guards.

"Things now began to get unpleasant and at the top of a rise we came on a belt of wire. The leading squadron got through all right, but the second had a bad time getting through from shell-fire, which they were able to get on just in time to catch them. The remaining squadron found another place and got through without much damage.

"In front of us was a long valley on the right of which was the wood before mentioned, and on the left the Guards' village. We set off down there as fast as we could go, jumping some small trenches in which was what seemed the last of the British Army, consisting of a Director of Ordnance stores and his clerks.

"It was good clear going down the valley, but at the end of it, about a mile off, was a deep sunken road full of huts and dug-outs into which the Hun had just arrived. It wasn't nice riding down here, but the men were wonderful, although they were losing a lot from rifle and machine gun fire and a certain amount of shells. A—— was killed here by a shell which landed almost under his horse. Both the C.O.'s horses were shot under him, one after the other, but we got down in the end all right.

"F—— who was leading, finding that he couldn't get over the sunk road, which extended 1,000 yards each way with a railway on the far side, dismounted and led his squadron off on foot towards the railway. He was killed here while getting his Hotchkiss gun going. The rest of the Regiment now came up, and the Hun having legged it out of the road to behind the railway where it was quite impossible to get at him mounted, we lined the road on foot and prepared to stop any further attempt on his part to advance.

"There was no one visible on our right; on our left we could see the Guards and tanks going for the village. The Guards took it in fine style, but the tanks had a bad time as there was a rotten little gun that kept getting direct hits on them and they went off like a firework.

"It was getting dark now, and after a bit our British Regiment came up on our right, which made things more secure and made a more or less continuous line, however thin, in front of the victorious Hun, who were a rotten

1917 lot really with the exception of their machine gunners. A whole crowd of them were coming out of the wood when we arrived, but they thought better of it at the last moment and melted away.

"We stayed there for the night, it freezing about 20 degrees, but the road had apparently been occupied by some R.E. who had run away early in the day and had left their rations and vast quantities of coats and blankets, which we were very glad of. We sent the horses away during the night and became Infantry.

"The Guards attacked on our left at 6.30 a.m. the next morning, and the Huns on our front ran into our trenches—a most miserable crowd. We stuck there all day, and the next night odds and ends began to arrive to strengthen the line, and during the night we were relieved by another Brigade after a very nasty dose of shelling."

19th Nov. On the 19th November the 2nd Cavalry Division had been moved up to the front. The 3rd Brigade bivouaced at Villers Faucon for the night, and at 1 p.m. on the 20th advanced to the Hindenburg support line about two miles west of Masnières in readiness to follow the 5th Brigade over the Canal, with the 4th Brigade in reserve, but night came on without any crossing having been effected. The Brigade remained in this position until 4.30 p.m. on the 21st, when the Cavalry advance was abandoned and it returned to Villers Faucon. On the 23rd the Brigade moved to Fins and on the morning of the 25th to Ribecourt. Here 200 men were left dismounted under command of Captain Tempest-Hicks,* and the remainder of the Regiment returned to Fins. There was no actual fighting except by the dismounted party, but the Brigade was under shell fire most of the day, the casualties of the 16th being five men wounded and three horses killed.

The Regiment remained at Fins until the 6th December, the dismounted party having rejoined on the 30th November. This had been badly shelled while in the trenches at Bourlon and had lost three men killed and six wounded.

Dec. On the 4th the Regiment had the unpleasant experience of having the camp bombed by airplanes, the casualties being Lieutenant Pargeter and six men wounded. Five horses were killed and 11 others badly damaged.

On the 6th December the Regiment marched to the camp at Bouchy and thence to billets round Bovelles, where it remained for the rest of the month, there being no military operations beyond the usual trench fighting during the winter.

On the 20th a dismounted party of eight officers and 201 men was sent to Hermilly.

Captain Cheyne was in command of the Regiment with the acting rank of Lieut.-Colonel, vice Lieut.-Colonel Eccles temporarily invalided from November 16th.

---

* A dismounted Brigade was formed from the 2nd Cavalry Division and sent to assist the defence of Bourlon Wood.

CHAPTER XLI.

JANUARY, 1918, TO JULY, 1918.

January 20th, the move of the 5th Army to the South. January 1st, the 16th goes into the trenches. January 28th, the 3rd Brigade sent to Amiens. March 1st, to camp at Brie. March 4th, to trenches at Vermand. March 11th, the Brigade returns to Brie. March 13th, the Brigade moves to Grandru. General position at resumption of hostilities. The 3rd and 5th Armies. German Armies and plans. March 21st, Second Battle of the Somme opens. March 22nd, Crozat Canal crossed by enemy. Orders of General Gough. General retreat of 3rd and 5th Armies. March 24th, Allied Council at Doulens. General Foch appointed C.-in-C. March 25th, Formation of Carey's Force. March 26th, Attack renewed. Further retreat. The 2nd Cavalry Division engaged west of Noyon. March 27th, Withdrawal to Compiègne. March 27th, the 2nd Division to Montdidier area. March 29th, the Division to Cattenchy. March 28th, the 5th Army broken up. General Gough's command ceases. His place taken by General Rawlinson and 4th Army. March 30th, Renewal of battle. The 2nd Division at Moreville. March 31st, Fighting between the Avre and Luce. The line re-established. April 1st, the withdrawal of the 2nd Cavalry Division. April 5th, Final German attack fails. The line stabilised. End of Second Battle of the Somme. April 7th, the Battle of the Lys. Successes of the enemy. April 21st, Fighting suspended. April 23rd, Tank fighting between the Somme and Ancre. April 25th, the Lys battle renewed. Loss of Mount Kemmel. April 29th, German attack finally defeated. Close of Battle of the Lys. The 2nd Cavalry Division during the Battle of the Lys. April 29th, March of the 2nd Division to Clety. May 5th, the Regiment moves into billets at Longvillers. May 27th, the attack on the French along the Ailette river and Third Battle of the Aisne. June 9th, Attacks on the Montdidier section and at Rheims. June 18th, Termination of major operations. The line stabilised. General result of the fighting from March 21st to June 18th.

Summary of Events, February to June, 1918.—February 24th, Brest Litovski Treaty signed; final withdrawal from the war by Russia. March 5th, Roumania makes peace. 21st, Second Battle of the Somme begins. April 7th, Battle of the Lys. 22nd, Zeebrugge harbour blocked. May 9th, Ostend harbour blocked. 27th, Commencement of offensive by Allies; 3rd Battle of the Aisne. June 15th, Defeat of Austrians on the Piave.

On the 20th January the 5th Army was moved from the Ypres section to the south end of the front on the right of the 3rd Army, and took up the line from Gouzecourt to the Oise. This move was made by order of the British Government in response to the urgent request of the French for an extension of the British line regardless of the remonstrances of Sir D. Haig, whose repeated requests for reinforcements from England were entirely ignored. The battle front to the extreme right, where the British line joined that of the French at Barisis some eight miles south of the Oise, was 125 miles in length, and of this Sir H. Gough's 5th Army held no less than 42 miles.

On the 1st January the Regiment again went into the trenches, nine officers and 200 men being sent into the front line east of Villaret. On the 6th the 3rd Brigade was relieved by the 5th Brigade and the 16th went into reserve at Vendelles, where the Regiment remained until the 6th, when it went into

1918 the intermediate line. This area was heavily shelled from the 6th to the 17th, two men being killed and six wounded. Trench service continued in one or other of the lines until the 28th January, when the 3rd Brigade was relieved by the Lucknow Brigade and sent by train to the back area south-west of Amiens. The casualties during this period were two killed and two wounded.

Mar. On the 1st March the Regiment moved to the camp at Brie. On the 4th the dismounted party went into the trenches at Vermand in relief of the Canadian Dragoons. Though the trenches were subjected to considerable shelling and airplane bombing there were no casualties, and on the 10th the party was relieved by infantry and returned by train to Brie. On the 13th the Brigade moved to Grandru in reserve to the 3rd Corps on the extreme right of the British line. This place was a village five miles north-east of Noyon and 15 miles due west of Barisis. This day Major Brooke took over the command of the Regiment from Captain Cheyne.

The inevitable resumption of active hostilities in the coming spring was regarded with considerable uneasiness by Sir D. Haig and his Generals. But scanty reinforcements had been received from England, for the Government, obsessed by the fear of a possible invasion, persisted in keeping a large Army in the country; the line had been unreasonably extended, and it was known that the Germans were daily being reinforced by Divisions drawn not only from the Eastern front, where the Russian collapse was complete, but even from Italy, Roumania, and Bulgaria. Sir D. Haig expected that the attack would be made against the point of junction with the French, but he did not venture to weaken the northern flank, for he could not be certain of this. As a defeat on that section would have had most disastrous consequences, the 3rd and 5th Armies were left to meet the possible offensive in the certainty of receiving little help from outside.

In March the 3rd Army, under Sir J. Byng, lay from just north of the Arras-Douai road to near Gouzeaucourt, with four Corps (15 Divisions), the front extending over about 40,000 yards. Sir H. Gough, with the 5th Army, had to cover a front of 72,000, or 41 miles, with 14 Infantry Divisions and two Divisions of Cavalry. The details of his position were as follows:—

From Gouzeaucourt to Roussoy lay the 7th Corps under Sir W. Congreve, four Divisions, covering 14,000 yards.

From Roussoy to Maissemy, covering the valley of the Omignon, lay the 19th Corps under Sir H. E. Watts, holding a front of 10,000 yards with three Divisions.

In front of St. Quentin, from the Omignon to the Somme, was the 18th Corps under Sir S. Maxse, four Infantry Divisions and the 1st Cavalry Division covering 18,000 yards.

From the Somme to Barisis, south of the Oise, lay the 3rd Corps, under Sir R. H. Butler, with three Infantry Divisions and the 2nd Cavalry Division in reserve, thus covering no less than 30,000 yards, nearly 20 miles, with a scanty force giving an average of scarcely one bayonet per yard! It was true that some 11 miles of this front, between Moy and the Oise, were supposed to be covered by marshes, but the spring had for once been dry, and these were everywhere passable for infantry and in many places for field guns.

The vital positions on the front of the 5th Army were the high ground at Essigny covering the Crozat Canal, at Holnon covering the valley of the Omignon, and at Roussoy, covering the valley of the Cologne.

The Generals commanding both the 3rd and the 5th Armies fully realised the danger that threatened them, and exceptional defences were prepared along their front. These were organised in three zones. First, the "forward" zone, a "line of resistance," protected by barbed wire and covered by a line of outposts. The line of resistance was strengthened at intervals of 2,000 yards by redoubts armed with machine guns, the spaces between them being covered by artillery. Further behind, at a distance varying from half to three miles, came the "battle" zone, prepared on the same principle as the line of resistance. Further back still lay the final defensive zone, but this had not been fully completed when the battle began. A strong bridge-head was in progress of construction covering Peronne. It must be borne in mind that the 5th Army did not come into the new position until the end of January and that the time, six weeks only, was far too short to permit of the completion of these elaborate defences, the third, the final, defensive line being especially weak.

The Germans had now on the Western front 192 Divisions, of which more than half were concentrated on the British front, and 64 of these were massed for the attack on the 50 miles covered by the 3rd and 5th Armies. For the first time, as Helferich told the Reichstadt, the whole German manhood was united in a single theatre of war, ready to strike with the strongest army that the world has ever known.

Ludendorff's plan was to attack the junction between the French and British Armies. Then having, as he confidently expected, made a breach, he intended to drive the British Army northward, holding the French meanwhile to their ground, and then having pinned Sir D. Haig into a corner with the sea behind him, to strike at the exposed French left flank, and rolling up their line to open the way to Paris. It was of the greatest importance to the German Command that this success should be gained before the American Army was in a condition to take the field, and Ludendorff told the Reichstadt that he was prepared to sacrifice a million men to ensure victory.

The British Commander-in-Chief was fairly well informed as to the movements of the enemy and knew that a very large force was being assembled along his front. By the end of February it was evident that these preparations were being especially intensified along the front of the 3rd and 5th Armies; by the end of the third week of March it became certain that an attack on this section of the line was at hand, and every possible effort was made to meet it, 12 Divisions drawn from other parts of the line being held in readiness to be sent at a moment's notice if necessary to the threatened position and means for their rapid conveyance arranged for. Eight of these Divisions were in fact sent before the end of March and the other four before the 9th April.*

At 2 a.m. on the 21st Sir J. Byng and Sir H. Gough were warned that the attack would probably be made that day. The forward zone was always ready, and at 4.30 orders were sent out to man the battle zone.† There was a dense fog which had come on during the afternoon of the 20th, and under cover of this the Germans had been moving troops up to the front. By dawn 37 Divisions had been assembled within 3,000 yards of the British outpost line along the front of over 50 miles between Croisilles and the Oise, and at 5 a.m. a tremendous bombardment was opened upon the whole Allied line from Rheims to the sea, and at eight the infantry attack began.

The fog, which lasted with scarcely a break for the next four days, entirely

---

* The 5th Army only received two of these Divisions, the 8th Division on the 24th, and the 35th on the 26th.
† These orders had been foreseen and even rehearsed in the 5th Army, and the order "Prepare for Battle" was issued on the 19th.

1918 paralysed the defence. The gunners, unable to see 50 yards to their front, fired aimlessly into the mist, while the enemy's artillery, firing at registered targets by the map, were but little incommoded, and the rifle fire, which by its rapidity and accuracy had done so much to bring victory in previous actions, was made ineffective. The outpost line was overwhelmed before the posts could even send back warning, the enemy being in many cases through their line and behind them before the men were even aware of his approach. In the same way the attack burst through the intervals between the redoubts of the second line, and without pausing to assault them, pressed forward to the attack of the battle zone, leaving them to be dealt with by the reserves. The redoubts maintained a stubborn defence as long as it was possible, but by night-fall nearly all of them had been silenced and taken.

21st Mar. By 11 a.m. the enemy was through the forward zone opposite La Fere on the right, and further north at Langicourt and Bullecourt.

By midday Hargicourt and Villaret had been lost and the battle zone pierced at Ronzoy, Essigny, Maissemy, and Benay. In the afternoon, south of St. Quentin, Quessy had been taken, and north of the last place, though the battle zone was still held between Benay and the Somme Canal, the troops were forced back to its last defences. On the north the battle zone of the 3rd Army had been entered at Noreuil and Longatte, but the Flesquière ridge was still held.

The fighting continued far into the night, and it was evident that the enemy was concentrating masses of fresh troops for a renewal of the attack on the next day. The general result was that the Flesquière salient was abandoned during the night, and the 3rd Army line reformed on the old Siegfried line to Havrincourt and Hermies, while Sir H. Gough was obliged to withdraw his 3rd Corps behind the Crozat Canal, and the right of the 18th Corps to the Somme Canal, the bridges over both being destroyed after the troops had crossed.

The 3rd Cavalry Brigade had been billeted in and about Grandru, as has been already stated, since the 13th, the remainder of the 2nd Division being in reserve further north. The troops had already been warned to expect an attack on the 21st, and a dismounted party had been told off and held in readiness to move. This party consisted of Major Cheyne, Captain Allen, Lieuts. Archer, Cox-Cox, Wodehouse, Stephens, Drabble, Pilkington, and Watson, and 208 other ranks.

The bombardment began at 10 p.m. on the night of the 20th, and at 4.30 a.m. on the 21st its increased intensity showed that the attack was impending.

At 2.30 in the afternoon orders were received to send off the dismounted party which marched to La Bretelle, from which place it was taken by motor cars to Le Pateau, the rest of the Regiment and the led horses remaining at Grandru. The enemy's attack, however, was made further to the north and the 16th were not engaged during the day. The dismounted party were posted in some old reserve trenches on the railway, and during the night the infantry in front of these was moved away further to the north.

22nd Mar. The enemy's attack was renewed at dawn on the 22nd, the fog being as thick as on the previous day. In the southern sector the enemy reached the canal at Jussy, where an attempt was made to cross by means of rafts. At 1 p.m. a crossing was effected at Quessy and later at La Montague and Jussy, but the further advance here was kept in check. In the centre Ste. Emilie and Hervilly were lost, but the latter was afterwards retaken, and here the attack was well held. Further north the enemy met with more success for Le Verquier, Villers Faucon, and Epèhy were lost and the troops were withdrawn in the evening to the third defensive line, Bernes—Bouchy—Nurlu and Equancourt, where the right of the 3rd Army rested.

The right of the 3rd Army was heavily engaged all day and Croisilles and St. Leger had to be abandoned late in the afternoon, but generally little ground was lost. South of St. Quentin, however, the third defensive line was penetrated, several gaps created, and practically all the attenuated line had been forced out of the third defensive zone by night-fall. The whole of the reserves had to be thrown into the fight and the troops were withdrawn to the last and final defences with the greatest difficulty. The 3rd Cavalry Brigade was not engaged during the day, though the rest of the 2nd Division had some stiff fighting about Jussy in conjunction with the 18th Infantry Division.

The led horses and the remainder of the 16th were not moved from Grandru, but at 6 p.m. a squadron was sent to support the dismounted parties as it was reported that some of the enemy's advanced troops had got over the canal in the fog. There was considerable firing in the outpost line, but the night passed quietly with this exception and no attack was made. The 16th, however, had the misfortune to lose two officers, Lieut. Stephens and Second Lieut. Sir J. Watson, who were killed in the outpost line, though this was not known until the 24th. Six other ranks were wounded, but none killed.

Sir H. Gough's first orders for the 23rd, issued at 11 p.m. on the 22nd, were to hold the Peronne bridge-head and the line of the Somme, but later, when the full reports of the day's results came in, coupled with the intelligence that large numbers of fresh troops were being massed in front of his shattered line, he decided not to run the risk of a defeat, which might easily be disastrous, by fighting in this exposed position. Early on the morning of the 23rd, therefore, he gave orders for a general retirement of the 19th Corps behind the Somme. The 7th Corps, further north, was directed to conform and to retire to the general line Doigt—Nurlu. This movement necessitated the abandonment of the Peronne bridge-head.

The 3rd Army line was also re-adjusted in conformity, contact being still maintained with the left of the 5th Army at Equancourt.

Early in the morning the enemy renewed the attack by crossing the Crozat Canal in force, and there being now a gap in the line near Ham the town was occupied at once by the German troops. Further north the withdrawal to the west bank of the Somme was successfully accomplished and the bridges having been previously destroyed all attempts to cross the river were repulsed with loss.

On the 3rd Army front the attack was on the whole well held though Le Bucquières and Beugny were lost, but at the point of junction near Equancourt a gap was opened between the 5th and 7th Corps into which the enemy pushed troops in spite of vigorous efforts to close it, and the 7th Corps was forced back from Peronne across the Tortille River, being obliged to retire because the 5th Corps (3rd Army) had been driven from its positions by a strong attack and this had uncovered its left flank. Every man that could be scraped up was pushed into the gap, including the cooks and the crews of derelict tanks.

Early on the 23rd advance parties of the enemy began to make their appearance along the Crozat Canal, and six Hotchkiss guns were sent off with an escort of 30 men to reinforce the 20th Hussars. At 3.30 p.m. the Regiment and the led horses marched via Baboeuf to Carlepont wood, where it bivouaced for the night.

Owing to the fog, which was denser than ever, there was great difficulty in maintaining contact between the various dismounted detached parties. During the early morning there were numerous patrol encounters and much machine gun

1918 fire. Before 10 a.m. the enemy had forced a crossing of the Canal at Menessis notwithstanding the desperate resistance of the dismounted parties of the 3rd Brigade, which were forced to retire first to Faillouel and finally to Villequier Aumont, five miles north of Chauny. By night-fall the 16th detachment had broken up into three parties. These were not got together again until the next morning when they eventually were collected at Bethencourt. The party was 24th ordered to remain at this place in support of the French, who were being moved Mar. up to the relief of General Gough's 3rd Corps. When the roll was called only 87 rank and file answered to their names, and it was discovered that Lieuts. Watson and Stephens had been killed on the 22nd. The Headquarters and led horses moved in the afternoon to Bailly, and before marching 75 led horses with an escort of 25 men were sent back to pick up the dismounted men. The casualties on the 23rd were 21 killed and 20 wounded.

In the area between the Somme and the Oise the attack re-commenced at dawn in a dense fog, and the 20th and 36th Divisions were driven out of Eaucourt and Cugny and obliged to fall back first to Villeselve and finally to Guiscard. Chauny also was lost in the afternoon, and during the night the French and British north of the Oise were withdrawn to the ridge above Crepigny covering Noyon.

The 2nd Cavalry Division was moved this day to Appilly, in the valley of the Oise, five miles due east of Noyon.

North of the Somme the German attack was pressed with great energy all day, and though the 35th Division and some composite battalions collected from the Albert district were coming up to reinforce the 7th Corps at Bray, the day's fighting resulted finally in a general retirement of the 7th Corps and the right and centre of the 3rd Army. Though the line of the Somme was still held north of Ham, Peronne and Clery were gone, and by night-fall the 4th, 5th and 7th Corps were holding with difficulty an irregular line with several gaps in it from Hem on the Somme to Bazentin, and thence north, by Grevillers, west of Bapaume, to Ervillers on the Bapaume-Arras road.

The casualties of the 16th on the 24th were seven men wounded among the scattered dismounted parties retiring from the Crozat Canal.

25th On the 25th the 7th Corps was placed under General Byng's command, and Mar. as the 3rd Corps, which was being relieved by the French was now under the command of General Fayolle, the 5th Army command was reduced to two Corps only—the 18th and 19th.

The main German attack this day was between Hem, on the Somme, on the 7th Corps, and further north to Ervillers, on the left and centre of the 3rd Army, and its result, after a day of hard fighting, was that the line was forced back to the Ancre river. The 7th Corps fell back to positions between Bray on the Somme to just east of Albert, the 5th Corps lay along the Ancre from Albert to Beaumont Hamel, the 4th Corps from Bucquoy and Ablainzevelle in touch with the 6th Corps at Boyelles, thus leaving a gap between Beaumont Hamel and Serre.

This withdrawal uncovered the left of the 5th Army, which was compelled to retreat also. In the course of the day Noyon, Guiscard, Nesle and Chaulnes were lost and the 19th Corps driven back to the line Hallencourt—Estrèes—Frise, and at night-fall, though still fighting obstinately, the line was practically broken into several pieces with numerous gaps, the point of junction with the French in the neighbourhood of Roye being dangerously weak.

The retreat of the troops north of the Oise necessitated the withdrawal of the Cavalry also, and at dawn the 2nd Division was ordered from Appilly to Pontoise, four miles south-east of Noyon. The led horses had been sent up from

Bailly and the dismounted parties were collected here and mounted again and a 1918 squadron formed with them, the 25 men for whom no horses had been provided being sent back on foot to Bailly. In the evening the squadron marched to Chiry on the Oise, where it remained for the night. The casualties of the 16th this day were 16 wounded.

The untoward events of the past week greatly disquieted both the Allied Governments. On the 24th Lord Milner was sent from London to Paris. On the 25th a conference was held at Doulens at which M. Clemenceau, Sir H. Wilson, and Lord Milner met General Pétain, the French Commander-in-Chief, and Sir D. Haig. Both Lord Milner and M. Clemenceau were of opinion that it was absolutely necessary to appoint a single Commander-in-Chief for the whole of the Allied Armies on the Western front. To this both Sir D. Haig and General Pétain assented, and after some discussion General Foch was selected for the post. The appointment was at once approved and ratified by the two Governments.

Meanwhile Sir H. Gough had begun to collect from the Line of Communication details of all kinds a new force for the protection of Amiens, which was now in imminent danger of attack. This was placed in the command of Major-General Grant, C.R.E. of the 5th Army, who at once commenced the repair of the line of the old defences running from Hamel, on the Somme, by Marceleave and Mezieres to Moreuil on the Avre river. The command of this force was subsequently transferred to Brigadier-General Carey of the Field Artillery as General Grant's services at C.R.E. could not be dispensed with. The 19th Corps was then ordered to retire to the line Le Quesnoy—Rosières—Proyart—Bray, at which last place it was to link up with the 3rd Army.

On the morning of the 26th the attack was renewed all along the line. 26th North of Albert the enemy were held, for though Colincourt was lost it was Mar. retaken in the afternoon, but further south, owing to a mistake as to the meaning of an order, the 7th Corps fell back to the line of the Ancre, the right resting in the evening at Sailly-le-Sec on the Somme, thereby uncovering the left of the 19th Corps north of Proyart.

Further south the attack was vigorously pressed all day from Nesle, the enemy's objective being the capture of Montdidier, where there was an important railway junction now being used for detraining the French troops which were being brought up as quickly as possible to reinforce General Fayolle's Army. Though much ground was lost during the day the Germans were still five miles east of Montdidier at night-fall, and the French, in conjunction with what was left of the 3rd Corps, were beginning to make themselves felt from the south-west on the flank of the attack, though they had been forced away from Roye where there was now a dangerous gap in the Allied line.

The 3rd Cavalry Brigade at Chiry received orders to move to Porquericourt, near Noyon, to stop the enemy's advance west from the town. The Brigade was engaged all day in an unsuccessful attempt to check the advance. The country was close, there being much wood and many wire fences. The enemy was well provided with machine guns, which were used with deadly effect, and the 16th were forced eventually to withdraw to Cuy. After this the Regiment was split up into two parties, one under Captain Tempest-Hicks retiring to Ellincourt, and the other under Colonel Brooke to Chetry. Eventually the Brigade was ordered to reform at Compiègne and in the course of the next day most of the scattered parties were got together there.

The whole of the 2nd Cavalry Division were hotly engaged during the 25th and 26th, and there were many casualties. The 16th casualties on the 25th and 26th were Second Lieut. Martin-Holland killed and Lieut. Hayes wounded,

1918 together with three other ranks killed and 37 wounded. There were a number also missing, but the greater part of these rejoined at Compiègne.

27th Mar. During the night the enemy had occupied Albert after driving out the rearguard troops in the town, but were unable to debouch from the place, and further north Ablainzevelle and Ayette were lost, but elsewhere the line of the 3rd Army was well maintained. South of the Somme the attack recommenced about 8 a.m. on the front held by the two remaining Corps of the 5th Army and the French. Proyart, Framerville, and Morcourt were lost, and though the important point of Rozières was held and the line maintained as far as Arvillers, Davenscourt and Montdidier itself were taken in the afternoon.

In the section immediately west of Noyon the French reinforcements had now become strong enough to deal with the attack, which indeed was not there very vigorously pressed, the main efforts of the enemy being directed against the junction of the Allied Armies about Roye and at Montdidier. The whole of the 2nd Cavalry Division was withdrawn during the day to Compiègne, where the scattered parties of dismounted men were collected and the led horses remounted.

28th Mar. On the 28th the 2nd Division and the Canadian Brigade left Compiègne at daybreak and made a forced march of 30 miles to the south-west of Montdidier, but on arriving it was found that the French had made a successful counter-attack and retaken the town. The 3rd Brigade halted for the night at Plainvillers and Chedoix. On the 29th the Division marched to Cattenchy, in the valley of the Avre river, about 12 miles south-east of Amiens.

The chief event of the fighting on the 28th was the determined effort made by the enemy on the line of the 3rd Army covering Arras. But the fog had now gone, the attack suffered very severely from the British Artillery at the outset of the battle, and after a hard day's fight the enemy was everywhere finally repulsed with very heavy loss. This action ended the attack on the 3rd Army, and for the next week there was nothing but some local fighting north of the Somme.

On the Amiens front, however, the situation was still very critical and much ground was lost. By night-fall the troops had been compelled to fall back to the line of the old Amiens defences, now manned by General Carey's force, which covered the city from Vaire, on the Somme, to Moreuil on the Avre.

Further south the French were forced back. Montdidier was again lost, and the line of the Avre only held with difficulty, the enemy having even gained a footing in the outskirts of Moreuil. But south of Montdidier the French troops held their own and even regained some of the ground lost during the previous day.

The British line by this time had been so much shortened that it was possible to withdraw some of the Divisions that had suffered most severely. The 5th Army was now definitely broken up and Sir H. Gough and his Staff were nominally sent back to superintend the construction of new defence lines,* his place at the front being taken by Sir H. Rawlinson and the Staff

---

* This was only a polite subterfuge on the part of the C.-in-C and a step to the recall to England that was impending.

The responsibility for the disaster to the 5th Army rested entirely with the War Cabinet in London, which had not only refused to heed the repeated demands of Sir D. Haig for more troops but had weakly yielded to the request of the French for the extension of the British line south of the Somme, notwithstanding his remonstrance. But it was necessary to find a scapegoat, and there were members of the Cabinet who had neither forgotten or forgiven Sir H. Gough for the part he had taken in the Ulster affair in 1914.

The despatch of the C.-in-C. of the 20th July, 1918, forms the best vindication of Sir H. Gough. It gives the following reasons for the retreat of the 5th Army:—

of the old 4th Army. The 3rd Corps also had been withdrawn from General 1918 Fayolle's command and ordered to Amiens, but the loss of Montdidier had necessitated a wide detour and it had not yet arrived.

The German attack was renewed on the 29th and Mèzieres was lost, thus 29th bringing the enemy close up to the Amiens defence line. Elsewhere the French Mar. maintained their positions.

During the night the enemy occupied the wood at Moreuil, and as a breakthrough at this point threatened to turn the right of the defence line it was urgently necessary to dislodge them. The 2nd Cavalry Division and the Canadian Brigade were hurried up from Cattenchy at daybreak, and the 16th, 30th 4th Hussars, and the Canadians were sent on to drive the Germans out of the Mar. wood. Supported by a company of infantry A and C Squadrons and the 4th attacked. A Squadron cleared the eastern edge of the wood, but C and the Hussars were held up by a heavy machine gun fire, and no further progress was possible. The enemy, however, were prevented from making any further advance and the position was held until 10 p.m., when the 16th and 4th were relieved and sent back to Thennes on the Amiens-Montdidier road, where they remained during the night. The 16th casualties this day were Lieuts. Maxwell and Wodehouse and one other ranks killed, Captain Allen* and 18 others wounded.

On the 31st the Germans attacked again between the Avre and the Luce. 31st The 2nd Cavalry Division was again engaged all day and had much fighting. Mar. Hangard was lost in the morning, but retaken in the afternoon. The fighting on this section continued all the next day, and finally the line was firmly reestablished, the enemy being driven out of Moreuil, while further south the French not only held their own, but re-captured much of the ground lost during the two previous days.

In the evening the British were relieved by the French, who took over the 1st line from Theunes southward, and the 2nd Cavalry Division was withdrawn, Apr. the 3rd Brigade to Paraclet.

The casualties of the 16th on March 31st and April 1st were five killed and nine wounded.

The 2nd Division suffered very heavy losses during this, the second, Battle of the Somme, the total casualties from March 21st to April 1st amounting to 70 officers and 2,000 other ranks killed, wounded and missing. The 16th lost five officers and 30 other ranks killed, and three officers and 109 other ranks

---

1.—The forces at the disposal of the 5th Army were inadequate to meet and hold so strong an attack.

2.—The time, seven weeks, it had wherein to complete the scheme of defence, was far too short.

3.—The thick fog of the 21st and 22nd March masked the fire of the guns, rifles, and machine guns, and this allowed the enemy to penetrate and turn the flanks of important localities.

4.—The dry weather had rendered the marshes of the Oise and the Somme useless as a protection to the over-extended line as was contemplated by the scheme of defence.

5.—It was impossible to reinforce the line of the 5th Army as an attack on other parts of the front might take place at any moment, the French in particular expecting one at Rheims.

(This last did take place later, with most disastrous results to their weakened line.)

Under these circumstances no Army Commander could have done more than Sir H. Gough. He maintained a losing battle with forces four times as numerous as his own for seven days with undaunted coolness, and the end of the action found his battle line still unbroken.

It was Mons and its retreat over again on a larger scale, and under considerably greater difficulties.

* Captain Allen was severely wounded while attempting to take a machine gun by himself, and afterwards died.

1918 wounded. The fighting was very severe, both about Noyon and Moreuil, and the Regiment displayed great gallantry under very difficult circumstances, many distinctions being gained both by officers and men. In the course of it the Regiment was practically destroyed as far as dismounted fighting was concerned, and at the end only one man to four led horses could be left mounted.

The 2nd Cavalry Division remained in billets in the Amiens area for the next ten days until it was moved north to the support of the 1st Army on April 10th.

On the 3rd the 16th moved to Camon, and on the next day the Leicester Yeomanry came in as a draft for the 3rd Cavalry Brigade, one squadron being sent to each of the three Regiments. Five officers and 48 men were posted to C squadron, but eventually this squadron was made up, both as regarded the officers and other ranks, entirely by the yeomen.

On the 10th the Brigade marched by Le Boile, Hesdin, Coyecque and Therouannes to Lynde, arriving there on April 13th.

4th Apr. No further attack was made until April 4th, when the fighting re-commenced between the Somme and Hangard, and with the French to the south of that place. This attack was repulsed with considerable loss to the enemy, though a little ground was lost by the French along the Avre.

5th Apr. On the 5th an attack was made north of the Somme, but without any result. The line was in effect now completely stabilised, the reserves having come up and the place of the old 5th Army taken by the 4th and the French, and the Second Battle of the Somme came to an end. Except that it was on a larger scale, the battle had followed the stereotyped lines, with the usual result—the utter exhaustion of the attacking troops and the gain of a quantity of perfectly useless territory, which was destined to be again lost in the inevitable counter-attack which followed.

7th Apr. The new line had scarcely been established before Von Ludendorff's second attack commenced. This was made on the front extending from about 10 miles north of Ypres to about 10 miles north of Lens covered by the 2nd and 1st Armies, with the intention of effecting a break between La Bassee and Armentières. Then after taking Bethune and forming a defensive flank along the La Bassée Canal to take Hazebrouck and Bailleul, thereby effectually separating the British and French and exposing the left flank of the last.

The attack was opened on the evening of April 7th by the 6th German Army under Von Quast on a line extending from the Lys to La Bassée (held by Sir H. Horne's 1st Army) with an intense bombardment, chiefly with gas shells. This continued without cessation until 7 a.m. on the morning of the 9th, when the infantry attack was launched in a dense fog. The first shock fell on the two Portuguese Divisions which were in course of being withdrawn from the front line. These were overwhelmed in a moment and the enemy at once pushed through the gap. The result of the day's fighting left the Germans in possession of all the ground up to the rivers Lawe and Lys, the last being crossed at Bac St. Maur. The important point of Givenchy was, however, held firmly.

On the 10th the line of attack was extended north of the Lys from Armentiéres to Hollebec by Von Arnim's 4th Army. The day's fighting left the enemy in possession of Estaires, Ploegstreet and Armentiéres, and well across the Lys, but Givenchy and the Messines Ridge were still intact.

On the 11th both Von Quast and Von Armim attacked on the whole of the salient from Givenchy to Hollebeke and made a further advance, Nieppe and Messines being lost.

On the 12th the German reserves were thrown into the battle and the British reinforcements also began to come up. These last consisted of six Australian 1918 Divisions, but as they could only come gradually into the line the situation continued to be very critical and the enemy's attack was barely checked after very severe fighting. On the 13th the attack was again vigorously pressed, particularly on the section opposite Bailleul. On the 14th Neuve Eglise was lost, on the 15th Bailleul. On the 16th Meteren and Wyteschaete were lost, but on the 17th an attack on Mount Kemmel was beaten off.

Fighting continued during the 18th, 19th and 21st, but the enemy met with little success, and by the 21st French troops had come up at Meteren and taken over part of the line which had become stabilised, and there was no further fighting of consequence until the 25th in this sector.

On the 23rd April an attack was made on the 4th Army between the Somme 23rd and the Ancre. The attack was made with four Divisions supported by the Apr. new German tanks, and for the first time British and German tanks fought each other. Under cover of the usual fog the enemy broke through the line and captured Villers Bretonneux, but here the advance was checked, and on the following day the place was retaken and the line restored.

On the 25th a new attack was made on the line in front of Mount Kemmel 25th at the junction between the French and the British. The action began with Apr. a heavy bombardment on the whole front between Meteren and the Ypres-Comines Canal, which was followed by the attack of nine Divisions, the capture of Kemmel being the objective. Mount Kemmel was lost by the French in the morning and the whole line forced back over a mile. On the 26th an attempt was made to retake Kemmel, which failed, and fighting continued all the next two days without any great change in the situation. On the 29th, after another bombardment, the enemy attacked again with eleven Divisions in mass formation, and after an initial success were finally repulsed with the loss of fully 20,000 men. This brought the Battle of the Lys to a close, though local combats continued all through the month of May. Von Ludendorff's plan had definitely failed for, notwithstanding his lavish expenditure of men, he had only succeeded in establishing a quite useless salient and had taken neither Hazebrouck nor Bethune, the capture of which was essential to its success.

The 2nd Cavalry Division was on the march northward when the Lys battle began on April 7th, and was ordered to proceed to Blaringhem, eight miles south-west of Hazebrouck, in support of the 1st Army. The 3rd Brigade was sent to Lynde, two miles further north, where it remained until the 18th, when it moved to Eecke. The three Regiments were stationed at several places in the neighbourhood until the 24th, relieving each other in turn in the occupation of the more exposed positions. There was some shell fire and airplane bombing, but no fighting, and the 16th had no casualties. On the 24th the Brigade returned to Lynde, and the 16th was sent to Blaringhem. On the 29th the 2nd Division marched to Clety, which was being evacuated by the French.

On the 5th May the Regiment marched to Longvillers, where it went into billets.

From the end of April to the 27th May there were no operations of any importance. Both the Allies and the Germans were engaged in making good the losses incurred in the battles of March and April and consolidating their new positions. But by the end of May Von Ludendorff had been able to fill up some 70 per cent. of the gaps in his depleted ranks, partly with men returned from hospital, and partly with fresh troops from Germany, and on the 27th May he began a new attack, this time on the line of the Ailette, from a point eight miles south of Chauny to Craonne, and thence by Berry au Bac and Berméricourt to north of Rheims.

1918   The line of the Ailette was held by the French 6th Army, four Divisions, to Craonne, thence south-east to Berméricourt by the British 9th Corps, four Divisions, which had been withdrawn from Flanders, "to rest!". Round Rheims was the French 5th Army and on its right again the 4th, extending into Champagne. Thus 30 miles from near Chauny to Berméricourt was held by eight Divisions only, and against them 25 German Divisions were massed for the attack.

27th May.   There was no warning of what was impending beyond some vague statements of prisoners taken on the 26th. At 1 a.m. on the morning of the 27th a bombardment of the line of the river began which was extended to the outskirts of Rheims, and at 4 a.m. the infantry attack commenced. With such a disparity of force the result was inevitable; the weak French line was overwhelmed in a moment, and before night-fall it had been driven across the Vesle. The British 9th Corps withstood the assault better and the enemy was held for some hours, but the retreat of the French had uncovered the left flank at Craonne, and though Berméricourt was held, the left was forced back to Fismes, where it linked up with the French.

    The attack was carried on without a pause during the next three days. On the 29th Soissons was taken, and on the 30th the enemy was across the Marne. Chateau-Thierry, however, was held and Rheims and its defences remained intact. Thus in 72 hours the whole of the gains of months of hard fighting were swept away. The Germans had made an advance of 30 miles, occupied ten miles of the Marne, and taken over 30,000 prisoners and 400 guns. The new front extended south-west from Rheims to Dormans on the Marne, along the river to Chateau Thierry, then turning sharply to the north to Poutoise.

9th June.   The line was now to some extent stabilised, but fighting continued until the 9th without any great advantage to either side. On that day a fresh attack was made by the enemy on 25 miles on the Montdidier section with 18 Divisions which resulted in an advance of about three miles on part of the front, and on the 18th Rheims was attacked on a front of 10 miles, but this last attack was defeated with comparative ease. With this the major operations came to an end for nearly a month, though a number of small local attacks were made from time to time both by the British and the French which met with some success.

    The general result of these actions were that the Germans had gained three great salients. On the northern flank the salient extended from a point 10 miles north of Ypres to 10 miles north of Lens. It had a base line of 30 miles with a greatest depth at a point 10 miles east of Hazebrouck.

    The centre salient had a base of 60 miles running from Arras to a point 12 miles west of Laon. The apex, just north of Montdidier, had a depth of 40 miles, the front running from Arras by Albert by Montdidier to the Aisne west of Soissons.

    The southern salient ran from the Aisne to Chateau Thierry, the apex, thence north-east along the Marne to Dormans, and thence to Rheims. The base line from west of Laon to Rheims was 25 miles, and the depth to Chateau Thierry 40 miles.

    This represented a vast gain in territory, including the important points of Albert, Montdidier, Soissons, and Peronne. In addition a great number of prisoners and guns had been taken and the unfortunate 5th Army practically destroyed.

    But these gains were much more apparent than real. The German front had been greatly extended and was now no longer covered by an intricate line of entrenchments. The southern salient was peculiarly difficult to hold as there were few railways and the greater part of the supplies had to be sent by 1918 a road from Soissons that ran parallel to the front. The losses in the field, too, had been enormous, reaching a total of at least a million men, and the troops were weary and dispirited, for the Allied line, though bent, was nowhere broken. On the other hand, the Allies were now thoroughly roused to a due sense of the danger. The Armies were for the first time united under the command of a single general of unquestionable ability in the person of Marshal Foch; all fears of invasion were abandoned and every available man was sent from England, upward of 400,000 being sent out in the course of July and August, and lastly every possible exertion was made to expedite the training of the United States Armies, twelve Divisions being now in the fighting line, though not yet formed into a distinct Army. Little as it then seemed to be, the battles of the Somme, the Lys, and the Marne were destined to be the beginning of the end and the final defeat of Germany.

CHAPTER XLII.

July 18th to November 15th, 1918.

New plans for offensive. July 18th, Attack of French on the southern salient. Success of attack. Aug. 8th, Attack by 4th Army. Disposition of Troops. The old Amiens Defence Lines regained. Attack by 1st French Army. August 9th, Attack by 3rd Corps. Fighting by the Cavalry. Attack by 3rd French Army. August 10th, Advance continued. August 18th, Attack by 10th French Army. General retreat of enemy. September 1st, Peronne regained. September 5th, 1st and 4th French Armies cross the Somme. September 12th, Attacks by General Byng and 1st U.S. Army. Further advance by 3rd and 4th Armies. September 24th, Advance resumed. Position of Allied Armies. September 26th, Attack by 4th French and 1st U.S. Armies. September 27th, Attack on Cambrai front. September 28th, Belgian attack. October 2nd, La Bassée taken. October 3rd, General Pershing drives enemy over the Suippe. October 8th, Attack by 3rd and 4th Armies. Cambrai taken. September 4th to 8th, Le Cateau, Laon, and Douai taken. Belgian and French attack. September 19th, General Allenby's victory in Palestine. September 20th, Belgians occupy Bruges. Lille evacuated. September 23rd, Austrian defeat. October 26th, Von Ludendorff resigns. November 3rd, Valenciennes taken. November 9th, Landrecies, Catillon and Quesnoy taken. October 10th, Ghent re-occupied. October 4th, March of 3rd Cavalry Brigade to Haspres. October 8th, The 16th sent to 22nd Corps, 1st Army. October 10th, The 16th cover advance. German attempts to procure armistice. Applications to President Wilson. Revolution in Germany. November 9th, Abdication and flight of Kaiser. German delegates meet Marshal Foch. Terms of Armistice. November 11th, Armistice signed. Surrender of Mons. The fighting early in the morning of the 11th. The last charge of the 16th. Fighting ceases at 11 a.m. and end of the War. The Regiment withdrawn to Harmignies. November 15th, The state entrance into Mons.

Summary of Events, July-November, 1918.—July 18th, Second Battle of the Marne. September 19th, Decisive defeat of Turkey in Palestine. 26th,

1918   Bulgaria sues for peace. October 24th, Decisive defeat of Austria by Italy. 29th, Austria sues for peace. November 10th, Mons retaken. 11th, The Armistice signed. End of the War.

Hitherto the offensive both of the Allies and the Germans had been conducted on similar lines and with the same futile results. Each attack had been made with the " break-through " as the objective. Each attack had been an initial success in that the hostile front line trenches had been first partially destroyed by artillery fire and then crossed by the assaulting infantry, and each attack had been eventually held up by the hostile reserves. The further the attack was pressed the more difficult it was to bring its own reserves into action and the stronger became the opposition. Then followed the counter-attack and the loss of part of the ground gained. The attacks, too, were made independently of each other, without any combined objective and at long intervals.

The offensive designed by the new Commander-in-Chief on the contrary was to make a constant succession of attacks at various selected points, each on limited front and for a definite objective, and to keep these going until he had got the enemy fairly on the move all along his line. The series of battles begun by Von Ludendorff in March had been originally devised on somewhat the same lines, but he made the vital mistake of making each attack on too great a scale and of not limiting his objectives. Thus he was only able to make four in all at comparatively long intervals. Each broke down by what may be termed its own weight, and ended in nothing more than the gain of quite useless territory and a great extension of the battle line.

The German attacks in the north were really far more dangerous than those on the Somme because they were on a smaller scale and delivered at shorter intervals. Had they been continued they might have had serious consequences, but his great offensive on the Somme had entirely used up Von Ludendorff's reserves and he was unable for the time to initiate new attacks. The result, therefore, was that the Allies were able to stabilise their battle line, which, notwithstanding the practical destruction of the unlucky 5th Army, was nowhere broken, but merely dented, while the victors not only incurred an enormous loss of men, but were left in an especially dangerous position. Though tactically successful, Von Ludendorff was left at the close of his great offensive in a far worse strategic position than he was when he began it.

The new Commander-in-Chief then began his offensive on that part of the German position which he considered the most vulnerable, the southern salient, and he attacked with confidence, knowing that the German Command had reached the end of their resources, while he himself grew daily stronger as the United States Divisions and the reinforcements from England came into line.

18th July.   The attack on the southern salient began on the 18th July on both its flanks by the 10th and 6th French Armies. It was immediately successful. By August 4th the salient was wiped out and the Germans driven back to the Vesle, the new front stretching from just east of Soissons to north of Rheims.

Meanwhile both the French and British had been engaged in local actions all along the line north of the Somme and at several points had materially improved their positions, while it became evident that the German Command was making preparations for a general retirement.

On the 8th August the next attack commenced. This was made by General Rawlinson with the 4th Army and the left wing of the French 1st Army on a front of 14 miles.

5th Aug.   The 1st, 2nd and 3rd Cavalry Divisions were ordered to Amiens to support the attack, and the 3rd Cavalry Brigade was reconstituted, the three regiments being assembled at Vron on the 5th August. Thence the Brigade marched to 1918 Pequiny, where the three Divisions were concentrated, arriving there on the 6th.

The following is a list of the officers who were with the Regiment when the final operations of the war began :—

        Staff—Lieut.-Colonel Brooke, D.S.O., M.C.
          Adjutant, Capt. Callender.
              Capt. Macdonald, Leicester Yeomanry.
      Medical Officer, Capt. Storey.
      Signal Officer, Lieut. Carlisle.
      Quartermaster, Capt. Connel.

A Sqdn.—Capt. Evans, M.C.	D Sqdn.—Capt. Tempest-Hicks, M.C.
Lieut. Thornton.	Lieut. Archer.
,, Pargeter, M.C.	,, Mowbray.
,, Pilkington, M.C.	,, Ryan.
2nd Lieut. Morris.	,, Deans.
,, Alexander.	,, Noakes.

       C Sqdn.—Capt. Hay, Leicester Yeomanry.
          ,, Pait ,, ,,
        Lieut. Browne ,, ,,
         ,, Brooke ,, ,,
         ,, Pym ,, ,,
         ,, Greig ,, ,,
         ,, Oldham ,, ,,

The plan of advance was for the 1st and 3rd Divisions to lead, with the 2nd in reserve. The 3rd Brigade formed the reserve of the 2nd Division. On the night of the 7th the Brigade marched via Amiens to Longeau and Glissy, taking position between these places, where they halted at 4 a.m. on the morning of the 8th.

General Rawlinson's force was distributed as follows :—

On his right the 3rd, 1st and 2nd Canadian Divisions, with the 4th in support.

In the centre the 2nd and 3rd Australian Divisions, with the 5th and 4th in support.

On his right, north of the Somme, the 3rd Corps, with two Divisions in line and one in support.

The three Divisions of the Cavalry Corps under General Kavanagh were massed east of Amiens, and in addition there was a special force of motor machine guns and cyclists with orders to operate along the Amiens-Roye road and a large number of tanks.

Every precaution had been taken to hide the movement of the troops into their positions, and there was no preliminary bombardment.

At 4.30 a.m. on the morning of the 8th an intense artillery fire was opened 8th on the whole front between the Ancre and the Avre rivers. This only lasted Aug. for five minutes, but it was sufficient to wipe out most of the enemy's defences. When the firing ceased the infantry advance began preceded by a long line of tanks.

The enemy was completely surprised and at first there was little resistance. By mid-day Démuin and Marceleave had been taken and the line was beyond the Albert-Montdidier main road; the Canadian Cavalry had even passed through the infantry and captured a train near Chaulnes. On the flanks, however, there was some hard fighting at Chipilly, Morlancourt, and Moreuil.

1918 Nevertheless by night the whole of the old Amiens defence lines had been cleared.

Meanwhile the 3rd Brigade had moved up to the Bois de Blangy at 10 a.m., and at 12.30 p.m. to Hangard, and thence to a valley south of Guillancourt, where the horses were watered and fed, after which the Regiment moved to the hill north of Caux. At 8.45 the Brigade returned to Guillancourt and bivouaced there for the night.

More than 13,000 prisoners, 400 guns and a great quantity of stores and ammunition were taken during the day.

The 1st French Army had been equally successful. The French attack began at 5 a.m. on a three mile front, and by night the line Pierrepoint, Plessier, and Fresnoy had been gained, with 3,300 prisoners and many guns, and the left was in touch with the cyclist corps on the Amiens-Roye road near Le Quesnoy.

9th Aug. On the next day a new attack was made by the 3rd Corps, together with a regiment of United States troops. This resulted in the capture of Morlancourt on the Ancre and of Chipilly, which had been retaken by the enemy in a counter-attack on the previous afternoon.

A further advance was made in the centre and in this the Cavalry Divisions took a prominent part. All three Divisions passed through the infantry line. The 8th Hussars (1st Division) took Meharicourt at a gallop, and a number of prisoners were rounded up and taken. The 16th were unlucky. In the afternoon A Squadron attempted to capture 50 machine-gunners in a wood between Vrehy and Beaufort, but were held up by a wired trench and being fired on by a number of machine guns from Harvillers were forced to come back after losing three horses.

At 6 p.m. the Regiment went forward through Warvillers, but after passing through the village it came under a heavy shell fire and further on between Warvillers and Rouvroy machine gun fire, and could make no progress. Ultimately the Regiment returned to Warvillers and remained there for the night.

This day the 16th had the misfortune of losing Captain Tempest-Hicks. He was riding at the head of his squadron when a shell struck the ground in front of him. The shell failed to explode, but as it ricocheted struck him full on the body killing him instantly. Captain Tempest-Hicks was one of the best officers in the Regiment. He had greatly distinguished himself on many occasions, and had already been three times wounded. His death was much regretted by the whole Regiment.

The other casualties this day were one private and two more were wounded. The village was badly bombed during the night but there were no casualties.

In the afternoon the 3rd French Army also attacked between Montdidier and Matz, and during the night reached Faverolles and cut across the Roye road, thus isolating Montdidier, which surrendered next morning. A large quantity of stores and ammunition was found in the town.

10th Aug. On the 10th the advance was continued along the whole front in co-operation with the French. In the morning the 16th moved to the Caux-Cayeau valley, but were again sent back to Warvillers. Here the Regiment was shelled by the enemy's heavy guns at long range, and three shells dropped right into it with the result that three men were killed and 12 wounded. At 8 p.m. it was sent back to a wood north of Beaufort, where 10 machine guns were taken, and bivouaced there for the night. The bivouac was again bombed at intervals during the night, but there were no casualties.

Fighting continued during the next two days without intermission, and by the evening of the 12th the infantry had reached the old German Somme defences of 1916 on a line west of Damery, east of Lihons, east of Proyart, and, north of the Somme, the west edge of Bray, while the French were on the line of the old Roye-Chaulnes defences. Attacks on the 13th showed that the enemy had been strongly reinforced and was prepared to fight on this line, so the Field-Marshal broke off the battle, having gained his immediate objective on this front.

The 3rd Brigade did no fighting during these days, but the Regiment, which remained in the Caix-Cayeux valley were bombed night and day by airplanes. On the 11th a bomb fell into the middle of the Regiment wounding five men and knocking over 18 horses. On the 13th, this bombing having become an unbearable nuisance, shelters were dug for the men. On the 15th the 3rd Brigade marched via St. Vaast to Le Pouchet, arriving there on the 17th. Here the Regiment remained in billets until the 21st.

The result of this battle was a general advance of 12 miles on the whole front. Twenty-three thousand prisoners and 400 guns were taken, and the enemy were in addition forced to evacuate a large extent of ground further south.

A series of attacks on all parts of the Allied front followed in rapid succession.

On the 18th an attack was made between the Oise and the Aisne by the 10th French Army, which advanced the line to within five miles of the Ailette, 10,000 prisoners and 200 guns being taken.

On the 21st General Byng with the 3rd Army attacked and recovered command of the Arras-Albert railway.

The next day the left wing of the 4th Army attacked and re-took Albert.

The enemy were now retreating all along the line and the advance was continued.

On the 25th the 1st Army attacked on each side of the Scarpe.

On the 29th August Bapaume was taken and a great depôt of stores found in the place.

On September 1st Peronne was regained and in the course of the next two days the enemy was driven across the Canal du Nord five miles west of Cambrai. On the 5th the 4th Army and the French 1st Army were across the Somme south of Peronne. During the following week the German retreat was continued followed closely by the Allies, without any fighting beyond rearguard actions, the one hope left to the German Staff being to establish their line for the winter along their old Siegfried defences, but on September 12th the retreat slackened and it became necessary to drive the enemy from his forward positions about Havrincourt and Epéhy. General Byng therefore attacked these with two Corps on the 12th and occupied Trescault and Havrincourt. On the same day the United States Army made its first appearance in the field as a separate force.* The 1st Army, commanded by General Pershing, attacked the St. Mihiel salient south of Verdun and after a battle of three days drove the enemy from all his positions, taking 15,000 prisoners and 200 guns.

During the five days following there were further advances made by the 3rd and 4th Armies terminating in the re-capture of Moeuvres. After this there was a pause in the operations until the 24th in order to bring up supplies and to prepare for what was expected to be the final blow. The final collapse of Germany was indeed now evidently at hand. On the 19th General Allenby decisively defeated the Turks in Palestine and in the ensuing operations destroyed the Turkish Army opposed to him by a brilliant use of his Cavalry,

---

* Three Corps had been so far engaged—one on the Marne and Ourcq, one on the Somme, and one on the Vesle.

1918 and on the 17th the debacle in Bulgaria commenced, terminating on the 26th by an armistice.

During these operations there had been many attempts made by the Cavalry to break through the enemy's infantry line, but these had been invariably frustrated by the fire of the machine guns, of which the Germans seemed to have an unlimited supply and which they used very liberally to cover their retreat. The German troops were still capable of making a good resistance when brought to bay, and this was especially the case with the machine-gun crews, though when actually retiring a great number of prisoners were taken, detached parties surrendering freely and there being many stragglers.

During September the 2nd Cavalry Division was broken up and the Brigades distributed among the several Corps. At the end of the month the 3rd Brigade was in reserve to the 1st Army and in camp at Inchy.

24th Sept. When the advance was resumed on the 24th the general position was as follows :—

The Belgian Army was north of Ypres. On the right of the Belgians was the 3rd French Army and General Plumer's 2nd Army extending to the Lys river. Then came General Birdwood's 5th Army facing Lille and Lens, General Horne's 1st Army opposite Douai, General Byng's 3rd Army opposite Cambrai, General Rawlinson's 4th Army facing St. Quentin.

Then came the French 1st Army under General Debeney extending the line to the Oise, General Mangin's 10th Army along the Marne and Ailette river, General Guillemat's 5th Army covering Rheims, General Gourand's 4th Army Champagne west of the Argonne, General Pershing's 1st United States Army between the Argonne and the Meuse river, the 2nd Army being near Briey.

The 3rd Cavalry Brigade was then at Inchy in reserve to the 1st Army.

Marshal Foch's plan was briefly for the Belgians to sweep the coast line to Ghent, the British to break the Siegfried line towards Cambrai, and the 4th French Army and the United States Armies to attack west of the Meuse in the direction of Mezières. In pursuance of this last design General Pershing's Army was secretly moved to the west bank of the Meuse and its place taken by the 2nd Army.

26th Sept. On the 26th Generals Gourand and Pershing attacked on a front of 40 miles and made an advance of from three to seven miles in depth.

The next day the 1st and 3rd Armies attacked on the Cambrai front and drove the enemy across the Canal du Nord, taking 10,000 prisoners and 200 guns.

On the 28th the King of the Belgians, part of the 3rd French Army, and two Corps of General Plumer attacked on a front of 20 miles south of Dixmude, making an advance of six miles and taking Comines and 10,000 prisoners. The same day the 10th and 5th French Armies attacked.

On the 29th the 4th Army attacked on the line Marcoing-St. Quentin and crossed the Schelde Canal, and following up the enemy the next day broke through the Hindenburg line at Bellenglise, Thorigny and Le Trouquoy.

From the 15th of July to the 30th of September the Allies had taken in all 250,000 prisoners, 3,600 guns, and 13,000 machine guns.

2nd Oct. On the 2nd October the enemy began an extensive retreat along the whole front south of Lens to Armentières. This was closely followed during the next two days, but on the evening of the 4th the resistance strengthened and it seemed as if a stand was intended, but the development of the further operations at St. Quentin and Cambrai obliged the Germans to resume the withdrawal. The final phase of the Allied offensive may be said to have now begun. On the 2nd La Bassée was taken by General Birdwood. On the 3rd General Pershing drove the enemy opposed to him over the Suippe river. On the 8th the 3rd and 4th Armies attacked on a front of 17 miles from Sequehart to the south of Cambrai in conjunction with the French Army on their right. The enemy made a good resistance at first, but was eventually driven from all his positions in disorder. Ramilies, Cambrai, and Bohain were taken, and by the evening of the 9th the troops were within two miles of Le Cateau. The Cavalry were at last able to operate with advantage on this section and were able to greatly harass the enemy's retreat, and to prevent the destruction of the railways.

1918

On the 10th the Chemin des Dames was seized by the French and Americans.

During the next three days the advance was pressed all along the front and Le Cateau, Laon, and Douai were occupied. On the 14th the Belgians, in conjunction with the French 3rd Army and the 2nd Army, attacked along the whole front from Dixmude to Comines. This attack was most successful, and by the 18th Ostend, Roubaix, and Turcoing were in the hands of the Allies, and Lille was evacuated by the enemy. By the 20th the Belgians were in Bruges and had extended their line to the Dutch frontier. The same day Denain was taken by General Byng.

On the 23rd Germany's last remaining ally was eliminated by the total defeat of Austria on the Piave river.

The retreat of the German Armies was now rapidly degenerating into a rout, while the Allied attacks were pressed with the utmost vigour along the whole front in order to give the enemy no time to establish a new entrenched line for another winter campaign. On the 26th the disheartened Von Ludendorff, unable to face the storm of indignation roused by his failure to justify his confident assurances of victory, resigned his post of Chief of the Staff.

During these operations the 3rd Cavalry Brigade had been obliged to merely watch the line of the infantry advance and remained in camp at Inchy until the 27th October, when a move was made to Buissy.

The advance continued to be pushed all along the line and the preparations for what proved to be the final blow were completed by the capture of Valenciennes by the 4th Canadian Division on the 1st November and the crossing of the Rhonelle by the 17th Corps and the 22nd Corps after some considerable fighting.

4th Nov.

After this defeat on the 3rd November the enemy withdrew some miles on the Le Quesnoy-Valenciennes front, and on the next day the decisive attack was commenced by the 4th, 3rd, and 1st Armies on a line of 30 miles, from the Sambre, north of Oisy to Valenciennes. In the centre of this line was the Forest of Mormal, and on the north the fortified town of Quesnoy. The attack was everywhere successful, and by the 9th the enemy was in full retreat. Landrecies, Catillon and Quesnoy were taken and the Sambre river was crossed at several places. On the 9th Maubeuge surrendered, and on the 10th the Belgians regained possession of Ghent. The French 1st Army moved in unison on the right of the British line and advanced as far as Guise. Twenty-five thousand prisoners and over 500 guns were taken. The 5th Army also captured Tournai, and the 2nd Army crossed the Schelde on its entire front during these days.

On the 4th November the Brigade marched by Marquion and Blecourt to Thun l'Eveque and thence by Haspres to Maing. On the 8th the Brigade was broken up. The 16th was attached to the 22nd Corps, 1st Army, and marched to Montigny. The next day an officers' patrol which had been sent to Camp Perdu to find the 11th Division reported that there seemed to be a possibility of using the Cavalry, and at 12.30 p.m. the Regiment, with a machine-gun squadron and D Battery R.H.A., proceeded by Eugenies to Camp Perdu, but

1918 owing to the bad state of the roads did not get there until after it was dark. A message was then sent on to the 22nd Corps Headquarters to say that the detachment intended to pass through the infantry line if possible, and orders were sent back to cover the advance of the 22nd Corps in the morning. On the 10th, therefore, the Regiment moved off in advance of the infantry, C Squadron covering the 11th Division, A the 56th, and D the 63rd. A machine-gun section went with each squadron and the remainder with the guns followed the centre column, the objectives being Havay-Maladrie and Villers St. Ghislain. There was little opposition, but the enemy were found to be holding the river with a line of machine guns placed at intervals of 300 yards.

10th Nov.

Eventually A Squadron forced a passage over the bridge at Haveng but was stopped at the cross roads just beyond it. Later on D Squadron got across the river and ejected the Germans from a sugar factory on the Bavai-Givry road, but was unable to advance over the higher ground beyond it. C Squadron was held up by enfilade fire but got over with the help of the guns. The Infantry then came up and the Cavalry were withdrawn. After a preliminary bombardment an attack was made by the 186th Brigade and the enemy driven off. The troops then halted for the night and at 4 p.m. the Regiment withdrew to L'Hermitage. The 16th lost 16 men killed and wounded in the day's operations.

11th Nov.

The next day was destined to see the end of the war though this was unknown to the troops. The destruction of the Hindenburg line at the end of September had convinced the German Staff of the hopelessness of continuing the war and representations were made to the Berlin Government urging it to negotiate an Armistice as soon as possible at any cost. The Imperial Chancellor and the Foreign Secretary both resigned on the 30th September and the Kaiser appointed Prince Maximillian of Baden Chancellor. President Wilson was chosen as the mediator, probably because he was thought to be what schoolboys would call the " softest " of the Allied chiefs. On the 4th October a Note was sent to the President asking him to take in hand the restoration of peace and the conclusion of an Armistice pending a discussion of terms. The Note further stated that Germany accepted the President's famous " Fourteen Points " as a basis of the proposed discussion. The Austrian Government also sent an identical Note. On the 14th President Wilson replied to the effect that the conditions of any Armistice must be settled by the judgment and advice of the military advisers of the Allied Governments. Further correspondence followed and on the 23rd October the President closed the discussion by refusing to take a separate position in these negotiations and re-iterating what he had already said in his Note of the 14th.

8th Nov.

Meanwhile events of the utmost importance were taking place in Germany. The rapid advance of the Allies, the demoralised condition of the German Army, the mutiny of the fleet at Kiel, and the terrible losses in the field had thoroughly awakened the nation to a true appreciation of the dangers of the situation. The shuffling diplomacy of the Government was swept aside in a burst of popular indignation, and on the 8th a " Workmen's and Soldiers' Council," as it was termed, decreed the abolition of the Bavarian dynasty. Similar Councils were formed in most of the larger towns and on the 9th Berlin followed the example and declared a Republic. The Imperial Chancellor issued a decree the same day announcing the decision of the Kaiser to abdicate and resigned his office after appointing Ebert his successor.

The next day the Kaiser himself left the Army Headquarters at Spa and took refuge in Holland and the Crown Prince followed his father's example.

On the 6th November the Rheichstag had nominated four delegates at the request of the Army Headquarters to discuss terms for an Armistice. Marshal 1918 Foch was appointed to represent the Allies with full powers. The German delegates met the Marshal in the Forest of Compiègne on the 8th and were presented with the Allied terms.

The terms of the Armistice were set out in 35 clauses. The principal stipulations as far as the Western front was concerned were as follows :—

1.—Cessation of fighting six hours after the signing of the Armistice (11 a.m. on the 11th November).
2.—Evacuation of Belgium, France, Alsace, Lorraine, and Luxemburg within 14 days.
3.—Repatriation of all inhabitants of the above countries within 14 days.
4.—Surrender of military equipment : 5,000 guns, 30,000 machine guns, 3,000 minenwerfer, 2,000 airplanes.
5.—Evacuation of all country on the left bank of the Rhine and the creation of a neutral zone six miles in width on the right bank of the river within 31 days.
6.—Occupation by the Allied troops of Mayence, Cologne and Coblentz with bridge-heads on the right bank of the Rhine at each place of a 19 mile radius.
7.—The Armistice to be accepted or refused by Germany within 72 hours of notification.

The German delegates at first remonstrated about the severity of the terms and asked for a provisional suspension of hostilities while they consulted the Berlin Government, but this was at once refused by Marshal Foch, and the terms were eventually sent by a courier to the Army Headquarters at Spa. Thence they were telegraphed to Berlin and the delegates were instructed by the German Provisional Government to accept them. At 5 a.m. on the morning of the 11th November the Armistice was signed and Marshal Foch sent an order to the Generals in the field as follows :—

"Hostilities will cease on the whole front as from the 11th of November at eleven o'clock. The Allied Troops will not, until a further order, go beyond the line reached on that date and that hour."

The morning of the 11th was cold and foggy. The Cavalry continued their advance at daybreak, covering the infantry columns. The 3rd Canadian Division had been fighting all night round Mons and at daybreak the town was taken, the whole of the garrison being either killed or captured.

During the night of the 10th orders were received by the 16th and the R.H.A. to cover the advance of the 63rd Division, the Advance Guard of the 22nd Corps, and to move off at daybreak. Accordingly the advance was continued to the line Villers St. Ghislain—Estinne au Val. There was little opposition up to this, but the enemy was found to be holding Estinne, and points on the Bray—Villers St. Ghislain road, and when driven from these retired to the north-east of St. Ghislain, where the advance was held up by artillery and machine guns. About 10 a.m. the R.H.A. Battery came into action. Lieut. Johnson then charged the machine guns with his patrol, but the enemy's guns opened fire on him at point blank range and every man and horse went down, though fortunately the actual casualties were limited to Lieut. Johnson and four men wounded. This spirited little affair was the final combat of the war as shortly afterwards orders were received to cease fighting at 11 a.m. just as the right squadron was preparing to charge the guns.

The D Battery, then with the 16th, were, however, ordered to fire a final salvo at half a minute before 11 o'clock. This battery of Horse Artillery was in action with the 16th on the morning of the day before the Battle of Mons,

1918 and thus fired the first and last shell of the war within a short distance of the same place.

At mid-day the Regiment withdrew to Harmignies, where it was billeted and hospitably entertained by such of the inhabitants as had survived the German occupation.

On the 15th two composite squadrons were sent to Mons, one of which, under command of Capt. Moubray, formed a special escort to General Horne, the Commander of the 1st Army, who was presented with the freedom of the city. The remainder of the Regiment marched to Grand Reng, where the two squadrons rejoined in the afternoon.

Here the 3rd Brigade was reformed.

On the 17th the general advance to the Rhine began, the 3rd Cavalry Brigade acting as advance guard, each regiment marching by a separate road.

The Brigade marched, with occasional halts, by Montignies, Charleroi, Warnant, Erzee, and Comblain to Ville, where it went into billets, Headquarters being at Ville, A Squadron at Ferrières, C at Filot, and D at Mye. Here the Regiment left the Brigade as it was now placed on the Roster for foreign service. There was much trouble with the transport during this march as the roads and bridges had been systematically destroyed by the retreating Germans. The roads were everywhere strewn with abandoned arms and equipment, and the inhabitants reported that great disorder and insubordination was apparent among the troops of the enemy, who were about two days' march ahead of the British Army. The Regiment marched into Ville from Comblain on the 22nd December, 1918, and remained in billets in that area until March 8th, 1919. During this period demobilisation was completed and the spare horses sold or transferred. On the 8th March the Regiment, now reduced to a cadre only, marched to Ensival, near Liège, and on the 16th proceeded by train to Antwerp, where it was sent to the Reception Camp. On the 22nd March the remnant of the Regiment with 50 horses embarked at Antwerp on the S.S. Menominee together with the Greys, 20th Hussars, 5th Lancers, 3rd and 7th Dragoon Guards, and the 3rd Brigade R.H. Artillery, and sailed for England under command of Lieut.-Colonel Brooke, the other officers being Capt. Callander, Adjutant; Capt. McConnell, Quartermaster; and Lieuts. Browne, Archer, and Pargeter.

After disembarkation the 16th were sent to Canterbury, where Lieut.-Colonel Brooke gave over the command to Lieut.-Colonel St. John on the 25th March.

In June the Regiment received orders to proceed to Syria. By this time the 16th had been reduced to 13 officers and 50 other ranks, and to bring the numbers up to something approaching full strength about 400 men were drafted into the Regiment. Of these about 100 were officially styled "Cavalry," but it was afterwards found that their only claim to the designation was that they had originally enlisted for that arm, but had eventually been posted to Infantry. After the war ended they were permitted to join the Cavalry if they wished to do so. The rest of the drafts were half-trained recruits.

To make things worse, owing to the short notice, the men had to be sent on furlough at once, and as they did not rejoin until a few days before leaving Canterbury, when the Regiment embarked all the men, except the original 50, were unknown to the officers and to each other.

APPENDICES TO CHAPTER XLII.

1.—Summary of Services of the 2nd Cavalry Division.
2.—List of Officers commanding Regiment 1914-1918.
3.—Casualty Lists. Officers killed in action during the War. Officers wounded. Names of other ranks killed in action, or died from wounds or other causes.
4.—Honours and Awards to Officers and other ranks.
5.—Names of Officers and other ranks mentioned in despatches.

APPENDIX I.

To All Ranks of the Second Cavalry Division.

Now that the Division is about to be broken up after a period of 4½ years since its formation, I wish to offer each one of you my heartfelt thanks for your services both individually and collectively. I do so, not only in my own name but in the names of the Divisional Commanders who preceded me.

While some of you enter into civil life, others remain at the helm, but wherever you may go, I would like you to keep with you a remembrance of the great part which has been played by your Division in the greatest of all wars. The Division has come through 4½ years of war without a stain on its character or a single regrettable incident, and as you will see by the account of its doings overleaf, it has come to the rescue of the Army at many a critical moment.

I hope that each one of you will always remember the good feeling which has kept us together during these years and carry the same into home life in England. Let us do this in memory of those we have unfortunately been compelled to leave behind; may their names never be forgotten.

THOMAS T. PITMAN, Major General,
Commanding 2nd Cavalry Division.

11th March, 1919.

The 2nd Cavalry Division was formed on 16th September, 1914, on the Aisne. It originally consisted of the 3rd and 5th Cavalry Brigades under command of Major-General H. de la P. Gough, C.B. The 4th Brigade joined the Division shortly after the capture of the Mont des Cats. This brilliant operation by the combined action of the 3rd and 5th Brigades first brought the Division to a prominent position as a fighting unit.

The Units in the Division have remained the same throughout the war with the exception of the Composite Household Cavalry Regiment in the 4th Cavalry Brigade, who were replaced by the Queen's Own Oxfordshire Hussars on 19th November, 1914.

The Division distinguished themselves in a contest against overwhelming numbers on the Wytschaete—Messines line from October 20th to November 1st, and later in the vicinity of Wulverghem until the end of the First Battle of Ypres.

In January and February, 1915, the Division had their first experience of regular trench warfare in the Ypres Salient, the first big mine of the war exploding under one of the trenches held by them.

In March they were in support at the Battle of Neuve Chapelle, the 5th Cavalry Brigade making the first attempt of Cavalry to break through the enemy's trench system. 1915

Shortly after returning to billets the Division was again hurried up to the Salient to take part in the Second Battle of Ypres, where the enemy launched poisoned gasses against us.

On 15th April, Major-General C. T. McM. Kavanagh, C.V.O., D.S.O., took over command.

Throughout the summer of 1915 large working parties were found for constructing defences in the vicinity of Kemmel.

On the 15th July, Major-General Sir P. W. Chetwode, Bart., C.M.G., D.S.O., took over command.

In September and October the Division was in support at the Battle of Loos.

The Division spent the first two months of the year in the trenches at Vermelles, when 1916 mining and countermining were of almost nightly occurrence.

1916   From June to September they were in support of the Second Army, which had been considerably weakened to find troops for the Battle of the Somme.

In September the Division moved South to the Somme, where they remained in vicinity of Dernancourt until the beginning of November.

On 16th November, Major-General W. H. Greenly, C.M.G., D.S.O., took over command of the Division.

1917   Early in the year the Division furnished strong working parties for railway construction, and in the begining of April took part in the Battle of Arras under very trying conditions for the horses.

From there they went into the trenches in front of Ronssoy. A most successful raid was carried out at Gillemont Farm, and a few days later a stubborn defence was put up when the Germans counter-raided the same position.

On November 16th, after a short spell in billets, the Division moved East to take part in the Battle of Cambrai. The mounted scheme having failed to materialise, a dismounted Brigade was formed, which had very heavy fighting in the defence of Bourlon Wood.

On the 30th November, when the Germans made their big counter-attack, the Second Cavalry Division assisted the Guards in restoring the situation.

They ended up the year by going once again into the trenches near Hargicourt.

There they remained until the end of January, and afterwards moved into the area around Athies.

In March, in order to meet the threatened German attack, the Division moved to the vicinity of Grandrue in support of the 3rd Corps.

1918   When the attack came on 21st March, the Division was immediately sent up in motor lorries to try and restore the situation. All units of the Division were engaged in very heavy fighting, especially on the Jussy canal, suffering heavy casualties.

On March 25th, the mounted Division was again reformed under command of Brigadier-General Pitman.

On the 26th they made a combined mounted and dismounted attack on the Bois des Essarts. This attack succeeded in holding up the Germans until the arrival of large French reinforcements.

From there the Division, to which was attached the Canadian Cavalry Brigade, made a forced march to Montdidier to support a reported break in the French line, and thence by another forced march to vicinity of Amiens, where the situation of the 5th Army was critical.

On the 30th March, the British line having broken, the Canadian Cavalry Brigade and 3rd Cavalry Brigade made a mounted attack at Moreuil Wood and restored the situation.

On the 1st April, the line having again broken, the whole Division carried out a brilliant dismounted attack at Rifle Wood under cover of their own artillery and machine gun barrage. The objectives were gained and the line restored, heavy casualties being inflicted on the enemy.

The losses of the Division from 21st March to 1st April were 70 officers and 2,000 other ranks.

The appointment of Brigadier-General T. T. Pitman, C.B., C.M.G., to command the Division with the temporary rank of Major-General was confirmed (dated March 29th).

From Amiens the Division was moved North to vicinity of Blaringhem and Flêtre to support the 2nd Army.

On 9th and 10th August the Second Cavalry Division took part in the successful operations in front of Amiens, which started the final battle of the war.

As soon as the war of movement commenced there was a general outcry for Cavalry, and the Division was split up on a front of three Armies. Playing a prominent part throughout the final operations, they had the satisfaction of knowing that nearly every squadron of the Division was well in front when the cease fire sounded on November 11th; one regiment taking part in the final attack on Mons, entered the town at the head of the Canadian Corps.

During the advance through Belgium after the armistice was signed, the Second Cavalry Division acted as Advanced Guard to the 4th Army.

APPENDIX II.

16TH (THE QUEEN'S) LANCERS.

LIST OF OFFICERS WHO HAVE COMMANDED THE REGIMENT DURING THE WAR AND GIVING APPROXIMATE PERIODS OF COMMAND.

Substantive Rank.	Name.	Acting Rank.	Period.
Lieut.-Colonel	MacEwen, M. L. (Period of Command terminated Dec. 19th, 1914.)		15-8-14 to 25-8-14.
Major	Eccles, C. J.	Acting	26-8-14 to 13-11-14.
Major	Campbell, C. L. K. (Died Mar. 31st, 1918.)	Acting	14-11-14 to 3-2-15.
Lieut.-Colonel	Eccles, C. J., D.S.O. (Gazetted Dec. 19th, 1914.)		4-2-15 to 25-5-15.
Brvt.-Lt.-Colonel	Campbell, C. L. K. (Died Mar. 31st, 1918.)	Acting	26-5-15 to 30-9-15.
Lieut.-Colonel	Eccles, C. J., D.S.O.		1-10-15 to 25-2-17.
Major	Shannon, W. J., D.S.O.	A/Lt.-Colonel	20-2-17 to 4-4-17.
Lieut.-Colonel	Eccles, C. J., D.S.O.		5-4-17 to 26-11-17.
Captain	Cheyne, J. L., M.C.	A/Lt.-Colonel	27-11-17 to 12-3-18.
Bt.-Major	Brooke, G. F. H., D.S.O., M.C.	A/Lt.-Colonel	13-3-18 to 25-3-19. 26-3-19 and onwards.
Lieut.-Colonel	Harris-St. John, C. E. St. J., D.S.O.		Ante-dated to 19-12-18.

C. E. HARRIS ST. JOHN, Lieutenant-Colonel,

Commanding 16th Lancers.

Canterbury; May 27th, 1919.

APPENDIX III.

16TH (THE QUEEN'S) LANCERS.

STATEMENT OF CASUALTIES—17TH AUGUST, 1914, TO 11TH NOVEMBER, 1918.

OFFICERS KILLED IN ACTION, WITH REGIMENT.

Rank.	Name.	Date of Casualty.
		1914.
Second Lieutenant	Macneill, W. M.	October 12th.
*Major	Dixon, C. M.	November 5th.
Captain	Macarthur-Onslow, A. W.	Ditto.
		1915.
Captain	Neave, A.	February 21st.
Lieutenant	Beech, R. A. J.	Ditto.
Lieutenant	King, N. W. R.	Ditto.
Lieutenant	Cross, D. R.	Ditto.
Captain	Nash, E. R.	February 22nd.
		1918.
Captain	Allen, J. E. R.	April 8th.
Second Lieutenant	Martin-Holland, G. R.	March 26th.
Lieutenant	Perceval-Maxwell, R. N.	March 30th.
Second Lieutenant	Wodehouse, Hon. E.	Ditto.
Lieutenant	Stephen, J. S.	March 22nd.
Second Lieutenant	Watson, Sir J., Bart.	Ditto.
Captain	Tempest-Hicks, C. E. H.	August 10th.

KILLED (ATTACHED R.F.C.).

		1916.
Lieutenant	O'Brien, T. D.	March 3rd.
Lieutenant	Arbuthnot, R. G. V.	

DIED IN ENGLAND.

Brigadier-General	Campbell, C. L. K.	
Captain	Adams, F. E.	
Lieutenant	Arbuthnot, M. A.	
Lieutenant	Russell, G. C.	
Lieutenant	Prosser, J.	

* Major Dixon had rejoined for service during the war and was second in command when killed.

ROLL OF OFFICERS WHO HAVE BEEN WOUNDED DURING THE WAR OF 1914 TO 1918.

Rank.	Name.	Date of Casualty.
		1914.
Colonel	MacEwen, M. L.	August 25th.
*Captain	Bellville, G. E.	August 25th.
Lieutenant	Tempest-Hicks, C. E. H.	September 14th.
Lieutenant	Cross, D. R.	October 16th.
Second Lieutenant	Aris, C. J.	October 12th.
Lieutenant	Clarke, J. G. W.	October 16th.
Major	Campbell, C. L. K.	October 30th.
Second Lieutenant	Wodehouse, Lord	Ditto.
Lieutenant	Beech, R. A. J.	October 19th.
Second Lieutenant	Davies, R. R.	November 5th.
		1915.
Lieutenant	Thornton, F.	February 20th.
Captain	Evans, H. L.	February 23rd.
Lieutenant	Allen, J. E. R.	Ditto.
Lieutenant-Colonel	Campbell, C. L. K.	February 22nd.
Lieutenant	Patrick, C. M.	Ditto.
Second Lieutenant	McBrayne, J. O.	April 27th.
Lieutenant-Colonel	Eccles, C. J., D.S.O.	May 3rd.
Second Lieutenant	Browne, J. B.	May 24th.
Lieutenant	Holmpatrick, Lord	Ditto.
Captain	MacGlashan, K. (R.A.M.C. att.)	Ditto.
		1916.
Second Lieutenant	Hayes, W. W.	January 20th.
Lieutenant	Davies, R. G. R.	February 4th.
Captain	Tempest-Hicks, C. E. H.	September 26th.
Captain	Aris, C. J., D.S.O.	November 16th.
		1917.
Lieutenant	Hayes, W. W.	November 29th.
Lieutenant	Carlisle, C. V.	Ditto.
Lieutenant	Pargeter, F.	December 4th.
		1918.
Lieutenant	Johnson, E. S. T.	March 29th.
Second Lieutenant	Cox-Cox, G. G.	Ditto.
Lieutenant	Hayes, W. W.	Ditto.
Captain	Allen, J. E. R.	April 1st.
Lieutenant	Johnson, E. S. T.	November 10th.

SUMMARY OF CASUALTIES—OFFICERS.

Killed	15
Wounded	25
Died of Wounds	2
Died of Other Causes	5

* Captain Bellville was dangerously wounded on the 25th August in the combat at Haspres, when the regiment rescued a French Convoy, losing the machine gun, smashed by a direct hit, and Captain Bellville and four men. He could not be removed as the surgeon considered so doing would be fatal. He was therefore left in the village and made prisoner.

ROLL OF WARRANT OFFICERS, N.C.O.'S AND MEN WHO HAVE BEEN KILLED IN ACTION DURING THE WAR OF 1914 TO 1918.

Regtl. No.	Rank and Name.	Date of Casualty.
		1914.
3621	Private Kemp, E. D.	September 6th.
2583	Corpl. Kerry, W. B.	September 8th.
5482	Private Leach, F. C.	September 12th.
2563	,, Deadman, E. T.	Ditto.
4683	,, Harvey, W. H.	September 15th.
710	Lce.-Sgt. Cooper, G.	October 12th.
5011	Private Jones, E.	Ditto.
4968	,, Richardson, E.	Ditto.
6133	,, Gibbons, J.	October 16th.
1572	,, Standing, A.	October 21st.
1454	,, Linfield, J.	October 23rd.
4525	,, Conlan, P.	October 30th.
668	Private Wiegold	Ditto.
53336	Sergt. Docwra, F.	Ditto.
3227	Lce.-Cpl. Topple, W.	November 5th.
4481	,, Bryant, W.	Ditto.
3092	,, Sturdy, R.	Ditto.
3225	,, Chapman, H. H.	Ditto.
3077	Private Syrett, H.	Ditto.
5995	,, Hughes	Ditto.
1389	,, Birmingham, G.	Ditto.
6258	,, Davison, T.	Ditto.
4752	Sergt. McDermott, H.	November 21st.
1234	Private Ramsay, H.	Ditto.
		1915.
5926	Lce.-Cpl. Parsons, E.	February 18th.
3270	Private Basson, W.	February 21st.
3838	,, Adam, C.	Ditto.
6006	,, Cutfield, T.	Ditto.
1017	Corpl. Annett, G.	Ditto.
5714	Private Alderson, C.	Ditto.
5685	Lce.-Cpl. White, W.	Ditto.
6302	Private Smith, T.	Ditto.
4937	,, Giles	Ditto.
4529	,, Jones, G. H.	Ditto.
316	Act.-Cpl. Jackson, A.	Ditto.
5402	Corpl. Liggins, P.	Ditto.
5595	Lce.-Cpl. Futrill, W.	Ditto.
5045	Private Lindsay, C.	Ditto.
7465	,, Rettie	Ditto.
3994	Private Brashier, H.	April 27th.
5182	,, Welbourn, E.	February 19th.
4165	,, Bannister, R. G.	May 2nd.
2973	Corpl. Tuddenham, R.	May 20th.
5064	Private Stratford, C. W.	May 19th.
2730	,, Mitcheal, J. L.	May 25th.
6749	,, Langdale, G.	Ditto.
1318	,, Haggar, C. R.	Ditto.
5680	Lce.-Cpl. Hill, A.	May 26th.
6844	Private Berry, B.	October 3rd.
		1916.
18043	,, Axford, F. R.	January 20th.
3060	,, Newborne, G.	January 26th.
		1917.
5202	Lce.-Cpl. Davies, S.	April 11th.
8485	Private Jones, J.	Ditto.
7277	,, Butler, G.	Ditto.
5237	Lce.-Cpl. Prytherch, S.	November 29th.
5076	Private Hill, S. G.	November 28th.
		1918.
1135	,, Frost, G.	January 13th.
13176	,, Neale, A.	Ditto.

ROLL OF WARRANT OFFICERS, N.C.O.'S AND MEN WHO HAVE BEEN KILLED IN ACTION DURING THE WAR OF 1914 TO 1918 (Continued).

Regtl. No.	Rank and Name.	Date of Casualty.
5213	Private Callow, B.	January 21st.
598	,, Marshall, J.	January 23rd.
7786	Trmptr. White, G. W.	March 21st.
6467	Private Flowers, M.	March 22nd.
6563	Lce.-Cpl. Panter, G.	March 23rd.
4843	,, Garn, T.	Ditto.
4733	Private Halls, A.	Ditto.
13071	,, McDonald, J.	Ditto.
4635	,, Flanagan, W.	Ditto.
13090	,, Andrews, H.	Ditto.
4835	Lce.-Cpl. Shipp, T. J.	Ditto.
9942	,, Fewster, E. A.	Ditto.
5068	Private Clark, G.	Ditto.
13198	,, Chick, F. C.	Ditto.
6692	,, Hobbs, A. R.	Ditto.
10141	,, Channing, S. C.	Ditto.
6461	,, Russell, H.	Ditto.
5040	,, Galvin, J.	Ditto.
5965	,, Read, F. H.	Ditto.
10938	,, Valder, E. W.	Ditto.
12523	,, Webb, R. J.	Ditto.
5088	,, Ambler, B.	Ditto.
2801	Corpl. Tillman, F.	Ditto.
5281	Private Hale, T. J.	Ditto.
11613	Private Simmonds, H.	Ditto.
10157	Corpl. Gale, G.	March 26th.
4944	Lce.-Cpl. Owen, A.	Ditto.
10103	Private Cantellow, R.	Ditto.
7541	,, Sheppard, F.	March 30th.
11637	,, Dabbs, H.	March 31st.
10647	,, Finch, J.	Ditto.
11456	,, Goodson, G. H.	Ditto.
11466	,, Jackson, J. W.	Ditto.
11628	,, Theobald, W. A.	Ditto.
30322	,, Plume, J.	August 9th.
11070	Private Kightley, H. T.	Ditto.
11438	,, Robinson, J.	August 10th.
926	Corpl. Baldry, A.	Ditto.
6135	,, Chenery, A.	November 10th.
5025	Trmptr. Fright, E. J.	November 11th.

KILLED IN ACTION WHILST SERVING AWAY FROM THE REGIMENT.

3861	Private Mead, F.	October 28th, 1914.
3026	Lce.-Cpl. Clover, E. W.	April 23rd, 1916.

ROLL OF WARRANT OFFICERS, N.C.O.'S AND MEN WHO HAVE DIED OF WOUNDS IN THE WAR OF 1914 TO 1918.

Regtl. No.	Rank and Name.	Date of Casualty.
		1914.
3287	Lce.-Cpl. Kemp, H.	October 23rd.
371	Private Martin, G. A.	October 27th.
4536	,, Arnold, W.	October 31st.
2538	Lce.-Sgt. Page, F. J.	November 5th.
3831	Lce.-Cpl. House, E.	November 6th.
7306	Private Martin, D.	November 23rd.
4063	Private Nightingale, A.	November 25th (whilst prisoner of war).
		1915.
283	Private Devine, W.	February 24th.
3884	,, Copsey, T.	May 25th.
638	Lce.-Cpl. Smith, T.	Ditto.
3749	,, Smith, J. T.	May 30th.
		1916.
5372	,, Reed, A.	July 11th.
6427	,, Hay, J.	October 7th.
4935	,, Baker, H.	September 12th.
898	,, Dumper, R.	November 8th.
		1917.
1438	S.S. Jackson, R.	April 12th.
6589	Private Elderkin, D.	April 14th.
6255	,, Ward, H. J.	April 17th.
5032	Lce.-Cpl. Purvis, J.	June 8th.
5363	Private Bulpitt, H. S. G.	June 21st.
6564	Lce.-Cpl. Russell, F.	July 2nd.
2857	Private King, B.	November 28th.
7572	,, Johnson, G.	Ditto.
5303	,, Green, A.	December 5th.
		1918.
5101	,, Barradell, A.	March 25th.
9839	,, Hislop, N. J.	April 9th.
2938	,, Hayden, A.	March 24th.
5236	Corpl. Humphries, E.	April 3rd (whilst prisoner of war)
13061	Lce.-Sgt. Maidment, C.	November 11th.
3591	Private Hargrove, C.	Ditto.
5000	,, Wybrow, J. E.	May 22nd.
5143	,, Hannaford, E.	April 2nd.
11897	,, Aldred, J.	June 2nd.

DIED OF WOUNDS AWAY FROM THE REGIMENT, ON SERVICE.

328	Private Crow, A.	November 1st, 1914.
4996	,, Wardle, A.	November 6th, 1914.
4873	R.S.M. Bell, J.	September 6th, 1916.
24075	Private Brown, W. H.	July 9th, 1917.

DIED FROM OTHER CAUSES DURING THE WAR OF 1914 TO 1918.

Regtl. No.		Rank and Name.		Date of Casualty.
				1914.
2809	Private	Redding, C. (Unofficial Report)		October 16th.
4192	,,	Greiner, C. W. H.	(on or since)	October 31st.
3839	,,	Kitchen, W.	ditto	Ditto.
4503	,,	Jordan, A. A.	ditto	Ditto.
3837	,,	Stephenson, F.	ditto	Ditto.
5756	,,	Mews, W. J.	ditto	Ditto.
4602	,,	Carver, E.	ditto	Ditto.
3638	,,	Smith, C.	ditto	August 29th.
				1917.
11415	,,	Hollister, C.		January 17th.
5214	Private	Wickwar, T. G. A.		August 23rd.
				1918.
31207	Sergt.	Hall, J.		November 14th.
5187	Lce.-Cpl.	Blissitt, A. S.	ditto	March 23rd.
5059	Private	Walsh, D.		October 25th.
10905	,,	Dunning, A. J.		November 17th.
				1919.
2225	,,	Morriss, H. G.		February 27th.
		DIED AFTER DISCHARGE.		
5060	Private	Elston, J.		
9901	,,	Southam, J. A.		
4516	,,	Fitzharris, M.M.		
6602	,,	Spink, C. H.		
10425	,,	Bartley, F.		

SUMMARY OF CASUALTIES—WARRANT OFFICERS, N.C.O.'S, AND PRIVATES.

Killed in action with Regiment	100
Died of Wounds	37
Died of Disease and Other Causes	20
Wounded with Regiment	368
Missing	14

APPENDIX IV.

16TH (THE QUEEN'S) LANCERS.

OFFICERS.   HONOURS AND AWARDS.   1914 TO 1919.

PROMOTIONS.

Rank.	Name.	Promotion.
T/Major-General	Babington, Sir J. M., K.C.M.G., C.B.	To be Major-General. Restored to the Active List, June 3, 1917.

K.C.M.G.

T/Major-General	Babington, J. M., C.B., C.M.G.	Jan. 1, 1917.
Lt.-General (T/Gen.)	Gough, H. de la Poer, K.C.B., K.C.V.O.	June 3, 1919.

C.B.

T/Brig.-General	Campbell, C. L. K. (Posthumous)	
Lieut.-Colonel	MacEwen, M. L.	Aug. 18, 1915.

C.M.G.

Major (T/Brig.-Gen.)	Campbell, C. L. K.	Jan. 1, 1917.
T/Lieut.-Colonel	Shannon, W. J., D.S.O.	June 3, 1919.
Bvt.-Lieut.-Colonel	Beddington, E. H. L., D.S.O., M.C.	Ditto.
Bvt.-Lieut.-Colonel	Howard, H. C. L., D.S.O.	Ditto.

O.B.E.

Lieut. A/Major	Loyd, R. L., M.C.	Jan. 1, 1919.

K.C.B.

General	Babington, Sir J. M., K.C.M.G., C.B.
General	Gough, Sir H. de la Poer

K.C.V.O.

Lieut.-General	Gough, Sir H. de la Poer

G.C.M.G.

Lieut.-General	Gough, Sir H. de la Poer

BAR TO D.S.O.

Capt. and Bvt.-Major	Howard, H. C. L., D.S.O.	Aug. 24, 1917.
A/Lieut.-Colonel	Brooke, G. F. H., D.S.O., M.C.	June 25, 1918.
Major	Shannon, W. J., D.S.O.	

BREVETS.

Rank and Name.	To be.	Date of Award.
Major Campbell, C. L. K.	Bvt.-Lieut.-Colonel	Feb. 18, 1915.
Captain Howard, H. C. L.	Bvt.-Major	Jan. 4, 1916.
Captain Beddington, E. H. L.	Ditto	June 3, ,,
Captain Brooke, G. F. H.	Ditto	May 3, 1917.
Bvt.-Major Beddington, E. H. L., D.S.O. M.C.	Bvt.-Lieut.-Colonel	Jan. 1, 1918.
Bvt.-Major Howard, H. C. L.	Ditto	June 3, ,,
Captain Graham, M.	Bvt.-Major	Sept. 4, ,,
Bvt.-Major Brooke, G. F. H., D.S.O., M.C.	Bvt.-Lieut.-Colonel	June 3, 1919.
Lieutenant Aris, C. J., D.S.O.	Bvt.-Major on promotion to Captain	Ditto.
Captain (T/Lt.-Col.) Graham, M.	Bvt.-Lt.-Colonel on promotion from Bvt.-Major	Ditto.

PAY.

Capt. and Qrtr.-Mstr.	McConnell, J.	Granted next higher rate of pay under the provisions of R.W., June 3, 1919.

D.S.O.

Second Lieutenant	Aris, C. J.	Nov. 9, 1914.
Lieut.-Colonel	Eccles, C. J.	Feb. 18, 1915.
Major	Shannon, W. J.	June 3, 1916.
Captain	Brooke, G. F. H., M.C.	Jan. 1, 1917.
Major	Earl of Dunmore, A. E., V.C., M.V.O.	Ditto.
Bvt.-Major	Howard, H. C. L.	Ditto.
Capt. and Bvt.-Major	Beddington, E. H. L., M.C.	June 4, ,,
Captain (T/Lt.-Col.)	Graham, M.	Jan. 1, 1918.
Captain	Holmpatrick, H. W., Lord, M.C.	Jan. 1, 1919.
Major	Macalpine Leny, R. L.	Ditto.

BAR TO M.C.

Lieut. (T/Major)	Clark, J. G. W., M.C.	June 22, 1918.
T/Major	Cheyne, J. L., M.C.	Sept. 3, 1918.

M.C.

Captain	Beddington, E. H. L.	Jan. 1, 1915.
Lieutenant	Brooke, G. F. H.	Ditto.
Lieutenant	Cross, D. R.	Feb. 18, ,,
Captain	Holmpatrick, H. W., Lord	June 23, ,,
Lieutenant	Archer, H. C.	June 26, ,,
Captain	Fraser, W. A. K. (C.I.H., att. 16th L.)	Jan. 14, 1916.
Lieutenant	Loyd, R. L.	Ditto.
Lieutenant	Tempest-Hicks, C. E. H.	Mar. 15, ,,
Captain	Cheyne, J. L.	Jan. 1, 1917.
Second Lieutenant	Robertson, J. H. (att. 16th L.)	June 4, ,,
Lieutenant	Arbuthnot, M. A.	Ditto.
Lieutenant (T/Capt.)	Clark, J. G. W.	Ditto.
Captain	Horn, T. L.	Jan. 1, 1918.
Second Lieutenant	Hollis, R. C. (att. M.G.C.)	Feb. 4, ,,
Captain	Storey, T. C. (R.A.M.C., att. 16th L.)	Apr. 21, ,,
Captain	Evans, H. L.	Sept. 3, ,,
Lieutenant	Pargeter, F.	Ditto.
Lieutenant	Wodehouse, J., Lord	May 31, ,,
Lieutenant	Johnson, E. S. T.	Nov. 11, ,,
Lieutenant	Johnson, E. S. T.	Jan. 1, 1919.
Captain	Orr-Ewing, J. (late 16th L.)	Ditto.
Second Lieutenant	Wodehouse, Hon. E.	Feb. 1, ,,

FOREIGN DECORATIONS.

LEGION D'HONNEUR.
CROIX DE COMMANDEUR.

Major-General	Babington, Sir, J. M., K.C.M.G., C.B.	1917.
Colonel (T/Brig.-Gen.)	MacEwen, M. L., C.B.	Jan. 19, 1916.

CROIX DE CHEVALIER.

Captain	Neave, A.	Oct. 11, 1914.
T/Lieut.-Colonel	Beddington, E. H. L.	July 14, 1917.

CROIX DE GRAND OFFICER.

Lieut.-General	Gough, H. de la Poer, and Croix de Guerre	

GRAND CROIX DE LEOPOLD.

Lieut.-General	Gough, H. de la Poer, and Croix de Guerre	

CROIX DE GUERRE.

Capt. and Bvt.-Major	Howard, H. C. L.	Dec. 8, 1916.
T/Lieut.-Colonel	Brooke, G. F. H.	May 11, 1918.
Captain	Tempest-Hicks, C. E. H.	Ditto.
Lieutenant	Cox-Cox, G. G.	Ditto.
Lieutenant	Brooke, G. T.	Ditto.
Second Lieutenant	Miles, J. J. A.	Ditto.
Major-General	Babington, Sir, J. M.	Nov. 26, ,,
Lieutenant	Arbuthnot, M. A.	Ditto.

ORDER OF SAVOY (Military).

Major-General	Babington, Sir, J. M., K.C.M.G., C.B.	1918.

CROCI DI GUERRA.

Major-General	Babington, Sir J. M., K.C.M.G., C.B.	1918.
Major-Bvt.-Lt.-Col.	Howard, H. C. L.	Nov. 29, 1918.
Lieutenant	Wodehouse, J., Lord	1918.

COMMANDER OF THE MILITARY ORDER OF AVIS.

Bvt.-Lieut.-Colonel	Beddington, E. H. L., D.S.O., M.C.	Oct. 24, 1919.

ORDER OF THE NILE, THIRD CLASS.

T/Lieut.-Colonel	Macalpine Leny, R. L., D.S.O.	Nov. 26, 1919.

ORDER OF WHITE EAGLE.

Lieut.-General	Gough, H. de la Poer	

ORDER OF CROWN OF ITALY (OFFICER).

Lieut.-Colonel	Howard, H. C. L., C.M.G., D.S.O.	1922.

MEDALS AND DECORATIONS, 1914-1919.

Warrant Officers, Non-Commissioned Officers and Men.

Regtl. No.	Rank and Name.	Date of Award.
	D.C.M.	
5043	Farr.-Staff-Sergt. Glasgow, F.	Nov. 3, 1914.
3225	Lce.-Corpl. Chapman, H.	Ditto.
866	,, Boyton, B.	Ditto.
4621	Private Larkin, R.	June 3, 1915.
1818	,, Waldron, S.	Ditto.
1809	Lce.-Sergt. Carr, K.	Ditto.
302	Sergeant Lawrence, E.	Apr. 4, ,,
2538	Lce.-Sergt. Page, F. J.	Apr. 1, ,,
3831	Lce.-Corpl. House, E.	Ditto.
1909	R.Q.M.S. Crocker, S. A.	Jan. 14, 1916.
5487	Sergeant Brown, D. H.	July 14, 1917.
5063	S.S.M. Groombridge, W.	Jan. 1, 1918.
973	Sergeant Howes, C. S.	Sept. 3, ,,
	BAR TO M.M.	
3217	Lce.-Corpl. Hanser, E., M.M.	June 27, 1918.
	M.M.	
1590	Corporal Bullock, R.	Oct. 10, 1916.
1463	Lce.-Corpl. Cain, W.	Ditto.
1481	Sergeant Fuller, G.	Ditto.
5491	,, Goodheart, O.	Ditto.
6180	Private Graham, J.	Ditto.
3217	Lce.-Corpl. Hanser, E.	Ditto.
4828	Private Swannell, S.	Ditto.
4801	,, Wade, C.	Ditto.
4919	Lce.-Corpl. Norris, J.	Mar. 12, 1918.
4956	Private Barrett, R.	Ditto.
2818	,, Beere, L.	Ditto.
6479	,, Sly, G.	Ditto.
4190	Sergeant Best H.	June 25, 1918.
1622	,, Deacon, W.	Ditto.
1085	Lce.-Sergt. Gunston, H.	Ditto.
7166	,, Horwood, S.	Ditto.
13114	Corporal Neely, S.	Ditto.
13221	,, Howard, F.	Ditto.
4065	Private Cutts, W.	Ditto.
4610	,, Trenfield, R.	Ditto.
1030	,, Wetherhead, E.	Ditto.
3215	,, Fitzgerald, E.	Ditto.
5103	,, Whyment, G.	Ditto.
5768	,, Degnan, L.	Ditto.
4621	,, Larkin, R., D.C.M.	Ditto.
5077	,, Lloyd, R.	Ditto.
5036	,, Richmond, J.	Ditto.
8580	,, Ford, H.	Ditto.
13104	,, Langford, E.	Ditto.
5418	Corporal Anderson, J.	Nov. 21, ,,
298	Sergeant Abbott, W. N. J.	Mar. 13, 1919.
13215	Lce.-Corpl. Chestney, W.	Aug. 20, .

FOREIGN DECORATIONS.

RUSSIAN CROSS. ORDER OF ST. GEORGE. THIRD CLASS.

| 7061 | ... | Private | Waldron, R. S. | ... | ... | Aug. 25, 1915. |

RUSSIAN CROSS. ORDER OF ST. GEORGE. FOURTH CLASS.

| 5663 | ... | Sergeant | Collyer, G. A. | ... | ... | Aug. 25, 1915. |
| 5237 | ... | Private | Prytherch, S. | ... | ... | Ditto. |

BELGIAN DECORATION MILITAIRE.

| 689 | ... | Sergeant | Gough, C. B. | ... | ... | Apr. 12, 1918. |

MEDAILLE MILITAIRE.

| 302 | ... | Sergeant | Lawrence, E. | ... | ... | Oct. 11, 1914. |
| 5578 | ... | ,, | Clarke, J. | ... | ... | June 25, 1918. |

BELGIUM CROIX DE GUERRE.

| 617 | ... | Sergeant | Keen, F. | ... | ... | Apr. 12, 1918. |

MEDAILLE D'HONNEUR. (avec Glaives en Argent.)

| 3840 | ... | Sergeant | Wright, G. | ... | ... | Jan. 28, 1919. |

M.S.M.

1256	...	Sergeant	Smith, H.	...	...	June 17, 1918.
330	...	,,	Bancroft, H.	...	...	Ditto.
6825	...	Private	Vaughan, M.	...	...	Jan. 1, 1919.
13089	...	R.S.M.	Wilson, A.	...	...	June 3, ,,
13117	...	S.S.M.	Lindsay, W.	...	...	Ditto.

ROYAL HUMANE SOCIETY. TESTIMONIAL ON VELLUM.

| 5150 | ... | Private | Samuels, G. | ... | ... | Apr. 18, 1916. |

APPENDIX V.

16TH (THE QUEEN'S) LANCERS.

OFFICERS MENTIONED IN DESPATCHES DURING THE WAR OF 1914 TO 1919.

Rank and Name.	Date of Mention.
Maj.-Gen. Babington, Sir J. M., K.C.M.G., C.B.	Eight times mentioned.
Lt.-Col. MacEwen, M. L.	Mentioned in Despatches by the C.-in-C. the Forces, Oct. 8, 1914.
Major Eccles, C. J.	
Major Campbell, C. L. K.	
Capt. Neave, A.	
Capt. Howard, H. C. L.	Oct. 8, 1914.
Lieut. Beddington, E. H. L.	
Lieut. Nash, E. K.	
Lieut. Cheyne, J. L.	
Lieut. Beech, R. H.	
Lieut. Tempest-Hicks, C. E. H.	London Gazette, Dec. 9, 1914.

OFFICERS MENTIONED IN DESPATCHES DURING THE WAR OF 1914 TO 1919 (Continued).

Rank and Name.	Date of Mention.
Lieut. Cross, D. R.	
Lieut. Davies, R. G. R.	
Lieut. Holmpatrick, H. W., Lord	
2nd Lieut. Isherwood, L. C. R.	
2nd Lieut. Wodehouse, J., Lord	
Lt.-Col. Eccles, C. J.	Mentioned in Despatches by the C.-in-C. the British Army in the Field, Nov. 20, 1914.
Major Campbell, C. L. K.	
Capt. Dixon, C. M.	
Capt. Onslow, A. W. M.	
Lieut. Cross, D. R.	
2nd Lieut. Aris, C. J.	
Major Shannon, W. J.	Mentioned in Despatches by the C.-in-C. the Forces in the Field, May 31, 1915.
Capt. Beddington, E. H. L.	
Capt. Howard, H. C. L.	
Capt. Horn, T. L.	
Capt. Hutton-Riddell, G., M.V.O.	
Lieut. Holmpatrick, H. W., Lord	
Lieut. Loyd, R. L.	
Major Macalpine-Leny, R. L.	Mentioned in Despatches by the C.-in-C. the Forces in the Field.
Capt. Howard, H. C. L.	
Lieut. Loyd, R. L.	
Lieut. McBrayne, J. O.	London Gazette, Dec. 31, 1915.
Major Shannon, W. J.	
Capt. Graham, M.	London Gazette, June 15, 1916.
Lieut. Callander, G. D.	
2nd Lieut. Hornyold, R. G.	London Gazette, Jan. 31, 1915.
Capt. Brooke, G. F. H., M.C.	Mentioned in Despatches by the C.-in-C. the Forces in the Field, Jan. 4, 1917.
Brig.-Gen. Campbell, C. L. K.	
Major Earl of Dunmore, V.C., M.V.O. (late 16th Lancers)	
Major Howard, H. C. L.	
Lieut. Wodehouse, J., Lord	
Lieut. Davies, R. G. R.	
Lt.-Col. Beddington, E. H. L., M.C.	Mentioned in Despatches by the C.-in-C. the Forces in the Field, May 15, 1917.
Major Earl of Dunmore, V.C., M.V.O. (late 16th Lancers)	
General Gough, Sir, H. de da P., K.C.B.	
Major Howard, H. C. L., D.S.O.	
Lt.-Col. Beddington, E. H. L., D.S.O., M.C.	Mentioned in Despatches by the C.-in-C. the Forces, Dec. 7, 1917.
Lieut. (T/Capt.) Clark, J. G. W., M.C.	
Capt. (T/Lt.-Col.) Graham, M.	
Major Harris-St. John, C. E. St. J., D.S.O.	
Bvt.-Lt.-Col. Howard, H. C. L., D.S.O.	
Major Macalpine-Leny, R. L.	
Lieut. Codrington, W. M.	Mentioned in Despatches by the C.-in-C. the Forces, Dec. 7, 1917.
2nd Lieut. Patrick, C. M.	
Major Shannon, W. J., D.S.O.	
Lieut. (T/Major) Aris, C. J., D.S.O.	Mentioned in Despatches by the G.O.C. the British Armies in France, Apr. 7, 1918.
Capt. and Bvt.-Lt.-Col. Beddington, E. H. L., D.S.O., M.C.	
Major and Bvt.-Lt.-Col. (T/Brig.-Gen.) Campbell, C. L. K., C.M.G.	
Major (T/Lt.-Col.) Howard, H. C. L., D.S.O.	June 1, 1918, by C.-in-C. Italy.
Capt. (T/Lt.-Col.) Graham, M.	London Gazette, Dec. 20, 1918.

Officers Mentioned in Despatches during the War of 1914 to 1919 (Continued).

Rank and Name.	Date of Mention.
Major Tuson, G. E., D.S.O. (late 16th L.)	
Lieut. Allen, J. E. R.	
Lieut. (T/Capt.) Davies, R. G. R. (att. M.G.C.)	
T/Lieut. Hornyold, R. G.	
Capt. Holmpatrick, H. W., Lord ...	London Gazette, Dec. 20, 1918.
Capt. (T/Lt.-Col.) Brooke, G. F. H., D.S.O., M.C.	
Lt.-A/Major Loyd, R. L.	
Capt. Murray, E. M.	
Bvt.-Lt.-Col. Howard, H. C. L., D.S.O. ...	Jan. 1, 1919, by C.-in-C. Italy.
T/Lt.-Col. Shannon, W. J., D.S.O. ...	
Bvt.-Major Brooke, G. F. H., D.S.O., M.C.	
Lieut. Aris, C. J., D.S.O. ...	
Bvt.-Lt.-Col. Beddington, E. H. L., D.S.O., M.C.	
Capt. (T/Lt.-Col.) Graham, M., D.S.O. ...	Mentioned in Despatches, Mar. 16, 1919.
Lieut. (T/Major) Clark, J. G. W., M.C. ...	London Gazette, July 5, 1919.
Lieut. (A/Capt.) Allen, J. E. R. ...	
Lieut. (T/Capt.) Ramsbottom Isherwood, L. C.	
Lieut. (A/Capt.) Davies, R. R. ...	
Lieut. (A/Capt.) Thornton, F.	
Bvt.-Lt.-Col. Howard, H. C. L., D.S.O. ...	June 1, 1919, by C.-in-C. Italy.

SUMMARY OF AWARDS.

Promotions	...	...	...	1	
K.C.M.G	...	...	...	2	
C.M.G.	...	...	...	4	
C.B.	...	...	...	2	
O.B.E.	...	...	...	1	
Bar to D.S.O.	...	...	...	3	
D.S.O.	...	...	...	10	
Bar to M.C.	...	...	...	2	
M.C.	...	...	...	22	
K.C.B.	...	...	...	2	
K.C.V.O.	...	...	...	1	
G.C.M.G.	...	...	...	1	
Brevets	...	...	...	10	
Legion D'Honneur	...	...	5		
Croix de Guerre	...	...	8		
Order of Savoy (Military)	...	...	1		
Croci di Guerre	...	...	3		
Mentions	...	...	...	81	
Order of Avis	...	...	...	1	
Order of the Nile	...	...	1		
Croix de Guerre (Belgium)	...	1			
White Eagle	...	...	...	1	
Order of Leopold	...	...	1		
Crown of Italy	...	...	...	1	

ROLL OF WARRANT OFFICERS, NON-COMMISSIONED OFFICERS AND MEN MENTIONED IN DESPATCHES DURING THE WAR OF 1914 TO 1919.

Regtl. No., Rank and Name.	Date of Mention.
4524 S.S.M. Pargeter, F.	Mentioned in Despatches by the C.-in-C. the Forces in the Field, Oct. 8, 1914.
4271 S.S.M. Archer, H.	
5121 Sergt. Lindsay, E.	
302 Sergt. Lawrence, E.	
2538 Corpl. Page, F.	London Gazette, Dec. 9, 1914.
710 Corpl. Cooper, G.	
2682 Lce.-Sergt. Roberts, A.	
5487 Sadd.-Corpl. Brown, D. H.	
1129 Lce.-Corpl. Jewkes, W.	
1481 Lce.-Corpl. Fuller, G.	
1256 Lce.-Corpl. Smith, H.	
1601 Lce.-Corpl. Holden, W.	
1869 Lce.-Sergt. Carr, R.	
3228 Lce.-Corpl. Beaumont, W. F.	
2638 Lce.-Sergt. Page, F. J.	Mentioned in Despatches by the C.-in-C. the Forces in the Field, Nov. 20, 1914. London Gazette, Feb. 16, 1915.
3831 Lce.-Corpl. House, E.	Mentioned in Despatches by the C.-in-C. the Forces in the Field, May 31, 1915. London Gazette, June 18, 1915.
4539 S.S.M. Norton, N. F.	
5122 Farr.-Sergt. Crossland, T.	
4963 Sergt. Pauley, W.	
510 Sergt. Wakefield, F.	
1645 Lce.-Corpl. Barton, A.	
3870 Lce.-Corpl. Brooks, W.	
3778 Lce.-Corpl. Kennett, W.	
5556 Private Adams, A.	
1589 Private Loscombe, J.	
5237 Private Prytherch, S.	
5578 Lce.-Cpl. Clark, J. W.	Mentioned in Despatches by the C.-in-C. the Forces in the Field, Dec. 31, 1915. London Gazette, Jan. 4, 1917.
3285 Private Taylor, G. C.	
5470 Private Thompson, J.	
5121 S.S.M. Lindsay, W.	London Gazette, May 15, 1917.
973 Sergt. Howes, C. S.	London Gazette, Dec. 7, 1917.
298 Corpl. Abbott, W. N. J.	London Gazette, May 20, 1918.
8 Farr.-Sergt. Arthey, T.	London Gazette, July 5, 1919.
13097 S.Q.M.S. Pauley, W.	London Gazette, July 5, 1919.

SUMMARY OF AWARDS.

D.C.M.	...	...	...	13
Bar to M.M.	...	...	...	1
M.M.	...	...	...	32
M.S.M.	...	...	...	5
Russian Cross of Order of St. George (3rd Class)	...	...	...	1
Russian Cross of Order of St. George (4th Class)	...	...	...	2
Belgian Decoration Militaire			...	1
French Medal Militaire			...	1
French Medaille D'Honneur			...	1
Belgian Croix de Guerre			...	1
Royal Humane Society Medal			...	1
Mentions in Despatches			...	34

1919

CHAPTER XLIII.

24TH JUNE, 1919—24TH NOVEMBER, 1920.

SYRIA AND PALESTINE.

Embarkation at Liverpool, 24th June. Landing at Port Said. Kantara. Port Said. Beyrout. March to Rayak. The Regiment sent by train to Homs. Unhealthy conditions at Homs. The camp moved. Evacuation of Syria. The march to Sarona. The Regiment sent by train to Belbeis. Embarkation at Suez, 24th November, 1920. Roll of the officers.

24th June On the 24th June the Regiment embarked at Liverpool in the S.S. Oxfordshire together with the Queen's Bays, both regiments being under orders to relieve Yeomanry in Syria, these being about to be demobilised.

The ship's orders were to land the troops at Beyrout, but the destination was subsequently changed by a wireless telegram to Port Said.

The Regiment disembarked at Port Said on the 6th of July, 12 officers and 463 other ranks, and on the next day the 16th were sent to the Base Depôt at Kantara, where there were still a large number of troops.

The Regiment remained in camp at Kantara for 10 days in order to draw horses and equipment to complete.

From Kantara the Regiment returned by train to Port Said, where it was inspected by Field-Marshal Lord Allenby previous to embarkation. After the inspection the officers and men embarked on the S.S. Abyssinia, the horses leaving by another ship in charge of a detached party, and sailed for Beyrout. There the Regiment went into camp on some waste land just south of the town. The horses arrived three days later.

On August 7th the Regiment moved by route march to Rayak, where it arrived on August 5th, the heavy baggage, with the advance party, having been sent to Homs, in Syria, direct by train in advance. On the next day one squadron and one troop proceeded by train to Homs, and by the 9th the whole Regiment had arrived there and joined the 10th Cavalry Brigade, which was commanded by a Brigadier-General of the Indian Army. The 10th Brigade belonged to the 4th Cavalry Division under Major-General Sir H. W. Hodgson. The other regiments of the Brigade were the 2nd Bengal Lancers, the 38th Central India Horse, and the Staffordshire Yeomanry, which the 16th was to replace.

The 16th went into camp on some low lying ground about three miles west of the town of Homs. This was bounded on the west by the river Orontes, and on the east by an irrigation canal.

The district round Homs was well known to be one of the most unhealthy places in Syria, yet by some strange perversity it was selected as a Cavalry Camp. The heat was not excessive as a cool land wind blew all day from the Lebanon, but it was infested by malarial mosquitoes to such an extent that within two months 65 per cent. of the men and seven out of 13 officers were in hospital with fever and had to be sent to the Casualty Clearing Hospital at Rayak, whence the more serious cases were sent to the Base Hospitals in Egypt. Very few of these men rejoined until after the Regiment was moved to Palestine.

Owing to this sickness, the shortage of officers and experienced N.C.O.'s, and the very indifferent horses issued to the Regiment, there was much difficulty in training the many recruits. There were also numerous guards to be

LIEUT.-COLONEL C. E. St. J. HARRIS-St. JOHN, D.S.O.
1918-1921.

found for Brigade Headquarters, Turkish prisoners of war, and the camp itself. 1919
The last had to be particularly strong on account of the local inhabitants being
most skilful thieves and constantly on the look out for rifles. One method they
tried was the firing of their rifles and guns in the direction of the camp night
after night, apparently in the endeavour to distract attention, while their
picked men stole into camp under cover of darkness. Some rifles stolen from
the Regiment while at Homs were recovered in Mesopotamia. It was very
difficult indeed to prevent the Arabs getting into the camp at night, as no wire
was available for use, and if they were caught and handed over to the local
authorities they had very little to fear, as Homs was under Arab jurisdiction.
As an instance, just before the Regiment arrived there, two men were caught
who had burgled an officer's tent, and stabbed the officer in bed when he
woke up. Luckily he was not seriously hurt. Their punishment was a fine
of £1 1s. each! During the latter part of our stay, guards for the camp were
found by the Hedjaz Army, and these proved trustworthy.

In October, 1919, the camp was moved to another site immediately to the Oct.
north of Homs. The reasons for this were the unhealthy nature of the first
camp and the danger of its being flooded when the rains broke. This second
camp was, however, little better than the first from the point of view of the
health of the Regiment, and everyone was greatly pleased when the news
arrived that Syria was to be evacuated in November. All ranks of the Regiment disliked Homs intensely. There were few British troops in the Garrison
with whom the men could fraternise, and there were no organised entertainments for them. There was some sand-grouse shooting and a little duck shooting on the lake of Homs, of which the officers took advantage, and some polo
on troop horses was started, but the difficulties in the way of organised games
or sport were very great.

On November 22nd the Brigade marched out of Homs in accordance with 22nd
the scheme for the evacuation of Syria, under the command of Colonel Hewlett Nov.
of the 38th Central India Horse.

For the march the strength was six officers (of whom one was a chaplain)
and 143 other ranks; it was necessary, therefore, to call upon the two other
cavalry regiments of the Brigade for assistance, so 100 horses were transferred
to each of them, and in addition they provided the whole of the drivers for the
transport. Even then the majority of the men led one or two horses.

The 16th, under command of Lieut.-Colonel St. John, with the other regiments of the Brigade marched at 7.30 a.m. on the 22nd November. The
rains had begun and roads had become nearly impassable. Even before the
Regiment had reached the Brigade rendezvous all the tents but five had to be
thrown away.

The line of march ran parallel to the Aleppo-Damascus railway, and the
troops did not get to Kosseir, the halting place for the night, until 7 p.m.,
though it was only a 17 miles march. The 16th then went on outpost, bivouacing in the wet, for it rained hard all the night.

The next morning the Brigade marched to Ras Baalbec, the 16th doing rearguard to the Brigade. The next day's march to Letwe was done in comparative comfort as the road, being close under the Lebanon mountains, was stony
instead of the usual sea of mud, and the 16th, being advance guard, got into
camp at Letwe at noon, but the following day's march of 17 miles to Baalbec
was worse than ever as it rained in torrents the whole day, and when the
troops crawled into the place after a march which took nine hours to accomplish, they had to bivouac in mud and water, and to make things worse the
horses kept breaking loose as the picket pegs would not hold in the soft ground.

1919
26th Nov.
3rd Dec.
On the 26th the Brigade arrived at Said Nail, where the troops halted for a much needed rest until December 3rd, when the Brigade marched to Ain Sofar. The road crossed the Lebanon Range and was a steep climb, rising to a height of over 4,000 feet. Several columns of French troops were passed on the way which were moving eastward.

Ain Sofar was quite a good town, possessing a good hotel and a number of substantial houses, and the Regiment had a comfortable night in billets.

The following day's march brought the troops to Beyrout. The town was full of plague at the time and the Brigade " camped " three miles south-east of the place, that is to say the troops lay down in the mud in their wet clothes, for it rained without ceasing the whole night, their only covering being bivouac sheets that were too short to cover them.

8th Dec.
They remained in this place until the 8th, when they marched 18 miles to a new camp, crossing on the way a stream three miles short of their destination by a very dangerous bridge. Here the horses were watered as there was no water nearer to the camping ground.

From this place the Brigade marched to Acre via Saida, Ain el Burak, Tyre, and Raisul Nakura, a distance of 62 miles, arriving there on the 12th. The Regiment halted for two days at Acre, where it rained without cessation the whole time, and on the 14th, still in rain and wind, marched along the shore to Haifa, where it was to entrain for Ludd.

14th Dec.

The work of entraining, in dirty cattle trucks, began at 6.30 p.m. When entrained it was discovered that no engine had been provided, and the train did not get away until 7.30 a.m. on the 16th. When Ludd was at last reached there was no shunting engine, and the horses remained another 12 hours in the trucks without food or water before they could be detrained. A few tents were served out, but the night was both wet and windy and most of them were blown down before morning.

18th Dec.
On the 18th the Regiment marched via Jaffa to Sarona. The weather was as atrocious as ever, and on arriving at the camping ground it was discovered that no preparations whatever had been made for the troops though a detachment of Engineers and the Advance Parties had been there six weeks.

Altogether the way in which this march was conducted was most discreditable to the General Staff all through, but notwithstanding the quite needless hardships to which the men, and the horses, had been subjected on the 26 days' march, only two men reported sick, and the horses came in in good condition and with only one sore back in the Regiment.

Many of the officers and men were still suffering from the malarial fever contracted at Homs. This fever was of so virulent a description that the medical authorities were afraid that it might spread to the other troops at the camp, and in June it was thought advisable to send the Regiment away to another station where there were no other troops. The Regiment was then ordered to move to Belbeis, to which place it proceeded by train from Ludd.

1920 June
Belbeis is on a branch line some 40 miles from Cairo. There was a permanent camp there, the place having been used during the war as a remount depôt, and there were covered stables, consisting of lean-to sheds, for the horses, but the officers and men were in tents. Here the Regiment had a much wanted rest for six months, and the place being dry and healthy, though very uninteresting, the effects of the fever were gradually got rid of and most of the convalescents rejoined from hospital.

In August orders were received for the Regiment to move to India during the next trooping season. This was very unexpected intelligence, as it was generally believed that no troops were to be sent out that year. The move

LIEUT.-COLONEL H. C. L. HOWARD, C.M.G., D.S.O.
1921-1925.

was originally intended to take place in September, but owing to the general disorganisation caused by a strike of the coal-miners it was delayed until November.

On November 23rd the Scots Greys came into Belbeis. The next day the horses and equipment were handed over and the Regiment went by train to Suez, where it embarked on the Transport "Field Marshal." A draft of time-expired men were left at Belbeis. These were sent to England later on.

Brevet-Lieut.-Colonel H. C. L. Howard, C.M.G., D.S.O., was in command of the Regiment; strength, eight officers and 326 other ranks. The names of the officers were as follows:—

Brevet-Lieut.-Colonel Howard, Commanding.
Capt. J. L. Cheyne, M.C.   2nd Lieut. R. M. Marter.
,, G. C. Barker.   ,, A. L. Leaf.
Lieut. G. G. Cox-Cox.   ,, W. H. F. Brunskill.
,, J. A. MacArthur-Onslow.

The 2nd Royal Dublin Fusiliers were also on the ship. The ship sailed on the 26th for Kurachee, where the Fusiliers were disembarked, and continued the voyage in the evening to Bombay, arriving there on December 11th. The 16th were disembarked and left by train for Lucknow the same day.

CHAPTER XLIV.

DECEMBER 12TH, 1920—JANUARY 17TH, 1925.

INDIA AND EGYPT.

The Regiment at Lucknow. Retirement of Lieut.-Colonel St. John, D.S.O. Lieut.-Colonel Howard, C.M.G., to command vice St. John. Visit of the Prince of Wales. Visit of Field-Marshal Sir W. Robertson. Amalgamation with the 5th Lancers, April, 1922. Roll of the officers. Favourable Inspection Reports. Inspection by the C.-in-C. India, General Lord Rawlinson. Orders to move to Egypt. The horses given over, February, 1924. Memorial tablet placed in the Church. The general health of the Regiment compared with 1890-96. The Regiment leaves for Egypt, relieved by 4th Hussars. Farewell Orders by G.O.C. U.P. District and others. Disembarkation at Suez, 19th March, 1924. Arrival at Cairo. Abbasia Barracks taken over from 9th Lancers. The Regiment remounted. Political disquiet in Cairo. Murder of Sir Lee Stack. His funeral. The Cavalry Brigade Horse Show. Visit of Lieut.-General Sir J. M. Babington. Retirement of Lieut.-Colonel Howard. His farewell order, January 17th, 1925. Lieut.-Colonel G. F. H. Brooke, D.S.O., M.C., to command vice Howard to H.P.

The Sixteenth relieved the 8th Hussars at Lucknow, but that regiment had already left the station and gone to Mesopotamia, taking their horses with them, and in consequence of this there were none to take over. On January 16th the first lot of new animals came in. These were 200 Australians from the Sehore Remount Depôt and were what were called "Trained remount

1921 riders," which meant that they had been ridden, but without bits or spurs, and had no training with arms. As most of the men were young and themselves untrained, and there were few instructors, a very difficult situation was created, particularly as many of the horses were, to put it mildly, rather "wild." Men and horses had to be trained together at the same time, and the results were not over satisfactory, a good many animals being spoilt in the process. On the 25th the Regiment was inspected by Lieut.-General Sir H. Hudson, G.O.C. Eastern Command. The troops were paraded mounted, but without arms or spurs, the horses being ridden in snaffles only and not moving out of a walk. On the 31st General Lord Rawlinson, C.-in-C. India, inspected the Regiment under similar conditions.

On the 17th February Lieut.-Colonel Harris St. John, D.S.O., was placed on retired pay on the expiration of his period of command. He was succeeded by Brevet-Lieut.-Colonel H. C. L. Howard, C.M.G., D.S.O.

From time to time more drafts of horses were received until the establishment was complete. All these were untrained with the exception of 30, mostly pack animals, which came from a disbanded machine-gun squadron at Meerut.

Up to October the Regiment was fully occupied with the individual training of the men and horses. During this period many new officers joined and drafts were received from England and from the disbanded 5th Lancers, 19th Hussars and 21st Lancers, so that by the end of October the Regiment was up to its full strength again.

On the 9th December H.R.H. the Prince of Wales arrived at Lucknow. The Regiment, together with "K" Battery R.H.A., formed his escort; the procession started from the railway station and proceeded to the Council Chamber, where H.R.H. received the address of welcome, after which H.R.H. was escorted to Government House, where he was received by H.E. Sir S. Harcourt Butler, G.C.I.E., K.C.S.I., Governor of the United Provinces.

After H.R.H. had inspected the Guard of Honour of the Queen's Royal Regiment, all the officers of the Regiment who were on parade were presented to him by the Commanding Officer, Lieut.-Colonel H. C. L. Howard, C.M.G., D.S.O.

On the 10th December the Lucknow Garrison was reviewed by H.R.H. the Prince of Wales.

During the three days which H.R.H. spent at Lucknow there were various functions and entertainments, among them being a Gymkhana Race Meeting and a one day Polo Tournament.

1922 After Christmas the Regiment went into camp at Nimsar, remaining there till the middle of January; this camp was four days' march from Lucknow, and three weeks' regimental training was carried out. This was the first regimental training which the Regiment had had an opportunity of carrying out since the war.

Owing to the horses not yet being fully trained, fast work could not be carried out, but the three weeks in camp was very useful experience for everyone.

On the 1st February, 1922, two squadrons under Lieut.-Colonel Howard railed to Delhi; strength—officers 9, other ranks 215, horses 225. These two squadrons formed part of the escort to H.E. the Viceroy, the Earl of Reading, G.C.B., G.C.V.O., on the occasion of the visit of H.R.H. the Prince of Wales. The remainder of the escort consisted of the 19th Lancers, H.E. the Viceroy's Bodyguard, and a battery of Field Artillery. The functions in which the two squadrons took part included the escort to H.E. the Viceroy from the station near the Delhi Fort, back to the Viceregal Lodge after H.E. had

Taken on the occasion of the Prince of Wales' visit to Lucknow, 9th December, 1921.

Lt.-Col. G. F. H. Brooke, D.S.O., M.C., Capt. J. B. Browne, Capt. R. G. R. Davies, M.C., Capt. G. C. Barker, Lt. H. A. Heber-Percy, Lt. H. F. Kendrick, M.C., Lt. R. M. Master, Lt. H. R. Moon, Lt.-Col. H. C. L. Howard, C.M.G, D.S.O. H.R.H The Prince of Wales.

received H.R.H. the Prince of Wales, and escorting H.E. the Viceroy to the Durbar which took place inside the Fort. The squadrons also lined the streets at Raisina, New Delhi, on the occasion of H.R.H. the Prince of Wales laying the foundation stone of the Lord Kitchener Memorial College.

The two squadrons were in camp at Kingsway, and one morning at about nine o'clock H.R.H. rode to the camp and walked round the lines with the Commanding Officer, and the officers were presented to H.R.H.

There was a ball at the Viceregal Lodge at which the ruling Princes in their magnificent robes and jewellery made a very fine sight.

The final of the Prince of Wales Commemoration Polo Tournament was perhaps one of the finest matches that has ever been seen, being between Jodphur and Patiala. At the beginning of the last chukka Patiala were leading by two goals, but Jodphur made this up and scored the winning goal just before time; it was a very fast game, and most exciting to watch.

On the 23rd February the two squadrons rejoined at Lucknow.

On the 28th February, Field-Marshal Sir William R. Robertson, Bart., G.C.B., G.C.M.G., K.C.V.O., D.S.O., came to Lucknow to stay for a few days with the Commanding Officer. It was a great pleasure to the Regiment to welcome the Field-Marshal, who had spent the first ten years of his service in the Regiment. As his visit was entirely private, no special parades took place, but the Field-Marshal addressed the Regiment one morning in the Regimental Theatre.

Army Order No. 133 of April, 1922, announced amalgamations of various cavalry regiments, amongst these being that of the 16th Lancers and the 5th Lancers, the latter to form one squadron, and the Regiment in future to be known as the 16th/5th Lancers.

The detailed instructions for this amalgamation were contained in Army Council Instruction No. 281 of the 25th May, 1922. By this instruction the 12th Lancers were to form a complete squadron, less any 5th Lancers then serving with the 16th Lancers, at home to be despatched to Lucknow to form the 5th Lancer Squadron. However, presumably owing to the expense which it would have entailed, i.e., the despatch of about 140 of all ranks from England, and the return to England of a corresponding number of 16th Lancers who would have become surplus, this first instruction was modified.

In the end, 32 other ranks of the 5th Lancers arrived at Lucknow on the 28th September, 1922. These, together with 21 other ranks who had previously served in the 5th Lancers, were posted to "D" Squadron, the remainder of the squadron being made up of 99 16th Lancers then in the squadron, which then became the 5th Lancer Squadron.

On the 29th September the Regiment became the 16th/5th Lancers.

The 5th Lancer officers who joined then or later were as follows:—Major H. A. Cooper, Captain J. C. Miles, Lieut. J. C. Biggs, M.C., Lieut. J. N. Bailey, Lieut. W. M. F. Bayliss.

During the period between the issue of the Army Order and the end of 1922 all officers were reposted to the amalgamated regiment in the London Gazette, with the exception of certain surplus officers who were retired or transferred under Army Council instructions to other regiments.

At the end of 1922 the roll of officers of the Regiment was as follows:—

Lieut.-Col. H. C. L. Howard, C.M.G., D.S.O.
Major H. A. Cooper.
Major and Bt.-Lieut.-Col. G. F. H. Brooke, D.S.O., M.C.
S. Major and Bt.-Lieut.-Col. M. Graham, D.S.O.
S.C.S. Major J. L. Cheyne, M.C.

Captain T. L. Horn, M.C.
Captain J. C. Miles.
Captain R. G. R. Davies, M.C.
S. Captain J. G. W. Clark, M.C.
S. Captain F. Thornton.
Captain R. Moubray.
Captain J. B. Browne.
Captain A. C. Macintyre.
Captain A. W. M. S. Pilkington, M.C.
Captain C. Nicholson, Adjutant.
Captain C. F. T. O'B. ffrench.
Captain and Q.M. J. McConnell.
Lieut. J. C. Biggs, M.C.
Lieut. J. N. Bailey.
Lieut. G. G. Cox-Cox.
Lieut. A. C. Byard.
Lieut. F. G. C. Noakes.
Lieut. E. Collins.
Lieut. W. M. F. Bayliss.
Lieut. A. L. Leaf.
Lieut. H. R. Moon.
2nd Lieut. G. J. R. Tomkin.
2nd Lieut. E. Wadham.
2nd Lieut. R. N. Fawcett.
2nd Lieut. J. A. H. Jephson.
2nd Lieut. A. B. Sullivan.
2nd Lieut. W. J. D. G. Johnston.

On the 23rd October, 1922, the District Commander, Major-General C. J. Deverell, C.B., inspected the Regiment on the conclusion of individual training; he expressed his great satisfaction at what he had seen, and noted a marked improvement since his last inspection.

A great deal of work had been carried out by all ranks during the summer to improve the training of horses and men, and by the end of this period the horses were fully trained and were fit to carry out galloping drill, which it had not been possible previously to do.

The scheme for camp this winter was the formation of a camp at Mohanlalganj (about 13 miles from Lucknow) in November, each squadron proceeding there in turn for ten days' squadron training, and the whole Regiment going out on the 10th December and returning on the 21st.

During the period the Regiment was in camp it was inspected by Major-General R. A. Cassels, C.B., C.S.I., D.S.O., Major-General of Cavalry.

At the conclusion of regimental training on the 14th February the Regiment was inspected by General Sir Havelock Hudson, K.C.B., K.C.I.E., G.O.C.-in-C. Eastern Command. He made the following remarks at the conclusion of his inspection :—

"I was much pleased with what I saw of the Regiment this morning. There was a marked absence of noise. The horses were in a hard condition, well in hand at all paces, consequently the drill was smooth and steady. I fully recognise the difficulties under which the Regiment has laboured in the past, young soldiers on partly trained remounts, constant changes in personnel due to fluctuating conditions of service, disbandments of some units and amalgamation of others. All the more, therefore, I congratulate all ranks on the manner in which these difficulties have been overcome, and the state of

Taken during Lord Rawlinson's stay at Lucknow, November, 1923.

Top Row.—Capt. J. McConnell, Lt. E. Collins, Lt. E. Wadham, 2/Lt. W. J. D. G. Johnston, Lt. R. N. Fawcett, 2/Lt. A. B. Sullivan,
Second Row.—Capt. J. C. Biggs, M.C., Lt. A. E. Byard, Lt. J. N. Bailey, Capt. C. Nicholson, Lt. F. G. C. Noakes, Capt. A. C. Macintyre, Capt. A. W. M. S. Pilkington, M.C.
Front Row.—Capt. J. B. Browne, A.D.C. to C.-in-C., Lt.-Col. H. C. L. Howard, C.M.G., D.S.O., Gen. the Lord Rawlinson, G.C.B., K.C.S.I., G.C.V.O, K.C.M.C., C.-in-C. in India, Maj. H. A. Cooper, Maj. T. L. Horn, M.C, A.D.C. to C.-in-C.

efficiency which they have now reached; a state which augurs well for the future of this fine regiment."

In the spring of 1923 Lieut.-Colonel Brooke proceeded to Weedon to be Chief Instructor at the Equitation School. Captain Davies proceeded home for employment at the Cavalry Depôt at Canterbury, but after a short period there he was posted as Adjutant to the Officers' Training Corps at Cambridge.

At the end of October, 1923, H.E. the Viceroy, the Earl of Reading, G.C.B., G.C.V.O., visited Lucknow. He arrived on the 29th October, when the Regiment lined the road from Hazratgunj to the Durbar at the Kaiser-Bagh.

At the end of November H.E. the Commander-in-Chief, General the Lord Rawlinson, G.C.B., G.C.S.I., G.C.V.O., K.C.M.G., arrived at Lucknow and stayed for a week with the Commanding Officer. On one morning H.E. walked round the lines, inspected the horses, men and stables, visited the institutes, etc.

A review was held on the 24th November by H.E. the C.-in-C. in which the Regiment took part.

A camp on the same lines as the previous year was held at Banthra (about 12 miles from Lucknow); squadrons each going out for ten days, and the Regiment from the 6th to the 20th December.

During the latter part of the summer orders had been received that the Regiment would leave India during the next few months. This move was caused by the recommendations of the Inchcape Committee, as a result of which the number of Cavalry Regiments in India was reduced from eight to six.

It was not until late in the winter that it was known definitely that the Regiment would proceed to Cairo to relieve the 9th Lancers at Abbassia at the end of the trooping season.

On the 1st and 2nd February, 1924, the Regiment was inspected by Major-General C. A. C. Godwin, C.M.G., D.S.O., Major-General of Cavalry.

1924

After this inspection the horses of the Regiment were broken up, and the bulk sent to the Remount Depôts at Babugarh and Saharanpur, and a certain number sent to other regiments. The reason for this was that the 4th Hussars, who were ordered to take the place of the Regiment at Lucknow, brought their own horses, Muttra being done away with as a Cavalry station. The horses of the Regiment therefore became surplus.

On the 25th February a memorial tablet to seven N.C.O.'s and men who died at Lucknow 1920-24, and to four officers, 51 N.C.O.'s and men, three women and nine children who died at Lucknow 1890-96, was unveiled by Colonel A. E. McNamara, C.M.G., D.S.O., Commanding 19th Indian Infantry Brigade. As no memorial to those who died during the previous tour of the Regiment at Lucknow was in existence, it was decided to include them in this memorial, erected in the Garrison Church.

A comparison of the numbers of deaths during these different periods is instructive, and shows great improvement has been made in medical science during recent years. In the old days in India the great scourge was enteric, but out of the seven deaths during the recent tour only one could be attributed in any way to enteric fever, the others being from heat stroke, accidents, pneumonia and cholera. The most noteworthy fact was that not a single man was left behind sick when the Regiment left India.

On the morning of the 3rd March the 4th Hussars arrived at Lucknow and took over the barracks, and on the same day the Regiment left in two trains for Deolali, where it remained for two days and then proceeded to Bombay and embarked on H.T. "Braemar Castle."

On the departure of the Regiment, the following farewell order from the G.O.C. U.P. District was published:—

> "I wish to express to all ranks of the 16th/5th Lancers my sincere regret at their departure from the United Provinces District, in which the Regiment has at all times set a high standard of all round efficiency in work and in sport. The Regiment will be much missed. I wish all in the Regiment the best of luck, and I hope that it may be my good fortune to serve with the Regiment again.
> "Sd., C. J. DEVERELL, Major-General."

A private letter to the Commanding Officer from General Deverell reads as follows:—

> "Your Regiment will be a great loss to India, and the United Provinces District in particular. It has been a great pleasure to have had the Regiment in my District, and I shall always be greatly interested in its future doings."

Extracts from other letters received by the Commanding Officer at various times may be of interest, and some of them are as follows:—

From Colonel-Comdt. L. C. Jones, who was our Brigade Commander at Lucknow, and who also commanded the cavalry at Delhi during the visit of H.R.H. the Prince of Wales:—

> "Delhi, 21-2-22.
> "Dear Howard,—Before we leave, I should like to tell you that your Regiment has made an excellent impression here. Their turn out and horsemanship was all that could be desired.—Yours sincerely,
> "Sd., L. C. JONES."

From H.E. Sir S. Harcourt Butler, G.C.I.E., K.C.S.I., Governor of the United Provinces, who left in December, 1922, to take up the appointment of Governor of Burma:—

> "I think that one of my greatest griefs in leaving Lucknow has been leaving all my kind friends in the 16th. I never met a nicer Regiment, and I do hope that we may meet again. I shall never forget your kind thought in sending the band to the station to play me off.
> "I won't say good-bye. It is au revoir, I am sure, and thank you ever so much."

From General Sir Havelock Hudson, K.C.B., K.C.I.E., who was G.O.C.-in-C., Eastern Command, during the first three years of the Regiment's stay at Lucknow, and who wrote on relinquishing his command in November, 1923:—

> "5-11-23.
> "It has always been a great pride and pleasure to me to have your Regiment in my command. They are all 'triers,' and I was always sure of a real welcome whenever I came to see you. With all good wishes for all good luck to you and your fine command."

All ranks were very sorry to leave Lucknow, where they made many friends, but as the move was made just before the hot weather the regrets were perhaps

THE REGIMENT'S WAR MEMORIAL
IN CANTERBURY CATHEDRAL.

not so great as they would have been had the move been made in the autumn.

The cavalry lines in Lucknow had not been modernised, and were exactly the same as when the Regiment was there in the early nineties; no electric light or fans had been installed, and each year it was said that it was going to be done the following year, but when the following year came the situation was still the same.

After the continual moves in 1919 and 1920 it was a great advantage to be settled somewhere for a few years, as it then became possible for training to be carried on without interruption and for the Regiment to be brought to a state of efficiency and fitness for active service.

At the same time, owing to the need for economy, in India there were no big manœuvres or training camps during the period which the Regiment could take part in. It was not possible to keep up to date as regards the latest modern developments; but at the same time the stay at Lucknow, anyhow for the first three years, fulfilled the first object of the unit becoming efficient. After the war most units had to be almost completely built up again, but this fact was recognised by the Commander-in-Chief and the various commanders, who devoted all their efforts for the first period after the war towards bringing units of all arms up to a proper state of efficiency.

During the stay in Lucknow the Regiment took part in all the various sports, polo, racing, football, and shooting.

The polo is dealt with separately; the most noteworthy success in football was the Regiment winning the Lahore Trades Cup in February, 1924, beating the following units in successive rounds:—

1st round ...	2nd Battalion	The Devonshire Regt. ...	1—0.
2nd round ...	2nd ,,	K.O.Y.L.I.	2—1.
Semi-final ...	1st ,,	Black Watch	2—0.
Final ...	2nd ,,	Notts & Derbyshire Regt.	1—0.

The Regiment arrived at Suez on the 19th March, and proceeded to Cairo on the 20th, taking over the new cavalry barracks at Abbassia from the 9th Lancers. Once again the Regiment found that it was not taking over a regiment of horses (this was owing to the 9th Lancers proceeding to Palestine and taking their horses with them). The Regiment was horsed by postings from three other cavalry regiments, the 3rd Hussars, 9th Lancers, and 15th/19th Hussars; these were old horses which had taken part in the war, and were of an average age of nearly 14 years. As they probably had been in many different units, and also never properly trained when they were sent out during the war, they were not as a whole a highly trained regiment of horses.

About 500 horses, all Walers, had been received in January from Australia, and the Regiment was issued with 105 of these. During the summer the principal training carried out was the training of these remounts and the improvement, as far as it could be done, of the older horses.

On June 7th, 1924, a Regimental War Memorial was unveiled at Canterbury Cathedral, where there were already two others, one to the officers and men of the Regiment who died during the Sikh Wars and the other to those who fell in the Boer War in South Africa.

A short service was conducted by the Dean of Canterbury in the presence of many of the officers, N.C.O.'s and men of the Regiment, in the course of which the Memorial was unveiled by Lieut.-General Sir J. M. Babington, K.C.B., K.C.M.G.

The summer of 1924 was uneventful in Egypt, but all the time the intrigues of Zaghloul Pasha and his Government against the British Authority were going on. The culmination of this was the assassination of the Sirdar, who died on the 20th November from wounds received the day previous.

On the 22nd November the Regiment took part in the funeral of H.E. Major-General Sir Lee O. FitzM. Stack, G.B.E., C.M.G., Governor General of the Sudan and Sirdar of the Egyptian Army, lining the road between the north and south Roda Island Canal Bridges, between Cairo and Old Cairo. At about 10 a.m., before the procession had passed, the Commanding Officer was informed by a Staff Officer that the Regiment was not to return to Abbassia after the funeral, but to go to the barracks of the 2nd Battalion the Duke of Wellington's Regiment, water and feed the horses, and await orders to escort H.E. the High Commissioner, Field-Marshal the Viscount Allenby, G.C.B., G.C.M.G., Colonel of the Regiment, later in the day. The Regiment reached Kasr-el-Nil Barracks at about 1 p.m., and was later ordered to be ready to move at 3.30 p.m. It was not until a little later that the Commanding Officer received the following letter :—

"The Residency, Cairo;
"22nd Nov., 1924.

"Dear Colonel,—Will you very kindly parade your Regiment in front of the Residency at 4.30 p.m. this afternoon—to escort H.E. the High Commissioner to the office of the Prime Minister.

"Yours sincerely,
"Colin Hindley, Major, A.D.C."

At 4.30 p.m. the Regiment was formed up outside the gates opposite the Residency, but there was a quarter of an hour's delay, and at 4.45 p.m. H.E. the High Commissioner, accompanied by Mr. Clark-Kerr, the Counsellor, and an A.D.C., drove out in a motor car. The procession, moving at a trot, proceeded to the offices of the Prime Minister, opposite the Houses of Parliament, where His Excellency got out and went in to interview Zaghloul Pasha.

The interview was short, and there was just time to re-form the escort when His Excellency came out and was escorted back to the Residency. On arrival at the Residency the Commanding Officer was ordered to go in and see H.E. the High Commissioner, who gave him orders to communicate his remarks to the Regiment; the gist of these remarks was published as a Regimental Order as follows :—

"H.E. Field-Marshal the Viscount Allenby, G.C.B., G.C.M.G., Colonel, 16th/5th Lancers, has ordered the Commanding Officer to inform all ranks that he was extremely pleased with the turn out and bearing of the Regiment when escorting him to the Prime Minister's House, and also to express his pleasure at being escorted by his own Regiment on such a historical occasion.

"The Commanding Officer has much pleasure in communicating this message, and wishes to add his own congratulations and appreciation."

The Regiment did not reach barracks till late in the evening, having been out for about 13 hours.

The occasion was a sad one—the funeral of a distinguished soldier and public servant who was brutally murdered,—but it was felt by all ranks that the Regiment had taken part in a historical incident which without doubt did more to raise the prestige of Great Britain than anything that had taken place in Egypt during the last few years, and which also without doubt had an effect all over that part of the Eastern world which was ruled by Great Britain.

LIEUT.-COLONEL GEOFFREY F. H. BROOKE, D.S.O., M.C.

It was noteworthy the manner in which H.E. the High Commissioner was received going to and from the house of the Prime Minister; he was greeted with marked respect by all the Europeans (many of whom were foreigners) in the streets.

The following orders were published :—

> "The G.O.C. has expressed his complete satisfaction at the smart turn out and bearing of the troops at the funeral of H.E. the Sirdar on the 22nd instant, and at the smoothness with which the arrangements made were carried out."

The following extracts from a letter from His Excellency the High Commissioner to the G.O.C. with reference to the funeral of H.E. the Sirdar :—

> "I was much impressed with the arrangements in the Church and in the streets, the bearing of the troops and the dispositions at the cemetery. My views are shared by all sections of the British and foreign communities represented. The conduct of to-day's ceremony reflects the greatest credit on all concerned. Please communicate this to the troops under your command."

On the 26th and 27th November the Cavalry Brigade Horse Show was held at Abbassia. This show comprised a number of skill-at-arms, jumping, etc., events for other ranks. The Regiment was very successful, winning the following events :—

Men's Jumping.—1st, L/Cpl. Church.
Remounts.—1st, Trooper Ogden; 2nd, Trooper Bemmer.
Remount Ride.—1st, Team.
Men's Lance, sword and revolver.—1st, Trooper Ellwood; 2nd, Trooper Fletcher.
W.O.'s and Sergts. Dummy Thrusting, sword.—1st, S.S.M.R.I. Fuller, M.M.
Men's Dummy Thrusting, sword.—1st, Trooper Fletcher; 2nd, Trooper Read.
Champion Man-at-Arms.—1st, S.S.M.R.I. Fuller, M.M.
Dummy Thrusting, lance.—3rd, R.S.M. Riddiford.

At the end of November Lieut.-General Sir J. M. Babington, K.C.B., K.C.M.G., and Lady Babington, arrived to stay the winter in Cairo. He was heartily welcomed by everybody and took part in many events, riding at the head of the Regiment again after 29 years in a march through the streets of Cairo. He also played polo on remounts in training chukkas and played goal for the officers against the sergeants at football.

On the 11th January Bt.-Lieut.-Colonel G. F. H. Brooke, D.S.O., M.C., arrived from England to take over command from Lieut.-Colonel H. C. L. Howard, C.M.G., D.S.O., on the 18th January. Lieut.-Colonel Howard, on handing over command, published the following order :—

SPECIAL ORDERS.
16th/5th Lancers.
Saturday.   CAIRO.   January 17th, 1925.

On handing over command, I desire to tender to all ranks my appreciation of their work, and my thanks for the splendid way in which I have been supported.

I am confident that the present excellent spirit and discipline, both in work and play, and your fine reputation, will be maintained.

I shall always be interested to hear of your doings, and to see anyone belonging to the Regiment.

I wish Lieut.-Colonel Brooke and the Regiment the best of luck in the future.

          Sd., H. C. L. HOWARD, Lieut.-Col.,
                       Commanding 16th/5th Lancers.

APPENDIX TO CHAPTER XLIV.

POLO.

The question as regards ponies on the arrival of the Regiment in India was a difficult one, and practically all the best tournament ponies were pre-war and consequently on the old side. During the war, naturally, very few ponies had been made.

The Regiment, like most others, had very few players with any experience. The cost of these tournament ponies was very high, and if they had been bought it would have meant that by the time a team was really got going the ponies would be too old. As many old beginners' ponies as could be found were bought, but they were not very plentiful. A number of green ponies were bought and trained, but here again there were few people available with sufficient experience to train them.

However, the Polo Club was started again and a stud of ponies got together, either old beginners' ponies or green ones.

By the time the Regiment left India in 1924 a fair number of very good ponies had been trained and the best were taken on to Egypt.

The Club was wound up early in 1924, and on balancing the accounts it was found that the total loss in capital was only £80; this result, considering that the club had to be wound up at an unsatisfactory time, i.e., before some of the young ponies had been fully made, was very satisfactory.

For the smaller tournaments which took place in various places before Christmas the policy was to try to make up as many teams as possible, so as to give the young players a chance of gaining tournament experience.

In November, 1922, the Regiment won the first tournament since arrival in India, this being the Royal Dragoons' Cup in the Lucknow Autumn Handicap.

At Christmas, 1922, a team went to Calcutta. This team consisted of Captains Pilkington and Moubray and Lieut.-Colonels Brooke and Howard. In the Ezra Handicap Tournament this team was beaten in the third round by the Queen's Bays (receiving four goals) by six goals to five.

In the I.P.A. Championship, in which were seven entries, the Regiment beat the 4th Dragoons in the first round by nine goals to two, and the Queen's Bays in the semi-finals by six goals to four. In the final the Regiment was beaten by the Viceroy's Staff by three goals to one, after a very good game; the Viceroy's Staff had beaten the "Tigers," consisting of three Patiala players with a handicap of nine each, and Count de Madre in the semi-final by eight goals to four.

Top Row.—Lt. E. Wadham, Lt. G. G. Cox-Cox, Lt. R. N. Fawcett, Lt. J. N. Bailey, Lt. W. M. F. Bayliss, Capt. C. F. T. O'B. ffrench, Capt. C. Nicholson, Lt. H. R. Moon, Lt. A. C. Byard, Lt. F. G. C. Noakes, Lt. E. Collins, Lt. J. A. H. Jephson, Lt. G. J. R. Tomkin.
Second Row.—Capt. J. McConnell, Capt. G. C. Barker, Capt. R. Moubray, Capt. J. C. Miles, Major H. A. Cooper, Lt.-Col. H. C. L. Howard, C.M.G., D.S.O., Maj. T. L. Horn, M.C., Capt. R. G. R. Davies, M.C., Capt. J. B. Browne, Capt. A. C. Macintyre, Capt. A. W. M. S. Pilkington, M.C.
In Front.—2/Lt. A. B. Sullivan, 2/Lt. W. J. D. G. Johnston.

For the Cawnpore Tournament in January, 1923, the Regiment entered three teams, and the subalterns, consisting of Messrs. Wadham, Bailey, Tomkin and Cox-Cox, were beaten in the final by the 15th Lancers.

Later in January, 1923, the Regiment won the 15th Hussar Cup in the Lucknow Tournament.

At Meerut in the Inter-Regimental Tournament the Regiment was defeated by the P.A.V.O. in the first round. The team consisted of Mr. Bailey, Captains Moubray and Macintyre, and Lieut.-Colonel Brooke.

In the Subalterns' Cup the subalterns were defeated in the semi-final by Hodson's Horse.

In November, 1923, for the Royal Dragoons' Cup at Lucknow, two teams of the Regiment reached the final, one team consisting of Messrs. Bailey, Wadham and Tomkin, and Captain Biggs, and defeating the other team consisting of Captains Pilkington and Browne, Major Horn, and Lieut.-Colonel Howard after extra time. In this tournament the Commander-in-Chief, General the Lord Rawlinson, G.C.B., G.C.S.I., G.C.V.O., K.C.M.G., brought his team to play, but they were beaten by the eventual winners.

At Christmas two teams went to Calcutta, one entering for the I.P.A. Championship and both for the Ezra Handicap Tournament. The team was defeated in the I.P.A. in the first round by the Viceroy's Staff, who eventually won the tournament. This team consisted of Captains Biggs and Pilkington, Mr. Bailey and Lieut.-Colonel Howard. The other team, consisting of Messrs. Cox-Cox and Tomkin, Captain Nicholson and Major Horn, won the Ezra Cup.

In January, 1924, the Regiment won the Cawnpore Tournament, the team consisting of Messrs. Bailey and Johnston, Captains Pilkington and Browne.

For the 15th Hussar Cup in January at Lucknow, the Regimental team, consisting of Messrs. Bailey, Tomkin, Cox-Cox, and Lieut.-Colonel Howard, were beaten in the final by the 4th Hussars. Two extra chukkas had to be played, and it was not until just at the end of the second that the 4th Hussars got away and scored a goal; our team had at least ten shots at the 4th Hussars' goal, but without any success.

This ended the Polo in India as far as the Regiment was concerned.

From a beginning of practically nothing the polo ponies had been gradually improving, and the result of the past season was—three tournaments won and the team just beaten in the final of the 4th. As in these four tournaments the finalist teams composed 12 different players, the results can be considered as satisfactory, and if the Regiment had remained in India for a longer period there is no reason why the results should not have improved.

The first tournament after arrival in Egypt was the Alexandria Summer Tournament in June. This tournament consisted of an open cup, which was won by the R.H.A., and a Handicap Tournament in two divisions, "A" Division being won by the R.H.A., and the runners-up being the Regimental team consisting of Messrs. Wadham, Bailey, Captain Pilkington and Lieut.-Colonel Howard.

The Alexandria Autumn Handicap Tournament in September was won by the Regimental team, consisting of Mr. Tomkin, Captain Pilkington, Major Horn and Lieut.-Colonel Howard.

The first tournament in Cairo was that for the Yousory Cup; teams limited to a handicap of not more than eight. In this tournament two Regimental teams reached the final, Mr. Moon, Captain Pilkington, Major Horn and Lieut.-Colonel Howard defeating Mr. Jephson, Mr. Bailey, Mr. Tomkin and Mr. Cox-Cox in the final after extra time. This match was practically the same as that played at Lucknow the year previous, with three players different, and the result was just the reverse.

For the Public Schools Tournament in November, the Old Etonians, Mr. Tomkin, Captain Pilkington, Lieut.-Colonel Howard, with Major Curtis (K.R.R.), defeated the Old Harrovians in the final, 5—4 (the Old Etonians received four goals).

Top Row.—Lt. J. A. H. Jephson, Lt. G. J. R. Tomkin, 2/Lt. A. B. Sullivan, Lt. F. Collins, Capt. C. Nicholson, Lt. A. L. Leaf, Lt. F. G. C. Noakes, Lt. W. M. F. Bayliss.

Second Row.—Capt. J. C. Biggs, M.C., Lt. G. G. Cox-Cox, Lt. J. N. Bailey, Capt. J. McConnell, Lt. A. C. Byard, 2/Lt. W. J. G. D. Johnston, Lt. R. N. Fawcett, Lt. E. Wadham.

Front Row.—Capt. A. W. M. S. Pilkington, M.C., Capt. J. C. Miles, Major H. A. Cooper, Lt-Col. H. C. L. Howard, C.M.G., D.S.O. Major T. L. Horn, M.C., Capt. F. Thornton, Capt. J. B. Browne.

APPENDIX I.

The Officers of the Regiment.
Continued from Vol. I. 1911 to 1925.

I.—The Colonels.
II.—Roll of the Lieut.-Colonels Commanding.
III.—The Annual Army Lists, 1911 to 1925.
IV.—Nominal Roll of the Officers, 1911 to 1925.

Colonel of the Regiment.

BABINGTON, James Melville, K.C.B., K.C.M.G., Lieut.-General. (Continued from Vol. I.) Served in the war with Germany, 1914 to 1918, in command of the 23rd Division from September, 1914, to October, 1918, being promoted Major-General and restored to the Active List for Service in the Field. Served in Italy October, 1918, to January, 1919, in command of the XIV. Corps. Was present at the decisive Battle on the Piave when the Austrians were finally defeated, where his suggestion of the occupation of the Island Grave di Papadopoli, carried out by troops under his command, materially contributed to the victory. Commanded the British Army in Italy from January, 1919, until demobilisation in March, 1919. Lieut.-General 1919. Eight times mentioned in despatches. K.C.B., K.C.M.G., Commander Legion of Honour and Croix de Guerre (France), Military Order of Savoy 1st Class and Croce di Guerra (Italy), 1914 Star, War Medal and Victory Medal.

Lieut.-Colonels Commanding.

GOUGH, Sir Hubert de La Poer, Lieut.-General, G.C.M.G., K.C.B., K.C.V.O.; Lieut.-Colonel Commanding Regiment, 1906—1911. (Continued from Vol. 1., p. 253.) Commanding 3rd Cavalry Brigade in Ireland at the outbreak of the war with Germany in August, 1914. Served in France and Flanders, August, 1914, to April, 1918. Commanded 3rd Cavalry Brigade at the Battles of Mons and Le Cateau and the subsequent Retreat. Commanded 2nd Cavalry Division, September, 1914, to April, 1915 Present at the Battles of the Marne and Aisne and the capture of Mont des Cats. Commanded 7th Infantry Division, April, 1915, to August, 1915. Present at the Battle of Festubert, May 17th, where his division broke the German lines. Commanded 1st Army Corps, August, 1915, to April, 1916. Present at the Battle of Loos, September, 1915. Commanded the 5th Army, April, 1916, to April, 1918. With 5th Army at first Battle of the Somme, July 1st to November 18th, 1916, the third Battle of Ypres, July 7th, 1917, and the Battle of Cambrai, November 20th. Commanded the 5th Army at the second Battle of the Somme, March and April, 1918. Promoted firstly Major-General and secondly Lieut.-General, for Distinguished Service in the Field.

Ten times mentioned in despatches, C.B. 1914, K.C.B. 1915, K.C.V.O. 1917, G.C.M.G. May, 1919; 1914 Star with Bar, War Medal, Victory Medal with Palm, French Croix de Guerre, Belgian Croix de Guerre and Order of Leopold 2nd Class, White Eagle with Swords, Order of the Sword 1st Class (Sweden).

MacEWEN, Maurice Lilburn, C.B., Brigadier-General; Lieut.-Colonel commanding Regiment, 1910 to 1914. (Continued from Vol. I., p. 253.) Served in command in the war with Germany, 1914. Present at the Battles of Mons and Le Cateau, where he was severely wounded, being incapacitated for further service in the field. Mentioned in despatches, Legion of Honour, 1914 Star and Clasp, War Medal, Victory Medal.

Employed during the remainder of the war in command of three several Brigades. While in command of the Thames and Medway Brigade at Chatham trained the detachments from the Battle and Cruiser Fleets and rehearsed operations for the landing at Zeebrugge. Retired pay 1918, with rank of Brigadier-General. Three times mentioned in despatches, C.B., Commander Legion of Honour (France), Cabalero Military Merit and of the Order of Isabella Catholica (Spain).

With regard to the operations at Zeebrugge the following extract from the Despatch, May 9th, 1918, of Vice-Admiral Keyes, commanding Dover Patrol shows the value of General MacEwen's services:—

"To Brigadier-General MacEwen and his staff at Chatham, who supervised the training of the officers and men from the Grand Fleet as if for the Royal Naval Division in France, is due much of the credit for the success, which resulted in great part from their whole-hearted co-operation."

ECCLES, Cuthbert, John, D.S.O.; Lieut.-Colonel commanding the Regiment, 1914 to 1918. Son of Major-General Cuthbert Eccles; born 1870. Gazetted Second Lieutenant 16th Lancers 1894, Lieutenant 1896, Captain 1899, Major 1909, Lieut.-Colonel to command vice MacEwen 1914. Served in France and Flanders in the war with Germany, 1914 to 31st December, 1917. Lieut.-Colonel Eccles was twice wounded, firstly in November, 1914, when he was severely wounded in the foot. Secondly on the 24th May, 1915, at the Sally Port at Ypres, when he was again severely wounded in the side and back. He rejoined October 1st the same year, but was again invalided to England in March, 1917. He rejoined in April, but he never fully recovered from the effects of the wounds, and in December he was placed on the sick list and was finally invalided out of the Service in December, 1918. He died on the 10th January, 1922. D.S.O., 1914 Star, War Medal, Victory Medal.

HARRIS-ST. JOHN, Charles Edward St. John, D.S.O.; Lieut.-Colonel commanding the Regiment, 1918 to 1921. Son of Charles Edward Harris-St. John of West Court, Finchampstead; born 1873. Gazetted Second Lieutenant 16th Lancers 1895, Lieutenant 1899, Captain and Adjutant 1902, Major 1910, Lieut.-Colonel to command vice Eccles, 1918. Served with the Regiment in the Boer War, South Africa, 1899 to 1902. D.S.O., Queen's Medal with five clasps, King's Medal with two clasps. Served in France with the Regiment February to April, 1915. Invalided home April, 1915. Served again in France as Assistant Military Secretary 5th Army July, 1916, to April, 1918, and 4th Army to May, 1918. Attached Staff 9th Corps May, 1918, to July, 1918, being present at the third Battle of the Aisne.

Mentioned in despatches. 1914 Star, War Medal, Victory Medal with Oakleaf. Holds also the Order of Military Merit of Spain. Commanded the Regiment in Syria and Palestine June, 1919, to June 20th, 1920. Retired on account of ill-health January, 1921.

HOWARD, Henry Cecil Lloyd; Lieut.-Colonel commanding the Regiment 1921 to 1925. Son of Colonel Henry R. Lloyd Howard, C.B., formerly Major 16th Lancers, of Wygfair St. Asaph, N. Wales. Born 1882. Gazetted Second Lieutenant 16th Lancers 1901, Lieutenant 1902, Adjutant 1906, Captain 1914, Bvt.-Major 1916, Major 1918, Bvt.-Lt.-Col. 1918, Lt.-Colonel to command vice Harris-St. John, retired, 1921. Colonel 1922. Passed Staff College 1911. On War Office Staff 1913 to 1914. Served in Boer War, South Africa, with the Regiment May, 1901, to May, 1902. Queen's Medal with four clasps. Served in war with Germany in France and Belgium 1914 to 1917, on Cavalry Corps Staff, and in Italy as G.S.O. 48th Division 1917 to 1918. Wounded November, 1919. Nine times mentioned in despatches, D.S.O. and bar for Conspicuous Gallantry at Messines; C.M.G. 1919, Croce di Guerra and Croix d' Officier Crown of Italy, 1914 Star, War Medal, Victory Medal.

A.A.G. G.H.Q. Great Britain February, 1919, G.S.O. 1st Cavalry Division Army of Rhine May to August, 1919, and to British Military Mission, Constantinople, August, 1919, to April, 1920. To command Regiment January, 1921, vice St. John, retired. Colonel 1922. To half-pay 1925. Asst.-Commandant R.M.C., Sandhurst, Sept., 1925.

BROOKE, Geoffry, F. H., D.S.O., M.C.; Lieut.-Colonel commanding the Regiment 1925. Son of John Monck Brooke, of Elm Green, co. Dublin, Ireland. Born 1884. Gazetted Second Lieutenant 16th Lancers 1903, Lieut.-Captain 1914, Brevet-Major 1917, Major 1920, Brevet-Lieut.-Colonel 1919, Lieut.-Colonel to command vice Howard to half-pay 1925. Served in France and Flanders through the war with Germany. Staff Captain 3rd Cavalry Brigade 1914, Brigade-Major 2nd Cavalry Brigade 1915, Brigade-Major Canadian Cavalry Brigade 1918. Commanded 16th Lancers March, 1918, to March, 1919, in the field, being in command during the severe fighting at Moreuil in front of Amiens at the close of the second Battle of the Somme.

Five times mentioned in despatches, Brevets of Major and Lieut.-Colonel, D.S.O. with clasp, M.C., French Croix de Guerre, 1914 Star, Victory Medal, and War Medal. Passed Staff College 1920, Chief Instructor Cavalry, Weedon, 1923.

LIST OF THE OFFICERS OF THE REGIMENT.

The following Rolls of the Officers have been compiled from the monthly Army Lists, and are not actual copies of them. Care has been taken to ensure accuracy as far as possible, but the official Lists issued during the war are not always correct as to dates and full Christian names. The dates after the names give the date of promotion to the rank then held, and are not repeated.

The full Christian names, where they can be ascertained, are given on first appointment to the Regiment.

The letters given after the names have the following meanings:—S., Staff; Y., Yeomanry; D., Depot; S.S., Signal Service; R.C., Reserve Regiment of Cavalry; M.G., employed with Machine Gun Corps; C.C., Divisional Cyclst Corps; T.C., employed with Tank Corps; F.C., serving under Air Ministry; C.O., serving under Colonial Office; F.O., serving under Foreign Office.

1911-12.

Colonel-in-Chief.
H.M. Alfonso XIII., King of Spain. K.G., G.C.V.O., Gen.

Colonel.
J. M. Babington, C.B., C.M.G., Hon. Maj.-Gen.

Lieut.-Colonel.
M. L. MacEwen   1910

Majors.
R. L. Macalpine-Leny
C. J. Eccles
C. L. K. Campbell
C. E. St.J. Harris-St. John, D.S.O., 1910

Captains.
C. F. Vanderbyl
A. Neave
G. E. Bellville
A. W. Macarthur-Onslow
F. E. Adams

Lieutenants.
W. J. Shannon
H. C. L. Howard
H. A. Reddie
G. D. Hall, S.
E. H. L. Beddington
G. F. H. Brooke, S.
J. Orr-Ewing, Y.
M. Graham, Adjt.
E. Copland-Griffiths
E. R. Nash
Lord Holmpatrick
J. L. Cheyne
T. L. Horn
H. L. Evans
R. A. J. Beech

Second-Lieutenants.
C. E. H. Tempest-Hicks
M. Daffarn
Robert Lindsay Loyd   1911
David Ronald Cross
John George Walters Clark

SPECIAL RESERVE.

Second-Lieutenants.
R. B. Longridge
W. M. Macneill
M. A. Arbuthnot
J. R. Collins   1911

Quarter-Master.
C. J. Aris

1912-13.

Colonel-in-Chief.
H.M. Alfonso XIII., King of Spain, K.G., G.C.V.O., Gen.

Colonel.
J. M. Babington, C.B., C.M.G., Hon. Maj.-Gen.

Lieut.-Colonel.
M. L. MacEwen

Majors.
R. L. Macalpine-Leny
C. J. Eccles
C. L. K. Campbell
C. E. St.J. Harris-St. John, D.S.O.

Captains.
A. Neave
G. E. Bellville
A. W. Macarthur-Onslow
F. E. Adams

Lieutenants.
W. J. Shannon
H. C. L. Howard
G. D. Hall, S.
E. H. L. Beddington
G. F. H. Brooke, S.
J. Orr-Ewing, Y.
M. Graham, Y.
E. Copland-Griffiths
E. R. Nash
Lord Holmpatrick, Adjt.
J. L. Cheyne
T. L. Horn
H. L. Evans D.
R. A. J. Beech
C. E. H. Tempest-Hicks

Second-Lieutenants.
R. L. Loyd
D. R. Cross
Reginald George Reyonalds Davies, 1911
John George Walters Clark

SPECIAL RESERVE.

Second-Lieutenants.
R. B. Longridge
W. M. Macneill
M. A. Arbuthnot
J. R. Collins
E. H. Barclay

Quarter-Master.
C. J. Aris

1913-14.

Colonel-in-Chief.
H.M. Alfonso XIII., King of Spain, K.G., G.C.V.O., Gen.

Colonel.
J. M. Babington, C.B., C.M.G., Hon. Maj.-Gen.

Lieut.-Colonel.
M. L. MacEwen

Majors.
R. L. Macalpine-Leny
C. J. Eccles
C. L. K. Campbell
C. E. St.J. Harris-St. John, D.S.O.

Captains.
A. Neave
G. E. Bellville
F. E. Adams
W. J. Shannon, Adjt.
H. C. L. Howard
E H. L Beddington, S.
Bertram Douglas Macculloch

Lieutenants.
G. F. H. Brooke, S.
M. Graham, Y.
E. Copland-Griffiths, Y.
E. R. Nash
J. L. Cheyne
T. L. Horn
H. L. Evans
R. A. J. Beech
C. E. H. Tempest-Hicks
R. L. Loyd, S.S.
D. R. Cross
R. G. R. Davies
J. G. W. Clark

Second-Lieutenants.
John Eric Russell Allen
Lionel Chas. Ramsbottom-Isherwood
Richard Rees Davies   1913
Frank Thornton
Robert Moubray
James Bernard Browne
Terence Donough O'Brien
Richard Nigel Percival-Maxwell
George Douglas Callander
Oswald Ernold Mosley
C. J. Aris. D.S.O.
William Warburton Hayes

Attached.
A. C. Stewart
James Gourlie

SPECIAL RESERVE.

Captains.
G Hutton-Riddell, M.V.O.
C. M. Dixon

Lieutenants.
Lord Holmpatrick
A. E. K. Henderson, D.
N. W. R. King

Second-Lieutenants.
R. B. Longridge
M. A. Arbuthnot
A. P. Mead, on prob.
C. V. Carlisle, on prob.
Wm. Meville Codrington, on prob.
O. C. Skinner, on prob.
C. M. Patrick, on prob.
A. C. M. Pym, on prob.
R. G. U. Arbuthnot, on prob.
Lord Wodehouse, on prob.
H. P. Conway, on prob.
F. de F. England, on prob.

List of Officers.

1914-15.

Colonel-in-Chief.
H.M. Alfonso XIII., King of Spain, K.G., G.C.V.O., Gen.

Colonel.
J. M. Babington, C.B., C.M.G., Hon. Maj.-Gen. (temp. Maj.-Gen.)

Lieut.-Colonels.
M. L. MacEwen, Col., 1914
C. J. Eccles, D.S.O. ,,

Majors.
R. L. Macalpine-Leny, S.
C. L. K. Campbell (temp. Lt.-Col.) (Bt.-Lt.-Col.) (temp. Brig.-Gen.)
C. E. St.J. Harris-St. John, D.S.O.
A. Neave 1914
W. J. Shannon, Adjt. 1915

Captains.
G. E. Bellville
H. C. L. Howard, S. 1914
E. H. L. Beddington, S. 1914
B. D. Macculloch ,,
G. F. H. Brooke ,,
M. Graham ,,
E. Copland-Griffiths ,,
E. R. Nash ,,
J. L. Cheyne ,,
T. L. Horn 1915
H. L. Evans ,,

Lieutenants.
R. A. J. Beech
C. E. H. Tempest-Hicks, S.S.
R. L. Loyd, S.S.
D. R. Cross
R. G. R. Davies 1914
J. G. W. Clark ,,
C. J. Aris, D.S.O., S. ,,
E. G. Case, R. of O. ,,
John E. R. Allen ,,
L. C. Ramsbottom-Isherwood, D. ,,
R. R. Davies 1915
W. M. Codrington, D. ,,

Second-Lieutenants.
Frank Thornton, R.C. 1914
Lord Wodehouse, S. ,,
R. Moubray ,,
J. B. Browne ,,
T. D. O'Brien ,,
R. N. Percival-Maxwell ,,
G. D. Callander ,,
C. V. Carlisle ,,
R. G. U. Arbuthnot ,,
O. E. Mosley ,,
W. W. Hayes ,,
H. C Archer ,,
Frederick Pargeter ,,
Frank Sibley Allen Sibley, R.C. ,,
W M. Reeves, R.C. ,,
H. F. Boles ,,
Lord Killeen ,,
Ralph Grandolph Hornyold, S. ,,
George C. Barker, R.C. 1915
G. T. Brooke ,,
John Prosser ,,

R. G. U. Arbuthnot 1915
John Stephen Stephen, R.C. ,,
John Clement Ryan (temp.) ,,
Lord Holmpatrick, Adjt., Capt. Spec. Res. 1914

Attached.
A. C. Stewart, Maj.
J. Gourlie, Capt.
W A. K. Fraser, Capt.
J. Leslie, Lieut.
G. H. Rhodes (temp. Lt.)
John O. MacBrayne (temp. 2nd-Lt.) 1914
J. J. Ryan (temp. 2nd-Lt.) 1914

SPECIAL RESERVE.

Captains.
G. Hutton-Riddell, M.V.O. 1914
C. M. Dixon ,,
Lord Holmpatrick, Adjt. 1914

Lieutenants.
R. B. Longridge R.C.
M. A. Arbuthnot, S. 1914
A. E. K. Henderson, D. ,,
N. W. R. King, D. ,,

Second-Lieutenants.
A. P. Mead, R.C. 1914
C V. Carlisle ,,
O. C. Skinner, R.C. ,,
C. M. Patrick, R.C. ,,
A. C. M. Pym, S. ,,
H. P. Conway, R.C. ,,
F. de F. England (on prob.), R.C. ,,
F. St. L. Greer (on prob.) 1915
G. T. Brooke ,,
D. G. Greig (on prob.), R.C. ,,

Quarter-Master.
J McConnell, Hon. Lt. 1914

1915-16.

Colonel-in-Chief.
H.M. Alfonso XIII., King of Spain, K.G., G.C.V.O., Gen.

Colonel.
J. M. Babington, C.B., C.M.G., Hon. Maj.-Gen. (temp. Maj.-Gen.)

Lieut.-Colonels.
M. L. MacEwen
C. J. Eccles, D.S.O.

Majors.
R. L. Macalpine-Leny, S.
C. L. K. Campbell (temp. Lt.-Col.), Bt.-Lt.-Col. (temp. Brig.-Gen.)
C. E. St.J. Harris-St. John, D.S.O., S.
W. J. Shannon, D.S.O.

Captains.
G E. Bellville
H. C. L. Howard, Bt.-Maj.
E. H. L. Beddington, Bt.-Maj.
G F. H. Brooke, M.C.
M. Graham, S.
E. Copland-Griffiths
J. L. Cheyne
T. L. Horn
H. L. Evans (temp. Maj.)
C. E. H. Tempest-Hicks, M.C. 1916

Lieutenants.
R. L. Loyd, M.C., S.S.
R. G. R. Davies, M.G.
J. G. W. Clark, S.
C. J. Aris, D.S.O., S.
J. E. R. Allen
L. C. Ramsbottom-Isherwood, S.
R. R. Davies
W. M. Codrington, S.S.
F. Thornton 1915
Lord Wodehouse, S. ,,
R. Moubray ,,
J. B. Browne 1916
R N. Percival-Maxwell 1916
G. D. Callander ,,
A. P. Mead ,,
C. V. Carlisle ,,
O. E. Mosley ,,
W. W. Hayes, R.C. ,,

Second-Lieutenants.
F. de F. England
H. C. Archer
F. Pargeter
F. S. A. Sibley (temp. Lieut.)
R. G. Hornyold (temp.) S.
G C. Barker, R.C.
G. T. Brooke
J. Prosser
R. G. U. Arbuthnot, M.G.
J. S. Stephen
J. C. Ryan (temp.)
D. G. Greig
Eric Seymour Thewlis Johnson 1916
Arthur William Milborne-Swinnerton-Pilkington, R.C. 1916
C. M. Patrick ,,

Claude Nicholson, R.C. 1916
Gordon Gerard Cox-Cox, R.C. 1916
Francis Noakes ,,
Hon. Edward Wodehouse, R.C. 1916
Stuart Maxwell Deans, R.C. ,,
Geoffrey Robert Martin-Holland, R.C. 1916
Lord Holmpatrick, M.C. Adjt., Capt. Spec. Res.

Attached.
J. Gourlie, Capt.
W. A. K. Fraser, M.C., Capt.
J. H. Robertson (temp. Lieut.) 1914
J. J. Ryan (temp. 2nd-Lieut.) ,,
C. M. Lazenby (temp. 2nd-Lieut.) 1915

SPECIAL RESERVE.

Captains.
G. Hutton-Riddell, M.V.O., S.
C. M. Dixon
Lord Holmpatrick, M.C., Adjt.

Lieutenants.
R. B. Longridge, S.
M. A. Arbuthnot, S.
A. E. K. Henderson, D.
A. P. Mead 1916
C. V. Carlisle ,,
O. C. Skinner, R.C. ,,
A. C. M. Pym, S. ,,

Second-Lieutenants.
H. P. Conway, C.C.
F. de F. England
G. T. Brooke
D. G. Greig

Quarter-Master.
J. McConnell, Hon. Lt.

List of Officers.

1916-17.

Colonel-in-Chief.
H.M. Alfonso XIII., King of Spain, K.G., G.C.V.O., Gen.

Colonel.
Sir J. M. Babington, K.C.M.G., C.B., Maj.-Gen., S.

Lieut.-Colonel.
C. J. Eccles, D.S.O.

Majors.
R. L. Macalpine-Leny
C. L. K. Campbell (temp. Lt.-Col.), Bt.-Col. (temp. Brig.-Gen.)
C. E. St.J. Harris-St. John, D.S.O.
W J. Shannon, D.S.O., S.

Captains.
G. E. Bellville
H. C. L. Howard, D.S.O., Bt.-Maj.
E. H. L. Beddington, D.S.O., M.C., Bt.-Maj.
G. F. H. Brooke, D.S.O., M.C.
M. Graham, S.
E. Copland-Griffiths
J. L. Cheyne, M.C.
T L. Horn
H. L. Evans
C. E. H. Tempest-Hicks, M.C.

Lieutenants.
R. L. Loyd, M.C., S.S.
R. G. R. Davies, M.G.
J. G. W. Clark, M.C., S.
C. J. Aris, D.S.O.
J. E. R. Allen (Act. Capt.)
L. C. Ramsbottom-Isherwood, S.
R. R. Davies, Adjt., R.C. 1917
W. M. Codrington, S.S.
F. Thornton
Lord Wodehouse, S.
R. Moubray
J. B. Browne
R. N. Percival-Maxwell
G. D. Callender
A. P. Mead, M.G.
C. V. Carlisle
O. E. Mosley (Empld. Comd. Depôt)
W. W. Haves
F. de F. England 1917
H. C. Archer ,,

Second-Lieutenants.
F. Pargeter
F. S. A. Sibley (temp. Lieut.)
R. G. Hornyold (temp.), S.
G. C. Barker
G. T. Brooke
J. Prosser
R. G. U. Arbuthnot, M.G.
J. S. Stephen
C. M. Patrick
J. C. Ryan (temp.), R.C.
D. G. Greig
E. S. T. Johnson
A. W. Milborne-Swinnerton-Pilkington
C. Nicholson

G. G. Cox-Cox
F. Noakes
Hon. E. Wodehouse
S. M. Deans
G. R. Martin-Holland
Robert Christmas Hollis, M.G. 1916
Fred Sparkes, C.O. ,,
George Albert Collyer ,,
Guy Campbell Russell, R.C. 1917
Gerald Archibald Drabble R.C. 1917
Sir John Watson, Bt., R.C. ,,
Richard Carr ,,

Attached.
W. A. K. Fraser, M.C., Capt.
J. H. Robertson, M.C., Lieut.
J. J. Ryan (temp. 2nd-Lieut.)
C. M. Lazenby (temp. 2nd-Lieut.)
A. C. G. Sparrow (temp. 2nd-Lieut.) 1916
T. F. Arnott (temp. 2nd-Lieut.) 1917

Special Reserve.

Captains.
G. Hutton-Riddell, M.V.O., R.C.
Lord Holmpatrick, M.C.

Lieutenants.
R. B Longridge. R.C.
M. A. Arbuthnot, M.C., S.
A E. K. Henderson, Empld. Comd. Depôt
A. P. Mead, M.G. 1916
C. V. Carlisle ,,
O. C. Skinner, S. ,,
A. C. M. Pym, S. ,,
F de F. England, R.C. 1917
E. M. Murray ,,
G. T. Brooke ,,
D G. Greig ,,

Second-Lieutenant.
H. P. Conway, R.C. (attd. Oxf. Yeo.) 1914

Quarter-Master.
J. McConnell, Hon. Capt. 1917

1917-18.

Colonel-in-Chief.
H.M. Alfonso XIII., King of Spain, K.G., G.C.V.O., Gen.

Colonel.
Sir J. M. Babington, K.C.M.G., C.B. (temp. Lt.-Gen.), S.

Lieut.-Colonel.
C J. Eccles, D.S.O.

Majors.
R L. Macalpine-Leny,
C L. K. Campbell (temp. Lt.-Col.), Bt.-Col. (temp. Brig.-Gen.)
C. E. St.J. Harris-St. John, D.S.O., R.C.
W. J. Shannon, D.S.O., t.c.
H. C. L. Howard, D.S.O. 1918

Captains.
G. E. Bellville (Offr. Cadet Bn.), S.
E. H. L. Beddington, D.S.O., M.C. (Bt.-Col.), S.
G. F. H. Brooke, D.S.O., M.C. (Bt.-Maj.)
M. Graham, D.S.O. (Bt.-Maj.), S.
J. L. Cheyne (Act.-Maj.)
T J. Horn, M.C.
H. L. Evans, M.C.
C. E. H. Tempest-Hicks, M.C.

Lieutenants.
R. L. Loyd, M.C., S.S.
R. G. R. Davies, M.G.
J. G. W. Clark, M.C., S.
C J. Aris, D.S.O., S.
J. E R. Allen (Act. Capt.)
L. C. Ramsbottom-Isherwood, S.
R. R. Davies, Adjt., R.C.
W. M. Codrington, S.S.
F. Thornton
Lord Wodehouse, M.C., S.
R. Moubray
J. B. Browne
R. N. Percival-Maxwell
G. D. Callander (Act. Capt. & Adjt.)
O. E. Mosley (Empld.) Min. of Munitions)
W. W. Haves
H. C. Archer, M.C. (Act.-Capt.)
F Pargeter, M.C. 1917
F. S. A. Sibley (Act. Capt.) (Offr. Cadet Bn.), 1917
R. G. Hornyold (temp.), S. 1917
G. C. Barker ,,
R. G. U. Arbuthnot, f.c. ,,
J. Prosser ,,
J. S. Stephen ,,
C. M. Patrick ,,
E. S. T. Johnson ,,
A. W. Milborne-Swinnerton-Pilkington, M.C. 1917
C. Nicholson 1918
G. G. Cox-Cox ,,

F. Noakes 1918
S. M. Deans ,,
R. C. Hollis, M.C., M.G. 1918
F Sparkes, C.O. ,,
G. A. Collyer ,,
G A. Drabble ,,

Second-Lieutenants.
Hon. E. Wodehouse
G. R. Martin-Holland
G. C. Russell, R.C.
Sir J. Watson, Bt., R.C.
R. Carr
James Arthur Macarthur-Onslow 1917
Julien James A. Miles ,,
E. Collins, R.C. 1918

Special Reserve.

Captains.
G. Hutton-Riddell, M.V.O., R.C.
Lord Holmpatrick, M.C.
E. M. Murray 1917

Lieutenants.
R. B. Longridge, f.c.
M. A. Arbuthnot, M.C., R.C.
A. E. K. Henderson, R.C.
A. P. Mead, M.C., M.G.
C. V. Carlisle
O. C. Skinner, f.c.
A. C. M. Pym, S.
F. de F. England, R.C.
G. T. Brooke
J. C. Ryan (attd. Res. Regt. 2nd K.E. Horse)
D. G. Greig
A. C. K. Lindsay-Stewart 1917

Second-Lieutenants.
H. P. Conway, R.C. (attd. Oxf. Yeo.)
O. H. Eustace-Duckett, R.C. 1918

Quarter-Master.
J. McConnell, Hon. Capt.

List of Officers.

1918-19.

Colonel-in-Chief.
H.M. Alfonso XIII., King of Spain, K.G., G.C.V.O., Gen.

Colonel.
Sir J. M. Babington, K.C.M.G., C.B., Hon. Lt.-Gen.

Lieut.-Colonel.
C. E. St.J. Harris-St. John, D.S.O. 1918

Majors.
R. L. Macalpine-Leny, D.S.O., Bt.-Lt.-Col. (Spec. Appt.)
W. J. Shannon, C.M.G., D.S.O., t.c.
H. C. L. Howard, C.M.G., D.S.O. (Bt.-Lt.-Col.), S.
E. H. L. Beddington, C.M.G., D.S.O., M.C. (Bt.-Lt.-Col.), S. 1918

Captains.
G. E. Bellville, S.
G. F. H. Brooke, D.S.O., M.C. (Bt.-Maj.)
M. Graham, D.S.O. (Bt.-Maj.), S.
J. L. Cheyne, M.C.
T. L. Horn, M.C.
H. L. Evans, M.C.

Lieutenants.
R. L. Loyd, O.B.E., M.C., S.S.
R. G. R. Davies, M.C., M.G.
J. C W. Clark, M.C.
C. J. Aris, D.S.O.
J. E. R. Allen (Act. Capt.)
L. C. Ramsbottom-Isherwood, S.
R. R. Davies, S.
W. M. Codrington
F. Thornton (Act. Capt.)
Lord Wodehouse, M.C., S.
R. Moubray
J. R. Browne
G. D. Callander (Act. Capt. & Adjt.)
W. W. Hayes
H. C. Archer, M.C.
E. Pargeter, M.C.
F. S. A. Sibley (Act. Capt.) (Offr. Cadet Bn.)
R. G. Hornyold (temp.)
G. C. Barker
C. M. Patrick
E. S. T. Johnson, M.C.
A. W. Milborne-Swinner-ton-Pilkington, M.C.
C. Nicholson
G. G. Cox-Cox
F. Noakes
S. M. Deans
R. C. Hollis, M.C., M.G.
F. Sparkes, C.O.
G. A. Collyer
G. C. Russell 1918
G. A. Drabble
J. J. A. Miles
J. A. Macarthur-Onslow 1919

Second-Lieutenants.
E. Collins
G. D. Callander, Lt. & Act.-Capt., Adjt. 1918
Richard Maurice Marter 1919
Alfred Lister Leaf ,,

SPECIAL RESERVE.
Captains.
G. Hutton-Riddell, M.V.O., R.C.
Lord Holmpatrick, D.S.O., M.C.
E. M. Murray

Lieutenants.
R. B. Longridge, f.c.
A. E. K. Henderson, R.C.
A. P. Mead, M.C., M.G.
C. V. Carlisle
O. C. Skinner, f.c.
A. C. M. Pym
F. de F. England
G. T. Brooke
J. C. Ryan
D. G. Greig
A C. K. Lindsay-Stewart

Second-Lieutenants.
O. H. Eustace-Duckett, R.C.
A. J. L. Hopkins 1919

Quarter-Master.
J. McConnell, Capt.

1919-20.

Colonel-in-Chief.
H.M. Alfonso XIII., King of Spain, K.G., G.C.V.O., Gen.

Colonel.
Sir J. M. Babington, K.C.B., K.C.M.G., Hon. Lt.-Gen.

Lieut.-Colonel.
C. E. St.J. Harris-St. John, D.S.O.

Majors.
W. J. Shannon, C.M.G., D.S.O.
H. C. L. Howard, C.M.G., D.S.O. (Bt.-Lt.-Col.), S.
G. F. H. Brooke, D.S.O., M.C., 1920 (Bt.-Lt.-Col.) 1919
M. Graham, D.S.O., 1920 (Bt.-Lt.-Col.), S. 1920

Captains.
J. L. Cheyne, M.C.
T. L. Horn, M.C. (Instr. Cav. Sch.)
H. L. Evans
R. G. R. Davies, M.C., S. 1919
J. G. W. Clark, M.C., Adjt. 1919
L. C. Ramsbottom-Isherwood ,,
F. Thornton ,,
Lord Wodehouse, M.C. 1920
R. Moubray ,,
J. B. Browne ,,
W. W. Hayes ,,

Lieutenants.
G. C. Barker
A. W. Milborne-Swinner-ton-Pilkington, M.C.
C. Nicholson
G. G. Cox-Cox
F. Noakes (Empld. Record Office)
S. M. Deans
J. A. Macarthur-Onslow
E. Collins 1919

Second-Lieutenants.
R. M. Marter
A. L. Leaf
Wm. Hubert Fawcett Brunskill 1919
Harold Rosslyn Moon 1920

SPECIAL RESERVE.
Lieutenant.
R. B. Longridge

Quarter-Master.
J. McConnell, Capt.

1920-21.

Colonel-in-Chief.
H.M. Alfonso XIII., King of Spain, K.G., G.C.V.O., Gen.

Colonel.
Sir J. M. Babington, K.C.B., K.C.M.G., Hon. Lt.-Gen.

Lieut.-Colonel.
H. C. L. Howard, C.M.G, D.S.O. 1921

Majors.
W. J. Shannon, C.M.G., D.S.O., t.c.
G. F. H. Brooke, D.S.O., M.C. (Bt.-Lt.-Col.)
M. Graham, D.S.O. (Bt.-Lt.-Col.), S.
J. L. Cheyne, M.C. 1921

Captains.
T L. Horn, M.C. (Instr. Cav. Sch.)
H. L. Evans, M.C., t.c.
R. G. R. Davies, M.C.
J. G. W. Clark, M.C.
L. C. Ramsbottom-Isherwood
F. Thornton, t.c.
R. Moubray
J. B. Browne
W. W. Hayes
G. C. Barker 1920
Alastair Campbell Macintyre ,,
Arthur Henry Talbot Chetwynd, O.B.E., M.C. 1921
Alec Clegg Smith, M.B.E., M.C. 1921
A. W. Milborne-Swinner-ton-Pilkington, M.C. 1921
C. Nicholson, Adjt. ,,

Lieutenants.
Hugh Allan Heber-Percy
G. G. Cox-Cox
H. F. Kendrick, M.C.
Arthur Charles Byard 1918
F. Noakes
S. M. Deans
J. A. Macarthur-Onslow
E. Collins
R. M. Marter 1921

Second-Lieutenants.
A. L. Leaf
W. H. F. Brunskill
H. R. Moon
Gerald Josselyn Royce Tomkin 1920
Edward Wadham 1921

Quarter-Master.
J. McConnell, Capt.

List of Officers.

1921-22.

16TH/5TH LANCERS.

Colonel-in-Chief.
H.M. Alfonso XIII., King of Spain, K.G., G.C.V.O., Gen. 1922

Colonels.
Sir J. M. Babington, K.C.B., K.C.M.G., Hon. Lt.-Gen.
Viscount Allenby, G.C.B., G.C.M.G., Col. L.G., Field-Marshal 1917

Lieut.-Colonel.
H. C. L. Howard, C.M.G., D.S.O.

Majors.
W. J. C. Shannon, C.M.G., D.S.O., t.c.
Henry Alexander Cooper 1919
G. F. H. Brooke, D.S.O., M.C. (Bt.-Lt.-Col.)
M Graham, D.S.O. (Bt.-Lt.-Col.)
J. L. Cheyne, M.C.

Captains.
T. L. Horn, M.C. (Instr. Cav. Sch.)
J. C. Miles 1917
R. G. R. Davies, M.C.
J. G. W. Clark, M.C.
F. Thornton, t.c.
R. Moubray
A. C. Macintyre
A. W. Milborne-Swinnerton-Pilkington, M.C.
C. Nicholson, Adjt.

Lieutenants.
Jervis Crosbie Biggs, M.C. 1917
James Nowell Bailey ,,
G. G. Cox-Cox
A. C. Byard
F. Noakes
E. Collins
Wm. Murray Forbes Bayliss 1919
R. M. Marter
A. L. Leaf 1921
H. R. Moon 1920
W. H. F. Brunskill 1921

Second-Lieutenants.
G. J. R. Tomkin
E. Wadham
J. A. H. Jephson 1921
Adam Burns Sullivan 1922
Walter John Duncan Goring Johnston ,,

MILITIA.
Captain.
J. M. Gordon-Dill 1919

16TH THE QUEEN'S LANCERS.
Captains.
H. L. Evans, M.C., t.c.

L. C. Ramsbottom-Isherwood
J. B. Browne
G. C. Barker
A. H. T. Chetwynd, O.B.E., M.C., f.o.
Conrad Fulke Thomand O'Brien ffrench 1920

1922-23.

Colonel-in-Chief.
H.M. Alfonso XIII., King of Spain, K.G., G.C.V.O., Gen.

Colonels.
Sir J. M. Babington, K.C.B., K.C.M.G., Hon. Lt.-Gen.
Viscount Allenby, G.C.B., G.C.M.G., Col. L.G., Field-Marshal, S.

Lieut.-Colonel.
H. C. L. Howard, C.M.G., D.S.O.

Majors.
H. A. Cooper
G. F. H. Brooke, D.S.O., M.C. (Spec. Appt.) (Bt.-Lt.-Col.)
J. L. Cheyne, M.C.
T. L. Horn, M.C. 1923

Captains.
J. C. Miles
R. G. R. Davies, M.C., S.
J. G. W. Clark, M.C., S.
F. Thornton
R. Moubray
J. B. Browne 1920
A. C. Macintyre
A. W. Milborne-Swinnerton-Pilkington, M.C.
C. Nicholson, Adjt.
C. F. T. O'B. ffrench 1922
J. C. Biggs, M.C. 1923

Lieutenants.
J. N. Bailey
G G. Cox-Cox
A. C. Byard
F. Noakes
E. Collins
W. M. F. Bayliss
A. L. Leaf
H. R. Moon
G. J. R. Tomkin 1922
E. Wadham 1923

Second-Lieutenants.
R. N. Fawcett
J. A. H. Jephson
Anthony Wm. Richard de Terrierès Mackeson
A. B. Sullivan
W. J. D. G. Johnston
Geoffrey Babington 1923

Quarter-Master.
J. McConnell, Capt.

MILITIA.
Captain.
J. M. Gordon-Dill

16TH THE QUEEN'S LANCERS.
Captain.
H. L. Evans, M.C.

1923-24.

Colonel-in-Chief.
H.M. Alfonso XIII., King of Spain, K.G., G.C.V.O., Gen.

Colonels.
Sir J. M. Babington, K.C.B., K.C.M.G., Hon. Lt.-Gen.
Viscount Allenby, G.C.B., G.C.M.G., Col. L.G., Field-Marshal, S.

Lieut.-Colonel.
H C. L. Howard, C.M.G., D.S.O.

Majors.
H. A. Cooper
G. F. H. Brooke, D.S.O., M.C. (Bt.-Lt.-Col.)
J. L. Cheyne, M.C.
T. L. Horn, M.C.

Captains.
J. C. Miles
R. G. R. Davies, M.C., S.
J. G. W. Clark, M.C., S.
F. Thornton
R. Moubray (Equitn. Sch.)
J. B. Browne
A. C. Macintyre
A. W. Milborne-Swinnerton-Pilkington, M.C.
C. Nicholson, Adjt.
C. F. T. O'B. ffrench
J. C. Biggs, M.C., C.O.

Lieutenants.
J N. Bailey
G G. Cox-Cox
A. C. Byard
F. Noakes (Garr. Adjt. & Qr.-Mr.)
E. Collins
W M. F. Bayliss
A. L. Leaf
H. R. Moon
G. J. R. Tomkin
E. Wadham
A. W. R. de T. Mackeson (attd. 17th/21st Lrs.) 1923
R. N. Fawcett ,,
J. A. H. Jephson ,,
A. B. Sullivan 1924
W. J. D. G. Johnston ,,

Second-Lieutenants.
G. Babington
Robert Macauley Fanshawe (attd. 17th/21st Lrs.) 1924
Raylton Dixon (attd. 12th Lrs.) 1924

Quarter-Master.
J. McConnell, Capt.

MILITIA.
Captain.
J. M. Gordon-Dill

INDEX LIST OF THE OFFICERS WHO JOINED THE REGIMENT AFTER 1910.

In this list the names are given alphabetically as far as the initial letter of the name is concerned. Subject to this the names are given in succession as they were first gazetted.

The date after the name is the date of the Army List in which the name first appears.

If an officer's name for any reason ceases to appear on the Roll of the Regiment and again he rejoins the name is given again under the date of rejoining.

A.
Allen, J. E. R., 1913-4.
Arbuthnot, R. G. U., 1913-4.
Archer, H. C., 1914-5.
Arnott, F. F., 1916-7.
Allenby, Viscount, 1921-2.

B.
Babington, G., 1922-3.
Barclay, E. H., 1912-3.
Browne, J. B., 1913-4.
Boles, H. F., 1914-5.
Barker, G. C., 1914-5.
Brooke, G. T. 1914-5.
Brunskill, W. H. F., 1919-20.
Byard, A. C., 1920-1.
Biggs, J. C., 1921-2.
Bayliss, W. M. F., 1921-2.
Bailey, J. N., 1921-2.

C.
Cross, D. R., 1911-2.
Clark, J. G. W., 1911-2.
Collins, J. R, 1911-2.
Callander, G. D., 1913-4.
Carlisle, C. V., 1913-4.
Codrington, W. M., 1913-4.
Conway, H. P., 1913-4.
Case, E. G., 1914-5.
Cox-Cox, G. G., 1915-6.
Collyer, G. A., 1916-7.
Collins, E., 1917-8.
Carr, R., 1916-7.
Chetwynd, A. H. T., 1920-1.
Cooper, H. A., 1921-2.

D.
Davies, R. G. R., 1911-2.
Davies, R. R., 1913-4.
Dixon, C. M., 1913-4.
Deans, S. M., 1915-6.
Drabble, G. A., 1916-7.
Dixon, R., 1923-4.

E.
England, F. de F., 1913-4.
Eustace-Duckett, O. H., 1917-8.
Evans, H. L., 1921-2.

F.
Fraser, W. A. K., 1914-5.
Ffrench, C. F. T. O'B., 1921-2.
Fawcett, R. N., 1922-3.
Fanshaw, R. M., 1923-4.

G.
Gourlie, J., 1913-4.
Greer, F. St. L., 1914-5.
Greig, D. G., 1914-5.
Gordon-Dill, J. M., 1921-2.

H.
Hayes, W. W., 1913-4.
Hulton-Riddell, G., 1913-4.
Holmpatrick, Lord, 1913-4.
Henderson, A. E. K., 1913-4.
Hornyold, R. G., 1916-7.
Hollis, R. C., 1916-7.
Hopkins, A. J. L., 1918-9.
Heber-Percy, H. A., 1920-1.

J.
Johnson, E. S. T., 1915-6.
Jephson, J. A. H., 1921-2.
Johnston, W. J. D. G., 1921-2.

K.
King, N. W. R., 1913-4.
Killeen, Lord, 1914-5.
Kendrick, H. F., 1920-1.

L.
Lloyd, R. L., 1911-2.
Leslie, J., 1914-5.
Lazenby, C. M., 1915-6.
Leaf, A. L., 1918-9.
Lindsay-Stewart, A. C. K., 1917-8.

M.
MacCulloch, B. D., 1913-4.
Moubray, R., 1913-4.
Mosley, O. E., 1913-4.
Mead, A. P., 1913-4.
MacBrayne, J. O., 1914-5.
McConnell, J., 1914-5.
Martin-Holland, G. R., 1915-6.
Murray, E. M., 1916-7.
Marter, R. M., 1918-9.
MacArthur-Onslow, J. A., 1917-8.
Miles, J. J., 1917-8.
Moon, H. R., 1919-20.
Macintyre, A. C., 1920-1.
Miles, J. C., 1921-2.
Mackeson, A. W. R. de F., 1922-3.

N.
Nicholson, C., 1915-6.
Noakes, F., 1915-6.

O.
O'Brien, T. D., 1913-4.

P.
Percival-Maxwell, R. N., 1913-4.
Patrick, C. M., 1913-4.
Pym, A. C. M., 1913-4.
Pargeter, F., 1914-5.
Prosser, J., 1914-5.

R.
Ramsbottom-Isherwood, L. C., 1913-4.
Reeves, W. N., 1914-5.
Ryan, J. C., 1914-5.
Rhodes, G. H., 1914-5.
Ryan, J. J., 1914-5.
Robertson, J. H., 1915-6.
Russell, G. C., 1916-7.

S.
Stewart, A. C., 1913-4.
Skinner, O. C., 1913-4.
Sibley, F. S. A., 1914-5.
Stephen, J. S., 1914-5.
Swinnerton-Pilkington, A. W. M., 1915-6.
Sparkes, F., 1916-7.
Sparrow, A. C. G., 1916-7.
Smith, A. G., 1920-1.
Sullivan, A. B., 1921-2.

T.
Thornton, F., 1913-4.
Tomkin, G. J. R., 1920-1.

W.
Wodehouse, Lord, 1913-4.
Wodehouse, Hon. E., 1915-6.
Watson, Sir J., Bt., 1916-7.
Wadham, E., 1920-1.

APPENDIX II.

Return of Warrant Officers, N.C. Officers and Men granted Commissions from 16th Lancers, 1914-18.

Regtl. No.	Name.	Date of Commission.	Regiment to which Commissioned.	Remarks.
2602	Andrews, W. N.	28— 6—18	3rd Essex Regt.	
4271	Archer, H. C.	12—11—14	16th Lancers.	
1141	Armstrong, C. Mc. D.	9— 9—16	10th K.O.Y.L.I.	
6145	Baillie, A.	23—10—15	R.F.A.	
803	Bareham, F.	6— 2—16	R.F.A.	
3646	Barrow, H. H.	6— 9—15	8th Royal Fusiliers.	
2817	Beaumont, N. A.	24— 9—18	3rd Manchesters.	
5009	Brill, F. W.	15— 1—15	5th Lancers.	
3021	Bruce, C. D.	26— 2—17	23rd Manchesters.	
5566	Budd, T.	28— 6—18	3rd Hants.	
3043	Brooke, G. T.	8— 3—15	16th Lancers.	
7475	Cargill, H. D.	8— 2—15		Not known.
1869	Carr, R.	8— 5—17	16th Lancers.	
4490	Clements, F. W.	14— 4—17	3rd Royal Welsh Fus.	
5663	Collyer, G. A.	24—12—16	16th Lancers.	
4629	Cooper, F.	6— 2—16	5th Berks.	
5716	Farley, H. W.	24— 1—15	8th West Kents.	
4854	Fitzpatrick, J.	12— 2—15	Manchesters.	
6878	Ford, W. E.	24— 9—18	Oxford and Bucks.	
5043	Glasgow, F.	25— 9—16	1st Gloucesters.	
3722	Gardiner, G. C.	1—10—15	Royal Irish.	
3119	Gamble, W. R.	6— 2—16	Yorkshires (P.W.O.)	
5491	Goodheart, O. F.	12— 6—16	1st East Kents.	
7699	Harvey, W.	28— 5—18	3rd Dorsets.	
5672	Haynes, J.	6— 2—16	Northumberland Fus.	
1414	Hollis, R. C.	5—12—16	16th Lancers.	
4088	Hawkins, J.	10— 7—17	12th Norfolks.	
157	Johnson, G. P. S.	5— 3—16	1st Royal West Kents.	
302	Lawrence, C.	6— 2—16	Northumberland Fus.	
636	Lloyd, J.	25— 9—16	8th Gloucesters.	
5105	McConnell, J.	1—10—14	16th Lancers.	
7060	Magoris, P. J.	10—10—15	R.F.A.	
2612	Martin, R. H.	3— 7—15		Not known.
492	Miles, J. J. A.	20— 9—17	16th Lancers.	
1632	Mills, G. C.	6— 2—16	11th West Yorks.	
5111	Mullins, F.	29—10—15	R.F.A.	
5682	Noakes, E.	26— 8—16	16th Lancers.	
1673	Nunn, F. J.	6— 2—16	17th Middlesex.	
4539	Norton, F. J.	6— 2—16	R.F.A.	
3690	Norris, F.	21—11—17	1st/4th Gloucesters	
5118	Parker, G. H.	29—10—15	R.F.A.	
4521	Pargeter, F.	12—11—14	16th Lancers.	
6265	Picker, L. C.	30—10—17	Essex.	
3851	Pitts, J. P.	13— 8—16	2nd Bedfords.	

Regtl. No.	Name.	Date of Commission.	Regiment to which Commissioned.	Remarks.
13177	Pinder, W.	27— 3—18	3rd Somerset L.I.	
3406	Pilley, E. C.	9— 9—16	10th K.O.Y.L.I.	
4036	Prosser, J.	10— 3—15	16th Lancers.	
3136	Reeve, W. N.	12—11—14	16th Lancers.	
7472	Roscorla, P.	15— 7—15	R.F.A.	
5504	Richards, W.	?	Territorial Force.	Not known.
5087	Ross, J.	26— 2—16	Royal Fusiliers.	
4451	Seal, E. J.	18— 7—16	Yorks and Lancs.	
7218	Slaughter, T. G.	4—11—15	R.F.A.	
7210	Sills, E.	25— 5—15	S. Res. of Officers.	
5104	Sibley, F. H. A.	12—11—14	16th Lancers.	
1968	Short, J. M.	19—11—16	2nd East Lancs.	
4678	Smith, H.	18—10—16	R.F.A.	
13148	Spoll, E. J.	9— 4—18	A.O. Corps.	
3632	Spendlove, W. H.	11—15	R.F.A.	
228	Spearing, J. G.	26— 2—17	9th Cheshires.	
758	Sparkes, F.	16—12—16	16th Lancers.	
5568	Strugnell, A. C.	14— 6—16	2nd Yorkshires.	
5252	Taylor, F. J.	6— 2—16	R.F.A.	
7054	Waldron, R.	10—10—15	R.F.A.	
7061	Waldron, R. S.	10—10—15	R.F.A.	
5941	Ward, H. S.	8— 3—15	A.V.C.	
3955	Webb, E. A.	19— 2—16	3rd/1st W. Somersets	
13206	West, S. R.	9— 4—18	6th Wilts.	
5852	Wharrie, W.	29— 5—17	Lincolns.	
13103	Williamson, C.	30— 1—18	3rd Essex Regt.	
5276	Willis, G.	15—10—17	3rd Worcesters.	
5564	Woodham, E. R.	6— 2—16	Norfolks.	

INDEX.

A.

Advance, Final, 99-103
Aisne, River, 57-9
Albert, H.M. King of the Belgians, 100
Allenby, Major-Gen. E. H. H., 18, 23, 30, 32, 95, 99, 122, 132
Amalgamation, 16th and 5th Lancers, 127
Ammunition, Shortage of, 69, 73
Antwerp, Siege of, 62-4
Armies, Distribution of, before Battle of Mons, 23-4
Armistice, 102-4
Aris, Lieut., 65
Asquith, Rt. Hon. H. H.: his Home Rule Bill, 2; his repudiation of Gough Memo., 10; his Cabinet, 16, 18; speech re shell shortage, 73.

B.

Bases: Amiens, 23; Havre, 23; St. Nazaire change to, 45
Battles: Mons, 28-9; Le Cateau, 33-7; Tannenberg, 43; Marne, 49-55; Aisne, 56-60; Nancy, 54; 1st Ypres, 67; Neuve Chapelle, 71; 2nd Ypres, 71; Loos, 74; Verdun, 76; 1st Somme, 76; Arras, 77; 3rd Ypres, 78; Caporetto, 78; Cambrai, 79-82; 2nd Somme, 84-91; Lys, 92-3; Ailette, 93-4; Amiens, 97-9
Beech, Lieutenant, Death of, 71
B.E.F. (British Expeditionary Force): Composition and staff, 19-20; embarkation and landing, 18; Retreat, from Mons, 29-49; move to North, 61
Belgian Army, Organisation of, 21-2; at Anwerp, 62-4; at Dixmude, 68; part in final advance, 100-1
Besseler, V., at Antwerp, 62
Breeks, Col., R.H.A., 5, 6, 13, 14
Bulow, V., at Mons, 28; Charleroi, 31; Mons Retreat from, 40-50; his orders to V. Kluck, 52-3
Byng, Sir J., Gen., at Vimy Ridge, 77; Cambrai, 79; his 3rd Army, 2nd Somme, 84-90; in final advance, 99

C.

Casualty Rolls: Mons, 29-31; Le Cateau, 37; Aug. 23rd-27th, 40-45; Aisne, 59; Naval Division, 64; Petit Morin, 53; total of B.E.F. Oct. to Dec., 1914, 68; mine explosion (16th L.), 70-1; Neuve Chapelle, 71; 3rd Cav. Div., 72; 2nd Cav. Div., 2nd Somme, 91; total during war, Western Front, 108-13
Cavalry Brigades, 1st, 2nd, 3rd, 4th, 5th, 19; 1st at Néry, 42; 4th at Néry, 42; 3rd, formation of, 26, 89, 97
Cavalry Divisions, 1st, 18, 97, 42
2nd Division, formation of, Gen. H. Gough, 60; Gen. Kavanagh, 71; Gen. Sir P. Chetwode, 73; Gen. Pitman, 95
Cavalry Regiments, 4th D.Gs., first shot of the war, 27
Greys at Peronnes, 27
15th Hussars, 30
9th Lancers, charge of, 30
Greys at Cerizy, 39
12th Lancers at Cerizy, 39
20th Hussars at Cerizy, 39
3rd Hussars at Néry, 42
11th Hussars at Néry, 42
Bays at Néry, 42
12th Lancers, charge of, 56
4th Hussars at Chassemy, 57
16th Lancers at Chassemy, 57
5th Lancers at Chassemy, 57
16th Lancers at Norwich, 1; Dublin, 2; Curragh, 4; the Ulster affair, 4-15; at Dublin, 23; embarkation and landing at Havre, 23; at Jeumont, 22; Binche, 26; Perronnes and Elouges, 27; Battle of Mons, 27-31; Le Cateau, 34-37; the Retreat, 38-49; Marne, 52-5; Aisne, 58-60; at Lime, 59; move to line of the Lys, 62; Mont des Cats, 65; Warneton, 65; Mount Kemmel, 66; trench fighting, 67; deaths of Major Dixon and Capt. Onslow, 67; mine explosion, 21st Feb., 1915; deaths of Major Neave, Capt. Nash, Lieuts. Beech, King and Cross, 71; affair at Ypres sally port, 72; to billets at Petits Preaux, 76; at Epehy, 77; at Battle of Cambrai and Bourlon Wood, 82; at 2nd Battle of Somme, 84-92; deaths of Lieuts. Stephens and Sir J. Watson, 87; death of Lieut. Martin Holland, 88; fighting at Moreuil; deaths of Capt. Allen and Lieuts. Maxwell and Wodehouse; the Leicester Yeomanry, 92; billets at Longvillers, 93; reassembly of 3rd Brigade for final advance, 96; roll of officers, 97; combats near Warvillers, 98; at Inchy, 100; combat at Haveng, 102; at Estinne, 103; the last charge and Armistice, 103; entry into Mons, 104; to Antwerp and Canterbury, 104; to Port Said, Syria and Homs, 122; march to Sarona, 123; to Belbeis, 124; to Lucknow, 125; amalgamation with 5th Lancers, 127; to Cairo, 121
Cerizy, Combat at, 39
Charrier, Major, Death of, 37-8
Chetwode, Sir P., Brig.-Gen., 19, 20, 73
Churchill, Right Hon. W., Ulster and Army, 2; at Antwerp, 62-3
Combats: Le Grand Fayt, 37; Lesing, 37-8; Cerizy, 39; Néry, 42; Taillefontaine, 43; Villers Cotterets, 43; Chezy, 56; Mont des Cats, 65; Warneton, 65-6
Contemptibles, Origin of name,
Corps, British: i, ii, iii, 18; iii, 41; iii, vii, 88; iv, v, vi, xix, 89
Cross, Lieut., Death of, 71

D.

Dallas, Col. A. G., at Antwerp, 62
D'Amade, Gen., 24-5, and following.
Doulens, Conference at, 89
Dixmude, 68

E.

Eccles, Col., at Ypres, wounded, 72, 74
Elouges, 27, 31
Embarkations for Dublin, 1; for Havre, 23; for England, 104; Egypt, Palestine, Syria, 122; India, 125; Egypt, 130

F.

Foch, Gen., made Commander-in-Chief, 89
Frameries, Fighting at, 30
French, Sir John, Field-Marshal, C.-in-C. B.E.F., 18-74; his remonstrances to War Cabinet, 69, 70, 73; his interview in Paris with Lord Kitchener, 43; his resignation, 74
French Armies, Organisation and distribution of, 24

G.

Gallieni, Commandant Paris, 51
Gas, Poison, 71, 72
German Army, Organisation of, 22; distribution, 24
Gough, Sir Hubert, Gen., Brigadier 3rd Cavalry Brigade at Curragh, Ulster and Army, 2-15; Mons, Le Cateau, and Retreat, 25-55; to command 2nd Cav. Div., 60; 7th Infantry Div., 1st Army Corps, 71; 5th Army, 76; at 2nd Battle of Somme, 84-92; to England, 91
Grierson, Sir J., Gen., his death, 20

H.

Haig, Sir D., Gen. commanding 1st Corps, 20; C.-in-C., 74
Hesse, Prince Max of; his death, 65
Hindenburg Line, 77
Hindenburg, V., Chief of Staff, 75
Hogg, Lt.-Col., 4th Hussars, 2-14; (Ulster and Army); his death, 43
Homs, Regiment at, 122-3

I.

Indian Army, 68
Indian Cavalry, 79, 80-2
Infantry Regiments:
  4th Middlesex and Royal Irish at Mons, 28
  Cheshires and Norfolks at Audrignies, 31
  Lancasters at Le Cateau, 35
  Gordons at Le Cateau, 36
  Connaught Rangers at Le Grand Fayt, 37
  Munsters at Fesmy, 37-8

J.

Joffre, Gen., French C.-in-C., 22, 25, 63; succeeded by Nivelle, 75

K.

Kaiser, Wilhelm, 16, 25
Kavanagh, Gen., to command 2nd Cav. Div., 71
King, The, Inspection by, 67
King, Lieut., Death of, 71
Kitchener, Lord, Field-Marshal, 18, 62, 63; death of, 65
Kluck, V., commanding 1st German Army, 24-60

L.

Lanrezac, Gen., French 5th Army, 24
Le Cateau, 33-7
Le Grand Fayt, 37
Leman, Gen., at Liége, 25
Lloyd-George, Rt. Hon., Minister of Munitions, 73
Longvillers, Regiment at, 93
Ludendorf, V., Chief of Staff,
Lucknow, Regiment at 125-9
Luxembourg, 24
Lys, Fight for line of, 61-8; Battles of, 92-3

M.

MacEwen, Col., 1-9; (Ulster and Army); wounded, 37
Macneil, Lieut., Death of, 65
Marne, Battle of, 49-55
Marwitz, V., Commanding German Cav. Corps, 24-55
Maubeuge, Siege of, 59
Memorials, War: Canterbury, 131; Lucknow, 129
Molke, V., Chief of German Staff, 22, 27, 58
Mons, Battle of, 28-9; entry into, 104
Mont des Cats, Combat at, 65
Moreuil, Fighting at, 91
Mormal, Forest of, 31

N.

Namur, Siege of, 29
Nash, Capt., Death of, 71
Naval Division, 62-4
Neave, Major, Death of, 71
Néry, Combat at, 42
Neuve Chapelle, Battle of, 71
Norwich, 1

O.

Officers, Rolls of, 97, 104, 125, 127

P.

Paget, Sir A. Gen., C.-in-C. Ireland (Ulster and Army), 3-15
Parker, Lt.-Col., 5th Lancers, 4-9; (Ulster and Army)
Polo; India, 134-5; Cairo, 135-6
Pulteney, Major-Gen., 41

R.

Rawlinson, Sir A. Gen., at Bruges, 63; 2nd Somme, 90
Robertson, Sir W. R., Qrtr.-Mastr.-Genl., B.E.F.

S.

St. John, Harris-, Lt.-Col., 16th Lancers
Seely, Rt. Hon., Col., Secretary for War, 7, 8, 10; (Ulster and Army)
Smith-Dorien, Sir H. L., Commander 2nd Corps, B.E.F.
Sieges: Liege, 18; Namur, 29; Maubeuge, 59; Antwerp, 62-64
Sordet, Gen., 24
Stephens, Lieut., Death of, 88

T.

Tempest-Hicks, Capt., Death of, 98
Tanks, 76, 79, 84; German, 93
Trench Warfare, Beginning of, 60-7; Flanders, 69; Attrition by, 72

U.

United States Armies, 95, 99, 100

V.

Villars Cotterets, Combat at, 43
Vimy Ridge, 77

W.

War, Causes of, 15; Declaration of, 16
Watson, Sir J., 2nd Lt., Death of, 87
Wormald, Lt.-Col., Death of, 39

Y.

Yeomanry, Leicestershire, 92, 97
Ypres, Battles, 62, 67, 78

www.ingramcontent.com/pod-product-compliance
Lightning Source LLC
Chambersburg PA
CBHW081204170426
43197CB00018B/2918